POST-CONTEMPORARY INTERVENTIONS

· Series Editors: Stanley Fish and Fredric Jameson

LUKÁCS AFTER COMMUNISM

LUKÁCS
AFTER COMMUNISM

EVA L. CORREDOR

INTERVIEWS WITH CONTEMPORARY INTELLECTUALS

DUKE UNIVERSITY PRESS Durham & London 1997

© 1997 Duke University Press
All rights reserved   Printed in the United States
of America on acid-free paper ∞
Typeset in Melior with Antique Olive Compact
display by Keystone Typesetters, Inc.

Library of Congress Cataloging-in-Publication Data
Corredor, Eva L.
Lukács after Communism : interviews with contemporary
intellectuals / Eva Corredor.
p.   cm. — (Post-contemporary interventions)
Includes index.
ISBN 0-8223-1754-0 (cloth : alk. paper).
— ISBN 0-8223-1763-x (pbk. : alk. paper)
1. Lukács, György, 1885–1971.   2. Philosophy, Marxist.
I. Title.   II. Series.
B4815.L84C686   1997
199'.439–dc20   96-34207
CIP

To the memory of my father and
to my daughter Livia who will carry on

CONTENTS

ACKNOWLEDGMENTS

This volume would not have been without the contributions of ten distinguished intellectuals who agreed to share with me their views and theories relative to György Lukács. For their fascinating ideas and their enthusiasm for the project I shall remain forever grateful. I also wish to express my sincere appreciation for the gracious reception I received from all at the time of the interviews, which took place during precious summer leave, Christmas holidays, in between taxing conference sessions, and even just days after serious surgery.

Fredric Jameson, who has been important to my work all along by his sustained interest in Lukács, again gave invaluable direction, from initial encouragement to the publication of this study within the series he edits with Stanley Fish. To both inspiring editors I wish to express my deep gratitude and admiration.

Reynolds Smith's immediate interest in the project opened the door to Duke University Press, my first choice for the publication of this book. His editorial talents also helped streamline the manuscript by eliminating some of my favorite fluff. Thanks Reynolds. I wish to thank my readers at Duke for their constructive comments. I appreciated Peter Guzzardi's patience and support in moving along the publication. Many thanks to my copy editor, Bob Mirandon, whose eagle eyes detected every needy syntax and checked hundreds of foreign accents. Pam Morrison, my final editor, was a true blessing. Her quiet expertise and—a rare quality that I came to value immensely—wise understanding of authors' pressures and frustrations, made the final stages of this publication as smooth sailing and pleasant as they could be. My thanks go to Cherie Westmoreland for her creative visual contributions to the text and the cover.

I am indebted to several friends and colleagues at my institution: to Katherine Dickson and Laura Nauta from the Nimitz Library for invaluable help with research, interlibrary loans, and indexing; to John Hutchins for leading me gently toward realizing a surreal trip to Brazil; to Ray Collinson and Chris Buck for troubleshooting my technological crises; to members of the administration and colleagues who were instrumental in providing me with a Faculty Incentive Award and a Naval Academy Summer Research Grant in 1994–95 that enabled me to complete my last interveiw and spend a quiet summer writing my introduction. Thanks for the many words of support and encourage-

Acknowledgments

ment extended to me by friends, colleagues, and even strangers—too many to be listed here but not forgotten. They often did wonders.

Finally, my special and deep-felt gratitude goes to my daughter Livia, who has been with me all along and whose gentle, continuous support and steady confidence in my work made this book possible. To her my indebtedness is greater than words can express. The warmth and joy that never ceased to come from her and her young family have given meaning to everything in my life.

LUKÁCS AFTER COMMUNISM

This book was inspired by the revolutionary events in Russia and Eastern Europe that began in 1989. The political and economic turmoil that followed prompted questions about the continued validity and legacy of György Lukács's critical theories to a world that had just experienced the apparent bankruptcy of communism, an ideology that had risen and now seemed to have died nearly simultaneously with Lukács.

In 1991 a visit to a major bookstore in Budapest, György Lukács's hometown, resulted in the discovery of only one book on the Hungarian philosopher and critic, Hungary's most noted intellectual in the twentieth century.* In Paris a few faithful such as Nicolas Tertulian continued to teach Lukács at the Ecole des Hautes Etudes en Sciences Sociales of the Sorbonne. In New York Lukács's original disciples busied themselves at the New School for Social Research, dissecting his work, uncovering its shortcomings, while reclaiming their chairs at the University of Budapest from which they had been ousted during the communist regime, swinging back and forth between East and West, and enjoying the windfalls of the new world order.

A few years after the initial political tremor, critical aftershocks appeared on the most recent register of books in print. A two-volume *Hungarian Studies on György Lukács* (Budapest: Akadémiai Kiadó, 1993) was edited by Lukács's newly liberated countrymen, for whom "it is striking to learn that Lukács's influence extends even to the United States" (ix). They also felt, somewhat naively, that because of relative linguistic isolation, only Hungarian research could fully account for Lukács's thought and "provide a more reliable image of Lukács than that currently reflected in the international scholarly literature" (ix). Unfortunately, little in the volume's nearly seven hundred pages would significantly affect the current understanding of Lukács's work in the West. Lukács, in fact, wrote most of his works in German, and they had been available to the West for several decades.

The more apocalyptic and sensationalist reactions to the end of the Soviet regime in Russia and Eastern Europe have no doubt provoked

---

*The complete works of György Lukács, in seventeen volumes, were published in German by Hermann Luchterhand Verlag, Neuwied and Berlin, between 1960 and 1984.

partisan reactions to Lukács's significance, particularly by those who never read or were only superficially familiar with his work. Still, concerns about the "fate" of Marxism, the presence of Marxism in a postmodern world, or "whither Marxism"* must be considered to fully assess Lukács's role in the critical discourse after the debacle of communism.

If, as Francis Fukuyama suggested, history has indeed come to an end with the elimination of the East-West polarity after the cold war, a historically based criticism such as Lukács's could hardly carry its past weight into the future. "Posthistorical" wars, however, have shown that ethnic, tribal, and nationalist conflicts must not necessarily follow a bipartisan pattern to explode into full-blown historical catastrophes. History has never exactly repeated itself but has progressed under always changing and changed forms. History and conflict continue to live, it would seem, as long as human beings attempt to coexist in society, whether in a family, a nation, or the world.

Similarly, visions of political correctness have been in constant flux. Invented by the left, allegedly hijacked by the right, the conflicting truths espoused by left and right reflect the confusion created by willfully antagonistic and often arbitrary party politics that have left people baffled and amused about what should be considered right or wrong. The contradictions also reveal the more serious need for globally acceptable human ethics. The collapse of communism constituted yet another failure in this endeavor. The necessity and the desire to invent a more just society remain.

Proposed remedies to the current crisis abound. Among those who do not flatly reject any inferences about the future based on theories of the past are critics who simply wish to update or supplement earlier visions.** They speak of new spaces to be considered. They indict "Eurocentric" approaches to global crises. New concepts of ethnocentrism, nationalism, ecology, racism, sexism, religious fanaticism today have exploded notions of the past that implied a harmonious human totality. While these critics wish to go beyond Marxism and expand its vision, they propose no radically new approach that would truly replace the former model.

*A good sampling of current views on such issues are contained in *Whither Marxism? Global Crises in International Perspective*, ed. and intro. Bernd Magnus and Stephen Cullenberg (New York: Routledge 1995); and in *Marxism in the Postmodern Age: Confronting the New World Order*, ed. Antonio Callari, Stephen Cullenberg, and Carole Biewener (New York: Guilford Press, 1995).

**See Gayatri Chakravorty Spivak, "Supplementing Marxism," *Whither Marxism?* pp. 109–19.

A certain intellectually militant Marxism also remains unshaken.* It differentiates itself from the failures of communism and still attempts to enlighten the world about Marxism's continuous truth. Its proponents do admit the need for constant self-criticism and the study of lessons learned from the past.

After a period of significant "forgetting" of Marx and Marxism, and at a moment when to their enemies they seemed finally and safely buried, Jacques Derrida suddenly "admitted" in 1993 that he too had been haunted by the specter of Marx.** This strategically correct admission, which has already prompted a plethora of critical jubilations, has been heralded as the wisdom of the present and the voice of the future. In fact, very little has changed with Derrida's newest manifesto. The philosopher has simply repeated an extravagant exercise in deconstruction begun in *Grammatology* (1967) by substituting in *Spectres de Marx* (1993) Karl Marx for Claude Lévi-Strauss and Jean-Jacques Rousseau. Derrida's delayed use of the name of Marx has resulted in a repetition of a "hauntology" that has not altered his views of the past and—despite its occasional intriguing ethicist and even messianic tone—holds no revolutionary promise for the future. Derrida has resurrected Marx at his own convenience to provide him with a proper burial speech that restates the pragmatically deferred erasure of Marx and that celebrates the nonrealization of Marxism. "Exit Marx, enter Derrida," as we could call it, is the trace of a specter, similar to Hamlet's father, that has haunted Derrida in his wishful dreams of (patricidal?) philosophical erasure.

In the midst of such theoretical and critical agitation among the disciples and foes of Marxism and communism, the significance of the work of György Lukács remains open to question. Lukács was called the first and foremost theoretician of Marxist aesthetics. The Marxist dimension of his work must therefore be scrutinized in a similar way as Marxism itself. Furthermore, it is important to determine which aspect of his work—whether it was indeed his Marxism—has contributed most significantly to the philosophical and critical thought of the twentieth century.

Lukács's life (1885–1971) and career (begun in 1904) span nearly nine decades. He lived in the midst of the turmoil of two devastating world wars. His private and professional lives were equally marked by

*Several of the critics interviewed for this study expressed a continued strong commitment to Marxism, in particular Michael Löwy, but also Fredric Jameson, Terry Eagleton, and Cornel West.

**Jacques Derrida, *Spectres de Marx* (Paris: Editions Galilée, 1993).

3

struggle and controversy. The son of a wealthy, ennobled banker, Lukács spent his life denouncing what he believed to be exploitative political regimes, capitalism and fascism, and inauthentic human values advanced by bourgeois society. Early in life, long before studying Marx, Lukács chose to devote himself to the study of social injustice as he observed it around him and as it appeared to him reflected in specific forms of art and literature. He wanted to understand reality and act upon it. Despite the bumpy road he had to travel through most of his career, a journey punctuated by political strife between East and West, Stalin and Hitler, and involving recantations of former works, Lukács saw his life become the embodiment of his ethics—"lived thought," as he described it in the title of his autobiography.

Already as a high school student at the Protestant gymnasium in Budapest, Lukács becomes cofounder of the experimental Thalia theater, which aims at being a people's theater. Its repertory includes plays by Ibsen and Hauptmann, considered to be socialist playwrights. At the same time he undertakes a systematic study of the philosophies of Kant, Dilthey, and Simmel.

After earning a doctor of law degree from the University of Kolozsvár, Lukács studies in Berlin under Simmel and composes his first major works, *The History of the Evolution of Modern Drama* and *Soul and Form*, both published in 1911. Lukács examines aesthetic forms for their capacity to express contemporary thoughts and feelings. In the course of his travels to Germany, Italy, and France, Ernst Bloch will convince Lukács to move to Heidelberg where Lukács establishes a close friendship with Max Weber and Emil Lask.

While studying in Budapest, Heidelberg, and Berlin, Lukács becomes steeped in the works of the great German classics: Goethe, Schiller, Hölderlin, Heine, Büchner, and Thomas Mann. His early writings reflect this indebtedness, but they already announce his personal interest in and confrontation with the philosophies of Kant, Heidegger, and Kierkegaard. Increasingly influenced by Hegel's objective idealism, but also critical of it, Lukács plans to write his aesthetics. In the light of Dostoevski's work, he intends to explore the relationship between ethics and a philosophy of history, but he soon abandons the larger project to condense his views in what became one of his most seminal works, *The Theory of the Novel* (1914–15). In it, Lukács investigates the origin of the genre of the novel and establishes theories of realism based on idealist notions such as intuition, inherited from the German Intellectual Sciences School (*Geisteswissenschaften*). At the same time, the book introduces the Hegelian, all-encompassing, historical outlook and man's role in the making of History.

During World War I, Lukács founds a Sunday Circle in which intellectuals and artists such as Arnold Hauser, Karl Mannheim, Béla Bartók, and Zoltán Kodály participate. In 1917 his important pre-Marxist essay, "Subject-Object Relationship in Aesthetics," appears in *Logos*. It puts forth a question, implicit in the essay's title, that will haunt Lukács throughout his life. Soon after writing this essay, Lukács in December 1918 joins Béla Kun's newly formed communist party; he becomes during the 1919 Hungarian Commune a superzealous deputy people's commissar for education who terrorizes the rich bourgeois with his socialist reform activities. Forced to flee to Vienna during the counterrevolution, when Horthy demands his extradition, Lukács is saved only by the strong intervention of a few noted intellectuals, among them Thomas Mann. This tumultuous period inspires Lukács to write his influential but highly controversial *History and Class Consciousness* (1923). It constitutes an amalgam of a materialized Hegelian theory and, for the first time, a Marxist theory that will provoke fierce attacks by both right-wing and left-wing politicians and force Lukács periodically to recant his work. The volume contains some of Lukács's most authoritative theoretical statements, among them his famous essay "Reification and the Consciousness of the Proletariat," which constitutes the foundation of Lukács's philosophical and political critique of institutionalized human exploitation. It announces the beginning of his lifelong struggle to resolve the dualism between subject and object, between man and the world, on the basis of an understanding of history as man's self-creation of the sociohistorical process, and an ethics founded on the fusion of consciousness and reality, theory and practice.

At the Marx-Engels-Lenin Institute in Moscow, Lukács becomes acquainted with Marx's 1844 *Economic and Philosophical Manuscripts* before the work's initial publication in the 1930s. He also sees Lenin's *Philosophical Notebooks*. The study of these texts has a major impact on his thought and prompts a modification of his views on Hegel, the subject-object relationship, epistemology, and the relationship between art and society. Art is seen as a tool in man's striving to objectify the senses; art is part of man's attempt to transform his world and himself through his own physical and mental labor; art is anthropocentric; aesthetic form is the specific, historical content of art that reveals the human distance from reality; a realist form represents the inner contradictions of a society, just as modernism reveals society's profound human predicament. For Lukács, great art reflects an understanding and provides a possible explanation of the crucial human problems of a given time. The main task of a critic is—and here

Lukács seems surprisingly close to Sartre—the elucidation, the "unveiling" to use the Sartrean term, of the relation between aesthetic form and reality.

During his exile from Nazism in the Stalinist Soviet Union (1933–44), Lukács composes his much-acclaimed *The Young Hegel* in a highly fruitful collaboration with Mikhail Lifshitz, with whom he also elaborates concepts of Marxist literary criticism. He writes *The Historical Novel* (1937) and numerous other essays on European art and literature, all of which were published after World War II. These constitute four thick volumes (4 through 7) of the Luchterhand edition of Lukács's *Werke*. In 1948 Lukács personally confronts Sartre and Merleau-Ponty and subsequently publishes a severe critique of the French existentialists' efforts to combine Marxism and existentialism. In 1954 in *The Destruction of Reason* he provides a fairly emotional and highly personal philosophical explanation of the rise of irrationalism and Nazism in Germany. After his problematic role in the 1956 Hungarian uprising, where he fought for a more orthodox Marxist rather than a more Western democratic government, Lukács retires from public political involvement and devotes his energy to publishing a critique of modernist literature, *Realism in Our Time* (1958), followed by two monumental two-volume statements, *Aesthetics* (1963), and *Ontology*, that he will not have time to complete before his death in 1971.

The sociopolitical upheavals of the late 1960s and early 1970s encourage the translation of many of Lukács's works into English, French, Italian, and most other major languages. His pre-Marxist and Marxist works inspire numerous analyses of man's concrete historical reality with the prospect of man's realizing both material and spiritual liberation. Hailed and attacked almost equally by both left and right, Lukács's theories have stirred reactions from virtually everyone. His critical work has been widely acknowledged as among the twentieth century's most brilliant and influential formulations of a historico-political methodology. In 1991 a comprehensive biography unearthed many of the personal and historical contingencies of an enormous body of work through which Lukács tried to adhere to his self-styled moral imperative: "I go to prove my soul." *

We are approaching the end of Lukács's century, but also the century of Einstein, Freud, the world wars, the development of nuclear power, computers, space travel, antibiotics, and the unresolved battles with cancer and AIDS. The successes and failures of twentieth-century intellectual effervescence have constantly enriched and altered our lives

---

* Arpad Kadarkay, *György Lukács: Life, Thought, and Politics* (Cambridge, Mass.: Basil Blackwell, 1991), p. 171.

and visions of reality. Just as nothing in the future will ever be the same as in the past, it would be absurd simply to *continue* Marxism, forcing our reality to fit the concepts elaborated for earlier societies. Such ultraconservatism would actually work against Marx's own revolutionary spirit. It would reduce Marx's and Lukács's visions and methodology to an ahistorical, absolutist straitjacketing of lives and societies. The collapse of communism in Eastern Europe and the former Soviet Union and the current problems with drugs and crime in an otherwise constantly more progressive postmodern world suggest that no social philosophy or ideology, not the communist subordination of the individual or the existentialist capitalization on the individual, have yielded entirely satisfactory models. Since the 1989 revolutions that were inspired by an admiration for American free culture, its free politics, and most of all its free market, Europe in particular has been struggling to help realize the dream of Western democracy for those who had fought it for more than half a century. A lesson we could derive from history is in fact a cautious skepticism toward most social systems with which nations have been experimenting. Even the meaning of democracy has required constant updating.

As noted, among Lukács's most seminal works is *History and Class Consciousness*,* which he wrote in 1923–24 during his transitional period from Hegel to Marx. Its most powerful chapter, "Reification and the Consciousness of the Proletariat" (pp. 83–222), contains what may go down in history as Lukács's strongest admonition for humanity: the necessity to guard against reification. In this work, intended to establish the unique revolutionary role of proletarian class consciousness in the fight for an egalitarian society, Lukács also addresses the origins of many philosophical, existential, and even psychological problems that have remained unresolved. He retraces the transformation of the original use value of human labor into a socially marketed, often fetishized commodity. He attempts to demonstrate how in modern times the natural and "organic" relationship between producer and product has been abolished and the human being made into an independent consumer object. The relation of human beings to their social function has been stripped of qualitative aspects to assume a purely quantitative, commercial value. Tying into his lifelong preoccupation with the Kantian subject-object predicament, Lukács speaks of the human subject who has had to surrender its natural link to its objective "being there" in society. An individual's lifetime is seen as rationalistically calculated

---

*György Lukács, *History and Class Consciousness: Studies in Marxist Dialectics*, trans. Rodney Livingstone (Berlin and Neuwied: Hermann Luchterhand Verlag, 1968). Page references to this work will be provided within the text.

and socially programmed, as if that life were an objective, calculable space within a mechanism, the sole raison d'être of which is to realize maximum capital gain. A more modern version of such Lukácsean theories could be found in today's "Total Quality Management," which is intended—perhaps for capitalist rather than humanitarian reasons—to counter the negative effects of mechanistic, isolated occupations that were captured so vividly some sixty years ago in Charlie Chaplin's interpretation of modern times.

Lukács locates the most alarming aspect of reification in the inability of individuals to recognize or even comprehend the arbitrariness and inhumanity of their own exploitation. The entrepreneur, the political or military master, or the head of an institution may succeed in using physical or intellectual labor within a scientifically established bureaucracy, a profitable technological environment, or a social or industrial mechanism, all of which appear legitimate and whose standardizations seem supported by law and society. In the process, human beings become metamorphosed into things, commodities, reified objects. If each individual's consciousness or intelligence is unable to see through such isolating and alienating reifications, the existing state of affairs can actually assume a ghostly objectivity and parade as unadulterated reality. The necessity to submit to isolated laws may not reveal the complete or relative irrationality of the total system. Gustave Flaubert's servant characters in *Madame Bovary* (Catherine) and *Un Coeur simple* (Félicité) could be analyzed as fictionalized examples of bourgeois reifications in the nineteenth century.

In the midst of reified situations, legitimate human crises may not be recognized, much less alleviated. Instead, questioning their occurrence could engender further suffering and punishment as a result of measures taken to protect the "order" of the establishment. Seemingly cohesive systems of laws could be purely formal, political, and economic rather than being legal and made to preserve justice. In the eighteenth century it was possible to establish the juridical basis of slavery when a proponent of slavery, "a 'Kantian' Hugo," argued that it "had been the law of the land for thousands of years and was acknowledged by millions of cultivated people" (p. 108). It would be fairly easy to identify such crises even today, for instance in some highly publicized sexual harassment cases, where the reluctance of certain judicial bodies to indict high-ranking officers or politicians may have led to harmful consequences to the lives and careers of presumed victims.

Arguments of reification could be made with regard to certain formalistic conceptualizations in the so-called exact sciences that have become immutable substrata to religious, philosophical, and, by extension, also "critical" givens (with regard to morals, social practices, the capabilities of women, etc.). Instituted reifications may be at the root of specifically human problems (the inability to eradicate crime and drug abuse, realize better health care, ensure sexual and racial equality) that have remained unresolved, while purely mathematical, rationalistic science and technology were able to leap ahead.

The problems Lukács confronts in his chapter on reification echo Fichtean views on the dark void that separates us from "origins," "truths," and "real" knowledge. He makes us aware of abstract substrata that still govern our perceptions and force us to continue our observations and experiments. He warns against adopting apparently fixed and objective laws for eternity. Many of Michel Foucault's theories on the reified power of discourse used to control judicial, medical, and sexual practices deal with similar problems. Even Jacques Derrida's deconstructions could be understood as a response to dilemmas of reification created by the linguistic system. Jean-Jacques Rousseau's critique of social institutions, culture, and civilization that supposedly have stripped man of his human essence could be seen as an admonition against the reification of human perversion.

Whether it is the purity of nature (Rousseau), art (Kant), the play instinct (Schiller), the view of the reality of history (Vico), the archaeology of discourse (Foucault), or the class consciousness of the proletariat (Lukács) that promises to save humanity from its self-created problems, the common denominator of these theories is a warning signal against the blind acceptance of diverse forms of reification that threaten to obstruct the normal course of life. Twentieth-century critics have denounced the fetishism of commodities, the dehumanization of labor, sexual exploitation, racial discrimination, rationalism, scientific arrogance, arbitrary laws, and the power of language as some of the reifying evils of society.

While according to Lukács reification can be overcome only by "constant and constantly renewed efforts to disrupt the reified structures of existence" (p. 197), other theoreticians are much less disturbed by the alleged social predicament. Some simply shrug it off. Seventy years after Lukács and in the midst of a plethora of pragmatist-linguistic-deconstructivist theories, Richard Rorty in 1993 deals with the "reification of language"* by rejecting the later Heidegger, who "continued his own quest for authenticity by attempting to win himself

*Richard Rorty, "Wittgenstein, Heidegger, and the Reification of Language," *The Cambridge Companion to Heidegger*, ed. Charles Guignon (Cambridge: Cambridge University Press, 1993). Page references to this work will be provided within the text.

a place in the history of Being—we could also say reifying himself!—
as the first postmetaphysical Thinker" (p. 349). Rorty pragmatically
prefers to side with Wittgenstein's later mocking attitude toward history, language, and philosophy—his escape from reification?—when
he comes "to see 'language' as referring simply to the exchange of
marks and noises among human beings for particular purposes, as no
more denoting a real essence than does 'game' " (p. 350).

Whether one shares in visions of reification or pragmatically wills
them away, as Rorty engaged to do, the term continues to evoke a negative experience. It implies the end of human vitality and authenticity.
It constitutes closure. Lukács perceived it as one of the evils of capitalism. In his essays on realism Lukács pointed to reifications that, according to him, existed and still exist in the bourgeois form of society.
In his analyses of contemporary fiction, drama, and art, he identified
reification as a phenomenon of his own time. Today, forms of reification persist in individual and organized systems of oppression and exploitation. Over the years the phenomenon has acquired a multiplicity
of signifiers such as "ethnic cleansing" and "sexual harassment."

In the 1990s traditional hierarchies and class structures seem to
have given way to more complex and less clearly differentiated social divisions. The historical, revolutionary role attributed by Lukács
to proletarian class consciousness appears to have shifted to groups
whose antagonistic strategies have been nourished by racial, gender,
ethnic, political, and religious inequities. Theories and systems have
changed in form, validity, and relevance. Yet many of Lukács's theories, such as reification, the fetishism of commodities, and irrationalism, continue to speak to us because they evoke dangers that individuals, groups, and whole countries still face.

At the same time we have to recognize that the fixation on or forceful
implementation of any one theory, including Lukács's own, could mis-
lead and in changed historical and social circumstances pose threats to
the freedom and happiness of the individual and of entire nations.
Theories can become reifications. Lukács made a point of cautioning
the reader in his 1967 preface to *History and Class Consciousness* that
orthodox Marxism is not the belief in this or that thesis; Marx's theses
might even be proven false. "Orthodoxy refers exclusively to *method*"
(p. xxvi). Inspired by such Lukácsean lessons, critics today have elaborated their own methodologies: Fredric Jameson developed his "cognitive mapping," Roberto Schwarz a "differential" reading of Lukács for
Brazil, and Cornel West his "messianic pragmatist philosophy." These
and other approaches will be discussed in this volume. They constitute
attempts to build on what is best in Lukács while trying to account for

the reality of the twentieth century. Thus, in the acute awareness of the potential ill effects of reified theories and dogmatic conclusions, we are still, even paradoxically, indebted to Lukács.

Any attempt at an ethical discourse, including Lukácsean theories of human life, culture, and society, must be careful to avoid closure and the dogmatic enactment of a telos or utopia. The guiding principle of such an attempt should be a self-critical process that is aware of its past history and present historicity. Ideally, it ought to engage in a mediatory process that moves between the constantly changing needs of the individual and similar transformations in the social sphere. It would have to find ways to balance the desire for individual freedom with a necessary, voluntary subordination of that freedom to the good of the larger community.

Such goals are not new. They preoccupied Lukács and are in fact shared by most religious philosophies and social contracts. The forms and means of their implementation, however, remain problematic. Today we interact within a new world order, within a global environment that extends to outer space, and within an increasingly nonhomogeneous population composed of "transgressive" human beings of more than a single entity; we are Irish Catholics, Chinese Americans, African Americans, and Russian Jews. Social interaction is to occur within the multiple microcosms of our daily lives, families, schools, and political and professional entities, without discrimination because of race, gender, age, or ethnic origin. It is a seemingly impossible task. We are still far from realizing the dream of the American melting pot. The most ingenious social and political propositions of the 1960s, made to assure racial equality and integration, are still at the heart of struggles over satisfactory solutions. Critical models based on post-Lukácsean thought frequently function only as abstract working concepts that echo Kantian ethics, Sartrean existentialism, and various lessons derived from Lukács's theories of realism, irrationalism, reification, fetishism, and exploitation. Still, their abstract, idealized vision may serve as an inspirational guiding principle in the fight *against* injustice and *for* equality and freedom. As such, they have value and significance.

In praxis, the intellectual framework provided by Lukácsean critical models can inspire textual analyses of narratives of history, politics, and fiction. Such models can be directed against economic and ideological slavery and abuse. Their ethics can prevent any unbridled individualism or "irrationalism," just as their clear focus on interactive relationships can defeat modernist situations in which the lonely individual—not unlike Lukács's "problematic hero"—falls prey to an impersonal and exploitative system. The framework based on Lukácsean models would not tolerate fascism. Since it deemphasizes the accumulation of power and opposes excessive control by a state, the interaction between individual and society could not allow the practice of Soviet-style communism. Nationalism could be included only in its rare form where it would truly represent the majority of a country's people, not just the politics and rhetoric of a ruling class. Nationalisms could function as individual players in the world economy and in international politics, but nationalistic communal groups, or nations themselves, eventually would have to recognize not just the advantages but the necessity of adhering to the global community. Post-Lukácsean critical models tend to advocate a new form of internationalism that has no permanent center which could assume power over others. Nothing and nobody could condone killing or being killed on the basis of differences in ethnic, religious, national, racial, or gender politics, which we have witnessed, more or less passively.

During his time Lukács encouraged the development of proletarian class consciousness as a means toward a more just and egalitarian society. Today, a similar kind of social consciousness should be required from all segments of the population. While Western society has become fairly well educated, relatively secure, and socially liberal, it will not have achieved true progress until moral standards have been elevated to equal heights: a goal that has been frustrating and eluding it. The question remains whether we will ever manage to allow or even to interest all human beings, including the very poor (the Brazilian subcultures or the American countercultures), drug addicts, criminals, and all exploited groups, to transform into morally and ethically acceptable, equal players in society. Yet the strength of a nation or an ideal global environment, it seems to me, should not be measured by the power concentrated in its elite leadership or the amount of its weaponry and capital wealth but rather by the quality of the daily life enjoyed by the majority of its citizens, if not by all of them. If new critical methods could help us achieve a fair, dynamic social exchange by which, say, 80 percent of the human population could live happy and productive lives, might we not assume that these would provide for the few who are unable, but not unwilling, to live up to the general standard?

Lukács's theories and his pre-Marxist and Marxist political and literary analyses—in spite of the critic's often unwieldy attachment to norms such as realism and totality—are based on similar questions of society and ethics. A guarantee to the majority of people of a fair and equal share in society constitutes the unity of Lukács's thought. In his lifelong investigations Lukács did not merely analyze human problems in their historical context or define cultural forms, literary and artistic, in relation to a socioeconomic subtext. In studying the human content of form, pointing out the value of irony in signaling human or social crises, in uncovering inauthentic values instituted for the purpose of human exploitation, in revealing the specificity of genres, systems, and social behavior, Lukács has provided us with models by which to approach and to try to understand our own reality. While instructing us about the past, Lukács has taught us ways to view and understand the present, and finally to act upon it ethically.

In reappraising Lukács's theories after the debacle of communism, it seemed appropriate to extend my investigation beyond books and to engage in an interactive critical exchange with contemporary theoreticians and philosophers who have shown ethical concerns and philosophical interests similar to those of Lukács but who constitute—a generation after his—the critical voices of the 1990s. The critics I invited to participate in this study were known to have been "touched" by Lukács, most of them at the outset of their careers. The project brought together ten recorded interviews that converged on a central topic, Lukács, but that crossed as many countries and disciplines as they did critical theories, methodologies, conceptual differences, and political positions. In our discussions of Lukács's and their own individual works, my intention was to identify and to ask the critics to reveal in this politically changed fin de siècle atmosphere the role Lukács may have played in *their* half century of intellectual autobiography.

Among those interviewed in France, Michael Löwy (Centre National de la Recherche Scientifique) remains the closest to Lukács and Marxism, while Jacques Leenhardt (Ecole des Hautes Etudes en Sciences Sociales), a disciple of Lucien Goldmann, recognizes more important influences than Lukács's on his thought and practice of the sociology of literature and art. Lukács's work continues to enjoy high visibility on the crossroads of Fredric Jameson's (Duke University) global journeys through critical theory. No other Lukácsean critic in the United States has engaged in such forceful dialectics between Marxism and all major contemporary critical theories as Jameson has. Peter Bürger's (University of Bremen) confrontations with modernism, the avant-garde, and most recently with Hegel frequently reach back to Lukács's theories, acknowledging both indebtedness and distance. George Steiner's (Cambridge University) comments reveal his personal experience and intense spiritual relationship with Lukács over the years. Cornel West (Harvard University), who has embraced Lukács in his messianic pragmatist philosophy, brings Lukács's theories alive in their relevance to problems of racial and sexual integration. A disciple and coauthor with Althusser, the noted anti-Hegelian Marxist, Etienne Balibar (Ecole Normale) speaks of the intellectual trajectory that has been leading him back to the discovery of the "subject of history" in Lukács. Terry Eagleton (Oxford University) engages in a lively dialectic on Lukács that has a definitely post-Althusserian and poststructuralist quality typical of his more recent intellectual processes. Susan Rubin Suleiman (Harvard University) brings to this study the critical dimension of a scholar of modernism, reader-response theories, and authoritarian fictions (*roman à thèse*), who is also a feminist and a recent observer of the postcommunist era in her (as well as Lukács's and my own) native Hungary. The interview with Roberto Schwarz (professor emeritus of the University of Campinas in São Paulo) reveals the dilemma of postcolonial critical discourse in the huge linguistic island of South America encompassed by Brazil. His surprising dialectics illuminate the usefulness and some of the paradoxes that result from misplaced Eurocentric theories such as Lukács's concepts of the proletariat, commodity fetishism, and realism within a Third World context.

What this study hopes to accomplish, then, is a mapping of Lukács's intellectual legacy for the critical discourse of the post-Soviet world of the 1990s. These interviews reflect the broad spectrum of the interdisciplinary appeal of Lukács's work. They also reveal a relativity of focus and some eclectic usage. None of the critics interviewed remained entirely with Lukács, nor did any one of them completely reject him. Implicit in their responses were signs of Lukácsean confrontations with contemporary, post-Lukácsean realities such as equal rights, racial integration, feminism, and the postcolonial and postmodern world. Informed by the post-Lukácsean plethora of linguistic, metaphysical, hermeneutic, scientific, and reader-centered theories, critics nevertheless brought into their discussions Lukács's conceptual framework to evoke problems of alienation, reification, and the individual in modern society. The relationship to Lukács's work in most cases was one of confrontation, admiration, sometimes fascination, and always a sense of indebtedness. The talents and intellectual creativity of the scholars, though, had quickly pushed them toward a *dépassement* on a critical and theoretical journey of their own. Their readings of Lukács were also subject-specific, conditioned by the individual's theoretical, political, ethnic, and racial context. Their dialogue with Lukács had often moved on both a conceptual and an emotional level but had left significant traces of difference in the thought processes of these "Lukácsean" scholars.

Perhaps not surprisingly, no critics interviewed for this study, diverse as they were in their interests and views, seemed much concerned with the recent blows to communism. It was a phenomenon, maybe a lesson, not a threat, and certainly not an end to their appreciation of Lukács's work. For all practical purposes, the crumbling of the Soviet regime was irrelevant to the current critical discourse. Lukács emerged essentially intact. At the same time, just as attitudes toward Lukács varied widely, the critics' appreciation of each other's work was anything but mutual and homogeneous. Yet all of them, even the fiercest anti-Marxists, paid tribute to the seminal importance of Lukács's theories in the development of their own intellectual positions.

It is impossible to categorize the critics' responses. Each one individually, and all of them together as a representative study, constitute an unprecedented critical assessment of Lukács's work by some of our leading theoreticians today. What they have in common is a subtle and thorough understanding of Lukács's theoretical concepts. They also share spontaneity, enthusiasm, and a discriminating interest—sometimes deeply critical—in the work of one of this century's most controversial figures. The majority recognized in Lukács not just an interlocutor and an inspiration, but a useful challenger, who either opened their eyes and minds to a new world or who simply introduced them to some form of creative beginning that had made a difference. By our entering into a critical dialogue with his time and history a generation later, Lukács's work has served his and our purpose. It is clear at the conclusion of this critical project that theoretical discourse today is neither ready to discard Lukács nor to stop at him.

Eva L. Corredor, August 1996

INTERVIEW WITH MICHAEL LÖWY

20 May 1991, Paris

ELC My main question today concerns György Lukács's theories and what has become of them after glasnost, the collapse of communism, and the opening of the East. As here in France you have certainly been, along with Lucien Goldmann, the one who has worked most extensively on Lukács, I would like to ask you how you view Lukács's theories now, whether you see them affected by the political upheaval and, if this is the case, then how you judge their present and perhaps future critical and intellectual significance. To begin, may I ask you to recall some of the influences that Lukács's theories have had on the development of your own critical work and thinking?

ML I devoted my doctoral thesis to Lukács's political evolution; it was published a number of years ago under a pretty strange title, *Toward a Sociology of Revolutionary Intellectuals: The Political Evolution of Lukács, 1909–1929* (Paris: Presses Universitaires de France, 1976).

ELC Much discussed in America.

ML Oh, really? Well the title of the English version was much better: *George Lukács: From Romanticism to Bolshevism* (London: New Left Books, 1979). This book has been translated into English, Italian, Portuguese, Swedish, and Spanish. I was inspired enough by Lucien Goldmann to devote my work almost exclusively to the young Lukács, from 1905 to 1929. There was a chapter on the post-1929 Lukács, for the most part to explain his connection with Stalinism. The main frame of my study was political, but in a more general context I tried to see how Lukács evolved from within the romantic anticapitalist culture of Central Europe (i.e., Germany and the Austro-Hungarian Empire). First he adopted a tragic vision of the world, then, starting with World War I and the Russian Revolution, he turned toward a utopian vision, and from there to the discovery of Marxism and to adhesion to the Communist Party. That is the itinerary I tried to follow, but to link it to the sociocultural context, that is to say, to the romantic culture and to the situation of the intellectuals in Central Europe. I tried to provide a sociology of culture. Basically, it is a Lukácsean analysis of Lukács's work.

ELC If I remember correctly, you said that Lukács was the intellectual par excellence of his period, that he was the paradigmatic intellectual of this historical moment.

ML I said he was paradigmatic of those intellectuals who committed themselves to Marxism, because Lukács was somebody who first established himself intellectually, and it is from this very complex intellectual formation that he turns toward revolution.

ELC If I remember correctly, you have also discussed the connection between Lukács and Lenin, and to judge from several communications that I have just heard at an American convention, I am under the impression that Lenin, and thus the connection between Lukács and Lenin, interests many intellectuals today.

ML That is not one of my central themes, but I dealt with it to the extent that, in the beginning, in 1918, when Lukács was already attracted by the revolution, when he had already found in the proletariat the messiah class of history, he was still very reserved toward and distrustful of the Bolsheviks, whom he found too authoritarian. But very rapidly, at the end of a lengthy debate on ethics, he will nevertheless rally to the Bolsheviks and communism. He is going to abandon his Tolstoian and somewhat rigorous ethics to accept a general dialectic vision, and that is when he decides to join communism. All the while, he remains focused on a viewpoint which is not quite that of Leninism in the sense that this viewpoint belongs to what we used to call "leftist communism" or "ethical communism." He remains attached to anarcho-syndicalist ideas that, for instance, make him reject parliamentarianism in a pretty categorical way. Thus, he defends positions that are not those of the majority of the communist movement. This is going to provoke a critical reaction from Lenin, who attacks those whom he calls the "leftists" and, in doing so, he then refers to Lukács. This was not a very important issue for Lenin. Lukács was only a lesser representative of this tendency, and Lenin insisted that communism be present in the parliament. Well, from that moment on, around 1921, Lukács evolves toward certain positions that are closer to what we could call "revolutionary realism," and *History and Class Consciousness* (1923) is an attempt to reconcile Rosa Luxemburg with Lenin. After 1924 there appears Lukács's book on Lenin, which is an attempt to explain, philosophically by way of dialectics, the significance of Lenin. This book is in complete conformity with Leninist orthodoxy but, curiously enough, immediately enters into conflict with the official interpretation of Leninism in the Soviet Union, which is that of Stalin. Let us just say that Lukács's *Lenin* immediately comes into total contradiction with Stalin's Lenin. Ironically, the moment at which Lukács becomes truly Leninist is also the moment at which his interpretation of Leninism enters into contradiction with the one of the primary Soviet officials (even if this is not especially obvious to everybody at the moment, I think it can be shown in the text). These are then the last moments of what we can call the "young Lukács."

ELC Thus you concentrate exclusively on the early Lukács?

ML That is correct, but I try to observe, even though briefly, what happens later and above all how Lukács reconciles with Stalin. I try to show the philosophical foundation of this reconciliation stemming from the following idea: in the young Lukács there is a very strong utopian tendency, a very strong ethical, moral, and utopian element of which the nucleus is the refusal of existing reality. Lukács has been influenced in this thinking by the Hungarian poet Endre Ady, who represents this very principle of refusal in all its splendor. Yet in 1926 Lukács experiences a highly traumatic event, his biggest moral, philosophical, and personal crisis. He is confronted with the dilemma of either "reconciling with reality" by accepting the Stalinist Soviet Union or breaking with the communist movement. This is a big dilemma. So he is philosophically going to justify his attachment to the movement in a very interesting article on Moses Hess, which appears in 1926. He criticizes Moses Hess as being a thinker who is too moralistic and utopian, who denies reality and does not understand that the principle of dialectics is the Hegelian "Versöhnung mit der Wirklichkeit," the reconciliation with reality.

ELC So he is actually criticizing himself.

ML Yes, he is criticizing himself. This is a break with his own past and a unilateral definition of dialectics as being the reconciliation with reality. In reality, dialectics are something else, they are precisely the tension between criticism and reality, between what is and what ought to be. From that moment on, he has found a philosophical legitimacy for his reconciliation with the Stalinist Soviet Union, and he will pursue it in the subsequent years while always retaining a certain autonomy and a certain distance.

ELC With regard to the methodology that he developed in *History and Class Consciousness*, how valid is it still today? Lukács said that even if the details and results of Marx's method were to be rejected, the Marxist scientific, analytical method would continue to retain its validity. This aspect of his theory should interest us today more than ever before.

ML I think that in *History and Class Consciousness* (1923) there are certain methodological, theoretical, and philosophical gains that remain useful today. And his definition of Marxism as being not just an assortment of dogmas and doctrinal systems, but as being first of all a *method*, is an idea which seems altogether profound to me. This is exactly what permits the assurance of the continuity of Marxism beyond the breakdown of a series of political and ideological structures without touching the profound significance of the method. And I think that the way in which he defines his method, with help of the category of totality, historical totality, remains entirely valid as a procedure to follow toward the understanding of how to act. And then, I think that certain of his analyses, such as the one of reification, retain all of their value. So in which ways do I feel we must go beyond Lukács? But that question is not really linked to the present moment. The questions I am asking myself about Lukács and his limitations are not based on glasnost or on the crumbling of the Berlin Wall. For me, the Lukács of *History and Class Consciousness* and the type of institutional Marxism that existed in the USSR and the Eastern countries are two completely different things. So what happens to one bears no consequence for the other. For me there is total contradiction between the Marxist spirit as it manifests itself in *History and Class Consciousness* and this type of mummified system, which was the official Soviet Marxism. There is no connection between the two. So, the fact that one of them has crumbled is great, and I rejoice in it, but that does not affect in any way what could be true or false in *History and Class Consciousness.* So, in my opinion, the question cannot be dealt with on that level. On the other hand, I find that *History and Class Consciousness* is limited in certain ways. For several years, for already ten years, I have been aware of certain limitations: a vision of history that is too linear, a vision of progress as something that is inevitable, a vision that is not critical enough of what I want to call modern civilization. This is where I feel the need not to replace but to *complete* Lukács, because certain things are altogether irreplaceable.

ELC You do not find him critical enough of modern civilization?

ML Yes, of modern civilization, not of bourgeois society, he is critical there, but one must go beyond bourgeois society to criticize aspects of what I call modern civilization, industrial civilization. The Frankfurt School's greatest contribution consists precisely of this: they took Lukács's *History and Class Consciousness* as their point of departure, but then went further by criticizing, in Horkheimer and Adorno's *Dialectics of the Enlightenment*, the instrumental reason and the logic born from modern civilizations and (above all in Walter Benjamin's work) the ideology of progress. There are a number of comments made by the Frankfurt School, and most importantly by Walter Benjamin and Marcuse, that I find extremely important. They consist of a series of critical thought developments inspired by the young Lukács that have been further enriched and given more depth by the Frankfurt School. I find these ideas very important since they allow us to tackle very current questions. I am thinking here mainly of the theme of reification but also of the combination of Marxist-Romantic criticism of capitalist civilizations, and even ecology. Starting with the work of Benjamin, Adorno, and Marcuse, we can confront ecological problems; while starting with Lukács's work, no, this is not possible. So such are the reasons why, in my opinion, we must not reject the enormous intellectual gains that are present in Lukács's work, but we must complete, advance, and enrich them.

ELC Does this affect his methodology as well? Is his historicism dated?

ML Yes and no. Historicism, with regard to its method, which consists of understanding each fact as a historical process and not understanding the economic, cultural, and political problems outside the contradictory movements of history itself, in historicity, is not dated; on the other hand, the concept that history has meaning, that it advances inevitably toward freedom or revolution, that is the part which seems out of date to me.

ELC What about dialectics? Must we maintain and continue them?

ML The dialectical method is absolutely irreplaceable. Only the dialectical method allows us to understand reality as a movement, where nothing is set, a movement founded on contradictions in which one can understand the parts only in their relation to their totality.

ELC You cling to the idea of totality, even though most critics rejected this concept in the sixties.

ML I know, I know; this idea is not in fashion today. Well, I think that part of this critique is interesting. It is true that to approach reality through the fragment, to see everything that is broken in reality through the fragment, to take the fragment as a monad, as a starting point to understand a social and cultural conjuncture, this can also be interesting, but for me these are moments to be integrated into an overall movement, that is to say, we cannot limit ourselves to the fragment. If the fragment is not taken as part of the whole it will inevitably remain sterile.

ELC You are continuing with Marxism?

ML Oh, yes, of course! Oh, yes!

ELC You do not find that it went bankrupt, that it was even affected by the collapse of communism in the East, and by the changes in the social reality and economic systems in the Eastern countries?

ML No! What went bankrupt according to me, was a pseudo-Marxism, an empty shell, an empty bureaucratic shell; there was no authentic Marxism in it. This is what went bankrupt. In my opinion, historically, it has been bankrupt for sixty years. The political system is collapsing now, but humanly, ethically, and philosophically, it has been bankrupt for sixty years at least.

ELC Ethically as well?

ML Yes, yes ethically. Since the establishment of the Stalinist regime, it has been morally finished.

ELC Before coming to France this spring, I reviewed the program of the last MLA convention in December 1990, and I thought that I was detecting a new tendency to replace the term "Marxism" with that of "economism."

ML That [economism] has nothing to do with it [Marxism]! These are people who have not read *History and Class Consciousness*, because the authentic Marxist paradigm is already in there and it is not economist at all. It is true that the dominant model of vulgar Marxism has been economist, but already *History and Class Consciousness* reflected this, and the Frankfurt School, which hails from Marx even if it is a heterodoxical Marxism, has nothing to do with this "economism."

ELC Do you find that the Frankfurt School has maintained more rigorous ethics than other Marxists, as for example Lukács?

ML Yes, yes. I think that one of the great superiorities of the Frankfurt School over Lukács is that they did not accept a reconciliation with Stalinism nor, for that matter, with the capitalist world. They maintained a position of refusal. That is the moral strength of an Adorno or of a Marcuse. Sometimes this refusal could become somewhat abstract and cut off from reality; I am thinking mainly of Adorno's later years when absolute refusal and pure negativity resulted in a meditation over aesthetics, incapable of understanding new political developments such as the student revolt. This is not the case with Marcuse, however. Marcuse is very close to the students' sensitivity and the revolt. But I am speaking of the Frankfurt School as a whole, containing this element of refusal and negativity that gives it a moral superiority, whereas Lukács accepted the party's pillory of discipline and all that it implies.

ELC What is your attitude toward Althusser, and more recently Habermas, the critical structuralism that is not the genetic structuralism of a Goldmann?

ML I have always had a very negative opinion of Althusserism. Althusser as a person was a very honest and upright individual, but his method, in my opinion, was simply the end result of a mechanistic and objectivist vision of Marxism, completely removed from the revolutionary, dialectical sources of Marxism. For me, structuralism is a complete dead end. I have always thought that Marxism would not make any sense if it were not understood as a dialectical, historicist method, and that is precisely what structuralism has rejected. As Althusser rejected historicism and humanism, in my opinion, he also emptied out Marxism of its essential component. There is nothing left but the trace of a sterile skeleton, a kind of metallic structure that does not help the human community to understand or to act in its best interest.

ELC An asignificant structure with regard to humans. And Habermas?

ML Habermas must not be confused or identified with Althusser! I think that Habermas is heir to the Frankfurt School, but at the same time he is somebody who has distanced himself from the spirit of the Frankfurt School. He is heir in the sense that he has maintained an element of criticism of modern civilization, which is very important and the most interesting aspect of his work; but I think that Habermas represents a certain form of regression with regard to the critical theories represented by the Frankfurt School. A regression to the extent that Habermas returns to the rationalism of the Enlightenment, the limits of which had been put into question by Adorno and Horkheimer. His program is simply to fulfill the Enlightenment's promise, whereas the program of the Frankfurt School is much more an autocritique of the Enlightenment. This autocritical dimension is diluted and practically disappears with Habermas; the Habermassian utopia is finally reduced to the idea of an ideal linguistic situation, founded on rational exchange. It omits everything that cannot be rationalized, everything that escapes the traditional rationalist framework. With regard to modernity, Habermas's position is much less critical than that of the Frankfurt School. It is more a restructuring of modern civilization than a critique that is directed toward the very foundations of this civilization, as is the case with Adorno and Benjamin.

ELC Is this where the influence of structuralism comes into play?

ML Structuralism, Parsons's sociology, and liberal thought. As a matter of fact, Lukács will reintegrate into critical thinking a series of elements that are exterior to it and thus produce something that seems to me somewhat eclectic: a kind of eclectic synthesis of critical theory and liberal rationalism. But I do not want to be too negative. I think that there is something authentic in this rationalist utopia which contains all the strengths and weaknesses of the philosophy of the Enlightenment.

ELC You have just spent the past several weeks lecturing in America. What subjects have you discussed? In what domain is your current research situated?

ML It so happens that my current work deals directly with Lukács. I have been working on this research for several years in collaboration with my colleague Robert Sayre, who is also a disciple of Goldmann and Lukács. I have been working with him on research about anti-capitalist romanticism, based on Lukács's work, and we are just in the midst of collaborating on a book that is a kind of general theory of romanticism, a sociology of romantic culture.*

ELC He wrote a book on the nineteenth century . . .

ML The book is called *Solitude in Society: A Sociological Study in French Literature*; it is a Goldmannian analysis of the French novel from the nineteenth and especially the twentieth century. For our current study we began with the Lukácsean concept of "anticapitalist romanticism," but we are going to criticize Lukács in two ways. First of all, this concept appears with the later Lukács, that is to say, starting with 1929–30, and continues through most of his subsequent texts. Anticapitalist romanticism is identified with reaction and reactionary thinking, with counterrevolution, and even with the culture that is preparing the way for fascism. But we are in complete disagreement with this. We consider this to be a false and unilateral conception of romantic culture. What we find interesting in Lukács is the idea that romanticism is in contradiction with capitalism. In fact, Lukács does not talk about romanticism. He uses the adjective "romantic." He speaks of a *romantic anticapitalism*. We have inverted the formula: we have replaced "romantic anticapitalism" with *anticapitalist romanticism*, and we have tried to explain that in its essence romanticism is a weltanschauung, a vision of the world; it is not just a literary school but a much broader phenomenon, since one speaks also of political romanticism and economic romanticism. . . .

ELC There is much talk about romanticism nowadays, right here in Paris. It seems to be in fashion.

ML There is an interest, especially a literary one, I believe. For us, romanticism is a vision of the world that opposes modern industrial and capitalist civilization in the name of certain values of the past, premodern, precapitalist cultural and social values. But that does not necessarily mean that it is a reactionary phenomenon because there also exists a utopian or revolutionary romanticism that does not aim at a *return to the past* but at a *detour leading through the past toward the future*. This starts with Rousseau and continues with Hölderlin, Fourier, Heine, William Morris, the young Lukács, and Bloch. There exists a whole history of this revolutionary romanticism, which is essential to us in order to wipe out this false vision according to which romanticism is synonymous with counterrevolution or reaction. So

*The results of this collaborative research of Michael Löwy and Robert Sayre have since been published as *Révolte et mélancolie: le romantisme à contre-courant de la modernité* (Paris: Payot, 1992).

that is where we categorically dissociate ourselves from Lukács, but we retain the idea that seems justified to us, which is the contradiction between romanticism and capitalism. We also pick up on Lukács's method in the sense that, according to us, one cannot understand romanticism without the category of totality, that is to say, that one must look at it in its historical context with regard to modern capitalist civilization in its entirety, as a reaction. Lukács's category of totality is very helpful to us here, both situating romanticism in a general historical, political, social, and economic context, that of capitalist industrial civilization as it develops since the end of the eighteenth century—the moment of birth of modern industrial capitalism—and trying to show that romanticism is still present today to the extent to which this type of modern bourgeois society continues to exist. The category of totality also helps us see romanticism itself as a *whole*, that is to say, *not* only as a literary school or a political movement, but precisely as something that has a totalizing dimension and a vision of the world that encompasses all cultural domains, be they religion, politics, art, etc. . . .

ELC Provoked by whom or by what?

ML Well, provoked by the crystallization of modern capitalist industrial civilization that first appeared at the end of the eighteenth century. Intellectuals, writers, artists, and, beyond that, other social categories react to this new dominant force by rejecting it in the name of certain values reminiscent of the past. This reaction assumes very different forms. We have proposed a typology that spans from reactionary Restorationist romanticism to utopian revolutionary romanticism. What they have in common is the refusal of quantification, of reification, of life's mechanization, of the disenchantment of the world; it is the totality of these characteristics brought in by the new civilization that is rejected. Romanticism is the cultural form that embodies this anticapitalist resistance inspired by the past—a very often too idealistic vision of the past. So, romanticism is a totality that is present in all spheres of the mind's life. Lukács's method thus serves us enormously, and his concept of romanticism as anticapitalist serves us as well; but we are in total disagreement with Lukács in his concrete analysis of romantic culture as a reactionary, counterrevolutionary, and prefascist culture. It is true that certain currents of romanticism will develop into fascism, and that fascism possesses romantic reactionary components; but this is only one aspect. To reduce romanticism to this single aspect is too narrow, unilateral, and thus false.

ELC You continue to attack capitalism, although it is establishing itself all over the world.

ML For us, that is more of a reason to do so! The more capitalism becomes universal, the only form of economic, social, political, and intellectual reality, the more its critique is necessary and timely.

ELC Do you have many friends and colleagues who share your anti-capitalist, Marxist view?

ML Yes and no. Let us just say that there are Marxists in French academia as there are Marxists everywhere in French society.

ELC Who are the ones who call themselves Marxists today?

ML There are some everywhere: at the university, in the unions, among students and youth.

ELC And yourself?

ML Yes, I consider myself a Marxist. Certainly, I am a heterodox, heretic Marxist, if you wish, but Marxist nevertheless. I think that Marxism needs certain external contributions, like romanticism for example, to enrich itself. Marxism needs to enrich itself continuously. Romanticism has raised certain questions that Marxism had not, so in this respect Marxism must continue to enrich and develop itself. The same goes for utopian socialism, which is very important. I am thinking of Fourier and the contribution of certain anarchists. I believe that the anarchists have understood the dangers of the State better than Marx. There are also the contributions of feminism, which was very little developed by Marx, and of ecology. So, I do not think we find all the answers in Marx. There is much to learn, especially from feminism and ecology.

ELC Do you work in the field of ecology?

ML Not directly. But I try to integrate it into what I am doing now. The aspect of the relationship of Marxism to nature is clearly present in our analysis of romanticism.

ELC It is indeed interesting that the great modern philosophers show hardly any interest in nature. In Sartre there is a total absence of nature, and the same goes for Marx.

ML So there is something new to be considered. Marxism does not make any sense if in its development it does not integrate all of these new questions, like the Frankfurt School was doing in its era by addressing the question of psychoanalysis. It was integrated by Marcuse, for instance, whose strength among other things stems from his articulation of Marxism and psychoanalysis. Thus, Marxism must not be seen as a closed system; that makes no sense. But at the same time there is a central nucleus in Marx, an element in his critical and dialectical method, in his revolutionary vision, which seems essential to me.

ELC Do you think that there is a future for Marxism?

ML I do not know. I cannot foresee the future, and I do not believe in a method that does. In this, I believe, Marxism has often made mistakes;

most Marxist predictions have not come to be. That we are able to predict the future scientifically, to me that is a totally false idea.

ELC Do you accept the idea of "imputed consciousness"?*

ML That I do, yes! I think that the revolutionary consciousness implied by the Marxist project *is* an objective possibility. But whether it is going to realize itself in the future, that I cannot predict. We can only try to bet on this. On this issue I certainly take sides with Goldmann, who stated that we can only put a wager on this subject. According to him, socialism is not a prediction or a certainty, it is a *wager*. So one must put a wager on the possibility of a socialist human community. It is a chance for the future that we cannot scientifically demonstrate, but to which we commit ourselves. So, this is the sense of my activity, a social, political, and cultural commitment stemming from a wager on the future of the human community.

ELC Is it an ethical and moral *engagement* for you, or is it primarily an intellectual interest?

ML For me, these things cannot be separated. Culture, ethics, and politics cannot separate themselves from each other. Everything that I write possesses an ethical, cultural, and political aspect at the same time.

ELC Do you feel rather isolated in this approach and in your point of view today in Paris?

ML At certain times I feel rather isolated. But there are a few friends who share similar ideas.

ELC And how are you received when you travel and give conferences in America?

ML I think that there is more of an interest over there.

ELC Do you speak of Lukács?

ML I speak about Lukács, romanticism, Walter Benjamin, and I am also working on another theme, the theology of liberation. But I am not

*"Imputed consciousness," or in Lukács's original language, "zugerechnetes Bewusstsein," is a term Lukács developed from Marx's famous passage in *The Holy Family*, where Marx discusses the historical destiny of the proletariat. The concept became one of Lukács's principal tools in his critique of society. Contrary to "real" consciousness, which is based on reason and logic but has a more observative function, "imputed consciousness" is seen as an agent of human freedom, a subjective indicator for an objective possibility toward the realization of the Marxist utopia, an anthropomorphic paradise, a classless society. Lucien Goldmann was one of the most fervent believers in the usefulness of the Lukácsean concept and developed it at length in *La Création culturelle dans la société moderne: Pour une sociologie de la totalité* (Paris: Editions Denoël, 1971). As evidenced by his subtitle, Goldmann attached great importance to the notion of *totality*. For all Hegelian Marxists such as Lukács and Goldmann, contrary to structuralist Marxists such as Althusser, the category of totality was crucial to the proper functionality (p. 134) of "imputed consciousness" as a critical instrument. Various critics have debated the claim to its scientificity.

saying that there are no people in France who are interested in these topics.

ELC What is the dominant critical current in France today? There was structuralism, then deconstruction, though Derrida, I believe, had more success in the United States than in France.

ML It is difficult to say. One good thing in France now is that there is no longer a dominant mode. Before, there was a kind of a wave that was submerging everything. Now there is more of a fragmentation of the cultural space that I find much better; that is to say, we see Derrida and his friends, Heideggerians, Marxists, liberals, Habermassians. I do not feel anyone dominating.

ELC Have you taken a position toward postmodern theories?

ML No, frankly, I have not worked much with that. It is very possible that at any given moment I shall work on that, but not at the present.

Translation by Eva L. Corredor with Yaël Fortier.

INTERVIEW WITH JACQUES LEENHARDT

18 May 1991, Paris

ELC In the 1960s and 1970s you dealt extensively with theories inspired by Marx, Goldmann, and Lukács. I therefore would like to ask you a few questions concerning these theories, and in particular Lukács's, to see what, according to you, has become of those theories today. Have Lukács's theories kept their relevance, do they continue to function as a critical instrument, or have they arrived at their end? Have they been wiped out by the reforms of Gorbachev, glasnost, and the collapse of communism in the Eastern and Central European countries? And you yourself, are you continuing to use them?

JL To answer this question, one must distinguish between several levels. The way you ask the question refers first of all to a political situation. You speak of glasnost, the transformation of the Central European and Eastern bloc; these extremely profound transformations concern the political life of Europe and the political life of the world. Personally, I do not believe that the transformations in the Soviet Union and in Eastern Europe had a direct influence on the growing detachment from communist politics and ideology. One could even say that the exact opposite is true. The detachment has grown slowly in Europe since the last war, in a long process that was born with the first signs of contestation before and after the war, much more pronounced after 1956 and the Soviet intervention in Hungary, and then again in 1968 and the intervention in Czechoslovakia, and again as a consequence of the rise of the Solidarity movement in Poland, which was a social movement with a strong religious component in opposition to the communist regime.

In short, I do not believe that one must focus one's attention on the most recent events in the Soviet Union in order to explain the gradual decline of the symbolic power of Marxism and communism. Moreover, one must make clear distinctions in the intellectual life of Europe between Marxism and communism and pay close attention to national characteristics, which in Italy or in France have led to very different intellectual developments from the ones in England or in Germany.

In the sixties, no doubt, there was in France a kind of revival of philosophical Marxism. This was a theoretical Marxism that subsequently gained some momentum around Louis Althusser and a group from the Ecole Normale. This renewed interest prompted a rereading of Marxism, which became very important within the framework of developing structuralist thought, but, I should like to stress, only within that framework. And we have seen its contents lose steam on their own at the same time as the structuralist movement was losing steam. It was thus a relatively circumstantial phenomenon, more philosophical than social and political in nature, important in the mid-sixties and at the beginning of the seventies, but that came apart rapidly thereafter.

ELC You see the revival of philosophical Marxism closely linked to structuralism. I don't see it that way. In the United States, for instance, Fredric Jameson was strongly critical of structuralism.

JL I believe that one must make a fairly clear distinction between what is happening in the United States and what is happening in Europe, in particular as far as the discussion around Marxism is concerned. In France, all intellectual movements developed on the basis of the existence, after World War II, of a very strong Communist Party, of a very broad allegiance of the intellectuals to the hope provided by communism and Marxism—the two being at that time largely interchangeable. Practically the whole intellectual world was intellectually and symbolically linked to the French Communist Party. It is this very strong symbolic presence, which owed much to the price the communists had to pay during the Resistance against Vichy and against Germany, that disintegrates little by little in the course of the fifties, sixties, and seventies. Consequently, the difference toward Marxist thought in France and in the United States is fundamental. In the United States, quite the contrary is true: the liberal intellectual movement had to establish itself on the memory of the McCarthy era and a witch hunt, in a climate that was quite different from the one in which the French intellectuals of that period basked. Therefore, one cannot interpret the Marxist "revival" in the United States within the same intellectual context as in France.

ELC But in the sixties and seventies—for example, in 1968—there is in France as well as in the United States a Marxist "revival" that dominates the revolutionary events.

JL No, I do not think at all that one can say that the social movements of 1968 were of Marxist inspiration. To begin with, the Communist Party—insofar as the Communist Party represents a Marxist position, and I would say it does not—was completely opposed to the 1968 movement. At best, it followed it belatedly, after a fashion, since there was an extremely strong social movement. The party was not a leader at all; it tried to catch up with the movement. That's all one can say about it.

The 1968 movement was fundamentally linked to certain crisis points in French society, which Marxism had enormous difficulties even noticing. French society remained quite traditional till the end of the fifties and the beginning of the sixties, because it had been predominantly agricultural for a fairly long time. Its traditional capitalism built on small family enterprises had trouble modernizing itself, particularly since France continued to wage colonial wars. As a consequence, France had to reinvest in an obsolete industrial apparatus owned by a ruling class that was both showing its age and was used to the captive market of the colonies. It is against this aging and this traditionalism that the new generations revolt, at a time when the colonial wars are over and when France has entered a period of rapid economic growth. It is within this context that something like an upheaval, a social trauma, occurs that escapes the mastery of traditional ideologies, including Marxism. Althusser's Marxist structuralism constitutes neither an explanation, nor a point of departure, nor a driving force of this movement.

ELC It was a movement against de Gaulle.

JL In a certain way against de Gaulle, no doubt, inasmuch as de Gaulle represented a great tradition, *the* tradition, but the foe was less the person of de Gaulle than a world that was outdated, a world that had come to an end.

ELC Are there still Marxists in France today?

JL Today, it seems to me, there are very few people who call themselves Marxists, for various reasons. One of these reasons is that a certain number of the fundamental teachings of Marxism, as an analytical method (here it is really necessary to distinguish between Marxism and communism), have been scattered everywhere and picked up even by declared anti-Marxists. On the other hand, a certain number of *political* concepts, as, for instance, the concept of class struggle, today appear outdated and in need of reformulation. Class struggle is no longer fashionable, if I may say so, which means that one tends to represent conflicts and struggles intellectually in a less antagonistic and less warlike manner than is suggested by revolutionary language. We believe today that oppositions should be settled through negotiations rather than direct confrontation. All this is obviously linked to forsaking the idea that there could be an alternative social and political system to capitalism.

ELC All this is less revolutionary, less extreme than it was in the sixties.

JL This is no doubt a less revolutionary vision. There is in France today a very obvious decrease of the utopian spirit, maybe temporarily, but that is not certain. New modes of dealing with the social and the symbolic spheres are establishing themselves and they do not favor revolutionary visions and global solutions. This is apparent in the worlds of both the workers and the intellectuals.

ELC Even in Mitterrand's politics?

JL Quite obviously in the politics of the politicians since, as far as they are concerned, they only reflect what is happening in society.

ELC Okay, but let's take a look at what moves the intellectual world and critical methodology today. Structuralism is more or less a thing of the past. Deconstruction has never occupied as much space in France as it has in the United States. What is happening to Marxist methodology? Has it been replaced? Is it still practiced today?

JL I would say that we live in an era that is quite difficult to characterize since, precisely, there are no more great, dominant currents. That is, we no longer have, as we did in the sixties and seventies, theoretical battalions offering a global vision. Marxism and other perspectives— from psychoanalysis to ideological or sociological analysis—find their most basic concepts put into question without any reassurance that rethinking these concepts would resolve a dilemma. This development renders the description of the intellectual situation extremely difficult if one wishes to continue thinking in terms of dominant currents.

ELC While visiting several bookstores in Paris, I observed what seemed like a certain revival of psychoanalytical interest. There are lots of books by Lacan in the windows.

JL If psychoanalysis, together with Marxism, was one of the dominant discourses in the sixties and seventies, I would not say that it still is today. It is *one* of the discourses, subject, as are all others, to conceptual revisions. It fell back upon therapeutic practice but in so doing is now discovering new convergences with disciplines such as ethology, sociology, anthropology.

ELC If we could come back to Lukács, I should like to ask a question of detail. Let us take, for instance, Lukács's theory of the novel or his theory of the historical novel. Have these theories maintained their relevance? Are there scholars today who continue to use them, appreciate them?

JL It is necessary to point out that Lukács has never been a dominant figure in France.

ELC He has nevertheless exerted a fair amount of influence on the French intellectual scene through Goldmann and, I would say, even through you, Michael Löwy, Nicolas Tertulian, and a few others.

JL I do not speak of the work of a few individuals. In the French intellectual debate Lukács has never played the role of a necessary point of reference. On the other hand, he has indeed had a substantial spokesman, Lucien Goldmann, who provided a reading of his work. This was already—and it is necessary to underline this—a *reading* of Lukács that, in itself, yes, constituted for some years an important point of reference. Thus, it is more the Goldmannian version of Lukács than Lukács himself that has had a fundamental influence in France. For instance, it is only fair to admit that Lukács's *Aesthetics*, in spite of Nicolas Tertulian's important book, has never been seriously discussed in France.

ELC I would not say "never." There have been conferences. You yourself organized an international conference in Paris on the work of Goldmann where there was much discussion of Lukács. There was an important and well-attended conference at Cerisy-la-Salle. . . .

JL No, no. Let's make sure that we understand each other correctly. When I say "never discussed," that does not mean that there have not been a hundred people who were seriously interested in Lukács.

ELC There have been numerous translations of his work.

JL His work has been widely translated. It is well known. But there have not been many Ph.D. dissertations, there has been little secondary literature, that is, there have been few books devoted to Lukács published in France. And when I say that he was not part of the discussion, I mean to say that there have not been any of those great debates that extend across the whole French cultural scene, in which one necessarily had to refer to Lukács. On certain points, surely, but that has remained, one must admit, limited to rather spotty discussions. *The Historical Novel* has been read by a few thousand people, but I cannot say that there has really been a large debate, as Adorno was the object of a debate, or as Habermas today is the object of a debate.

ELC Habermas, one could say, has been rather strongly influenced by Lukács.

JL Certainly, many people have been influenced by Lukács, but there exist several Lukácses, fragmented by the moments at which he was read: he was read within the anti-irrationalist debate; he was discussed in the perspective of the debate on socialist realism; he was discussed with reference to *The Theory of the Novel*, more particularly through the reading Goldmann provided of it and which I myself have often discussed. I am forgetting, of course, the polemics with Sartre on existentialism. Finally, there was Goldmann's book on *Lukács and Heidegger*, certain elements of which may have been taken up in the debate on Heidegger.

ELC Does Lukács have an importance today? You yourself, do you in your present scholarship refer to the work of Lukács?

JL I have read him widely, continue to read him, and, even though I do not quote him very often, he has certainly had great importance for me. I claim several paternities: Goldmann, of course, Lukács, Bakhtin, but also the theoreticians of aesthetics, philosophers such as Ricoeur or Deleuze, certain elements that derive from the German tradition, be it Adorno, Köhler, Jauss, or Habermas. All of this, then, constitutes a fairly complex patchwork that allows me to carry out my work as I please, of course. I think one has to note as well that, for my generation, the great philosophico-sociological tradition has been completed—I do not say contradicted, but completed—by everything that has been elaborated in the universe of semiotics, in discourse analysis, in the more precise definition of what a literary and argumentative text is in its procedures and in its forms. There is now a difference of perspective, which means that starting with Bakhtin, Barthes, Foucault, and all of French semiotics, one has noted a renewal and a relative displacement of certain questions that—in my case, at least—have never resulted in an abandonment of the great philosophico-sociological questions: they appear reexamined by way of a more precise analysis of the functioning of the textual object, the literary object, and the genres in the cultural universe altogether.

ELC When Goldmann died, in 1970, there were rumors that he had possibly committed suicide because, the rumors went, he had realized that his theories had failed.

JL That's an absolute idiocy and requires a poor knowledge of Goldmann, who knew happiness only when engaged in polemics and the task of having to convince.

ELC Are there people today who say that Lukács's theories have failed? That Lukács was completely mistaken? That his theories have no validity or that they are outdated? To what extent are Lukács and his theories rejected today, if they are?

JL I like the way you ask the question because it reflects a point of view, which to me appears completely wrong, namely, that theories would have or ought to have eternal validity. I believe that theories function, that they are a way of synthesizing, rendering coherent a perspective one adopts at a given moment, in a given historical, literary, philosophical, or political context. Consequently, to say that Lukács is not valid simply means positioning oneself in 1991 in a relation to texts that had been written in 1910, in 1914, in 1923, or in 1960. Philosophy and theoretical discourse, within the realm of the human sciences, are always discourses that fulfill a function in relation to the moment they are produced. I therefore absolutely refuse to proceed to a kind of ahistorical, atemporal devaluation of these theories. To say that Lukács was wrong is, necessarily, either stating that he was wrong in relation to us, today, and that is therefore, to a large extent, a stupidity; or it means inducing a historical analysis of the context and pretending that, in that context, his theory was absurd. This would require a completely different type of analysis; but I hasten to say that the echo produced, for instance by *The Theory of the Novel*, at its time and since, demonstrates in itself that it was replete with pertinent significance. I believe that *The Theory of the Novel* corresponds in an extremely fine and rich, lucid, and interesting manner to a moment in the evolution not only of literary production but of the more general questioning of values in Western society. It constitutes a brilliant way of summing up numerous debates of the nineteenth century and questions asked at the beginning of the twentieth century. Lukács, at that moment, maybe did not have the most "modernist eye," maybe he did not know, as other theoreticians did, how to wager on the future of literature. To make up for it, he made political wagers; he wagered on things that made a lot of sense at the time, and, as far as I am concerned, it is in that light that I want to evaluate him. As such, his theory remains interesting because it provides a perspective, even if it is not *the* eternal perspective.

ELC In fact, I am asking the question mainly with respect to methodology since a few years ago in the United States we experienced a revival of interest in historicism. It became known as the New Historicism. The New Historicists, naturally, claimed to have renewed the historical method of analysis. In Lukács's *History and Class Consciousness* we find the statement that even if the results obtained through Marxist analysis are no longer valid, the Marxist historicist methodology will always retain its value and usefulness.

JL I think it is tragic that certain periods tend to forget that the historical dimension is a fundamental dimension of all human and cultural processes. During the structuralist phase, we noted the bracketing of this historical dimension; this bracketing often appeared as absolute blindness. On the other hand, we have to admit that the structuralist period, maybe precisely because it built its foundation on the forgetting of history, allowed us to enter much more profoundly into the analysis of the very functioning of texts.

Today we therefore have to take up again—or continue, since I personally have never abandoned the historical perspective—the analysis of the production of social, literary, or artistic forms. However, we need to be aware that these forms themselves, inasmuch as they seem from a certain point of view linked to specific conjunctures, can and must also be read sub specie aeternitatis. By eternity I mean here at the same time the basic structures of social communication, the "traditional" forms of art or literature, and the "mental structures" to which Goldmann, following Piaget, attributed not only a precise social function, but a more profound anthropological grounding. As far as I am concerned, without being eclectic, I am in favor of an articulation of the discourse—which constitutes the true challenge for theory today—that would take into consideration at the same time the very long anthropological period, the long historical and sociological period *and* formal specificity. The challenge is not in the choice between history and structure. It is necessary, as Goldmann used to say—and in this I remain completely Goldmannian—to be a "genetic structuralist," which means study the structures but also observe how these structures are the result of sometimes very long, sometimes very short processes.

ELC I am glad you commented on this because I noticed this approach in all your works and in particular in *Lire la lecture* (Read the Reading). You summarized the principles of this methodology in *Pour une sociologie de la lecture* (Toward a Sociology of Reading),* where you outlined again the comparative study you completed with your Hungarian colleague, Pierre Józsa. Rather than analyze the text, you used sociocritical methodology to analyze the reader. Does your present work proceed in the same direction?

JL I should like to respond on two levels. First, as to my theoretical position, the preoccupation with the reader, with what occurs in the act of reading, is part of my general position toward literature. I believe that a vision, let's say a structuralist-genetic vision—that is, a historical and textual one—must necessarily take interest, as I did for instance in *Lecture politique du roman* (A Political Reading of the Novel),** in the conditions that produced the text and in the form of the text, but also— and this is the topic of several studies published since then—in the ways in which the text is perceived and understood by those who read it. I think we have to admit to ourselves that, if there is literature, this is not only because there are writers to write it, but it is because there is a general function of literature in society, a function to produce the objects of our imagination. In democratic societies in particular, in which the social link is constantly threatened by the power that each single individual possesses, creative fiction and its reading fulfill no doubt a

*Jacques Leenhardt and Pierre Józsa, *Lire la lecture: Essai de sociologie de la lecture* (Paris: Le Sycomore, 1982); Leenhardt, "Les effets esthétiques de l'oeuvre littéraire: Un problème sociologique," *Pour une sociologie de la lecture: Lectures et lecteurs dans la France Contemporaine* (Paris: Editions du Cercle de la Librairie, 1989).

**Jacques Leenhardt, *Lecture politique du roman: "La Jalousie" d'Alain Robbe-Grillet* (Paris: Les Editions de Minuit, 1973).

function of orientation for the reading individuals. Those individuals, beyond the entertainment and through it—because reading is a play with the imaginary—look in their reading for models of relationships with oneself and with others, for exemplary figures of the construction of the social link. This construction takes place, naturally, first of all in the family and in real social relationships, but it also occurs through the reading of the experiences of others by the intermediary of the whole process of knowledge and identification that accompany the act of reading. I therefore believe that in a study of literature one has nothing to gain from omitting a reflection that takes into consideration the totality of the process, from production to reading, while passing through the text. That is my theoretical point.

Now I am responding to the second half of your question concerning the orientation of my research at the present moment. Yes, I continue my research on reading. I have recently, in collaboration with Martine Burgos, at the request of the Council of Europe, conducted an investigation on reading in three European countries (Germany, Spain, France), using the methodology close to the one I had used with Hungary and Peter Józsa in the book *Lire la lecture*, which you mentioned. The question was to understand how the same text, whatever the coherence of its literary structure, whatever the coherence of its field of reference, and whatever the coherence of its set of values, becomes transformed by the act of reading, especially when this act unfolds in different historical, cultural, or social contexts. In the background of these investigations there is obviously a more general questioning that could be very roughly stated as: why is there literature? why have our democratic societies developed in particular a genre called the novel? and what is the role of this genre in the establishment of our democratic societies?

ELC You should reread Lukács. He will provide you with answers to many of your questions. Why and how does the novel develop from the epic? Why have people started to philosophize? and so on.

JL I find *some* answers in Lukács. I find there an incentive to do research, but I must nevertheless admit that the answers Lukács proposes remain very general and philosophical, and that his analysis of the novel as a form, contrary to the hypotheses advanced by Bakhtin, seems, according to me, to rely excessively on the governing concept of a former ideal society that has been degraded. I, on my part, do not believe we should think in terms of degradation of former models. The way I see it, society establishes, at each moment of its history, the conditions of its survival and its transformation. You may tell me that in Lukács, too, we find a prospective vision of society, particularly in

History and Class Consciousness. You will note, however, that in his theory of the novel, the retrospective vision prevails and that, moreover, Lukács himself is critical of it in his later work. I would nevertheless fully agree with you that these are questions that have not escaped Lukács's attention, although he has not truly examined them as such. When I use the word "truly," I want to stress that in a study of reading it is necessary to conduct empirical research, otherwise one runs the great risk of jilting the literary values we have been taught at school. That's what distinguishes me from the school in Constance that carries out a very interesting theoretical work on the position of the reader in the text but invents its own reader. I, on my part, try to do my work on real readers, to whom I propose a text, which they read, and it is them that I later question in order to learn what happened in their reading.

ELC I am again coming back to one of my principal questions: in this new research that you are conducting, you do not in any way identify with Marxism?

JL Look at my publications since the 1960s. You will, from time to time, find a quotation of Marx, but you will never catch me—including the sixties, although that was very fashionable at that time—referring to Marxism as such. I think that the Marxism of Marx has been profoundly integrated into the various sociological conceptualizations. His influence is therefore considerable. On the theoretical level, I don't think I want to single him out as such, not any more than Weberism or Durkheimism. It seems to me that we still need to think today—and I even believe that this is urgent—without falling back on theoretical bodies, fundamental as they might be—which had social and cultural objects and intentions toward these objects that can no longer appear to us under the same features.

ELC Does Marxism exist in France today?

JL There is talk about a return to Marxism in the near future? How fortunate! I myself have neither exalted nor condemned Marxism. The reading of Marx remains one of the most stimulating for the mind engaged in critical analysis. I believe that Marxism represents a fundamental moment in the conceptualization of society, the establishment of society in the nineteenth century. We witness at that time the breaking up of a social order that was governed by what is called the ancien régime. It was necessary to reconstruct a social order, that is, rebuild in a clear and coherent manner the elements of society. In the course of the eighteenth and the nineteenth centuries, society experiences fundamental transformations—industrialization, urbanization—which tear the population away from its traditional environment, its traditional beliefs, and exploit it in an absolute manner. This brings about great confusion, great disorganization within society. Thinkers, philosophers, and politicians throughout the eighteenth and nineteenth centuries reflect upon these questions, starting with Montesquieu and Rousseau. Then come Saint-Simon and Fourier, Comte and sociology. Marx takes his place within this stream of thought, which will be overdetermined by his vast knowledge of the social and economic development of England at the time of the Industrial Revolution. Marxism, as a discourse about society, aims at reorganizing society according to a logic that takes into consideration the conflict between classes, seen as a conflict of interests and a conflict with regard to functions in production. There have been other ways of conceiving its reorganization: Durkheimism, that will appear soon thereafter, or Weberism. These two systems will establish themselves in different contexts and, above all, will concentrate on relationships other than the conflict between classes. The reason for this may be that they minimized the class conflict or that it did not appear to them telling enough to provide a global explanation and, above all, a point of departure for a reorganization. One must insist on the fact that they all were searching for a determining social causality, a determination at the highest level of the social system in its entirety. I believe that that period has reached its closure, at least epistemologically, and that in that respect, Marxism has aged as have the other systems. In that sense your questioning, which leans on the transformations that have been shaking the Soviet bloc, is pertinent. Everybody today is aware of the necessity to "think" society—if it is still appropriate to use the singular within the planetary and communal social space in which we live—according to new organizational modalities. We therefore have to find, to invent concepts and an epistemology that conform to the contemporary experience of the social. But I myself would not say, as does Baudrillard, that the social is dead. It has changed and is changing because we never cease transforming it.

ELC So what happened to the scientificity of the Marxist method? Goldmann used to insist on the scientificity of his Marxist methodology, particularly with reference to the concept of "imputed consciousness."

JL Not really that much happened, after all. Goldmann sought to affirm a rigor but not a scientificity. That's a discourse you find rather in Althusser. Goldmann claimed at one point to have accounted correctly for 90 percent of the texts he had analyzed, but as the Marxism after Marx is concerned, he always stressed that it had swayed between a determinist (Engels) and a dialectic position. Since he felt he belonged to the latter, he would indeed judge it more "scientific," that is, more apt to account for the human reality. There is no doubt a metaphoric aspect to the use of the word scientific that goes back to the age-old debate over the nature of "truth" in the human sciences and the "exact" sciences. I believe it is preferable to speak of analytic rigor rather than science, since there is necessarily, when one uses the word science, a confusion—which some entertain with a certain complacency—with the natural sciences. These are nomothetic sciences, that is, sciences that produce laws. I do not believe that there are permanent laws of society. The ways in which societies function force us continuously to redefine the parameters and the very concepts used in sociological inquiry. That is the reason why, as far as I am concerned, I use very sparingly—in fact not at all—the notion of scientificity in the human sciences. They are called "human sciences"; it is only proper to insist more on the word human than on the word sciences.

ELC In browsing through the most recent program of the MLA convention I found a rather curious thing: people who formerly would speak of "Marxism" seem to have replaced the term, while speaking within the same context, with "economism." Have you noticed a similar practice in the current critical discourse in France?

JL No. I do not find this tendency in the theoretical discourse of the social sciences in France. Economism is a way of presenting the elements used for social interpretation in a hierarchical fashion that gives priority to economy. One can thus rightfully accuse our politics of being tendentious toward economy. All those who have governed us, including the socialists, have given in to this tendency. Marxism itself can be perceived as an economism when it asserts the extreme deterministic power of the economy. In that respect, indeed, it appears as a partner of economic liberalism. They are partners in sharing the idea that human behavior is determined by the stakes of economic interest. This constitutes the foundation of a general consensus on the stakes, on the basis of which liberalism and Marxism can become opponents with regard to methods and distributions. But we must point out as well that there is a strong critical tendency in Marx against this consensual basis. It can thus ignite the revolutionary spirit, which always rises again and often in contradiction to the realistic handling of the class struggle, in particular in the case of political parties that originate from Marxism.

As to the political and social debate in France, I would say that, on the contrary, in the face of the economism which presupposes the almightiness of economic reasoning—which certain people believe governs all the problems of society—there has been developing a countertheory that insists heavily on human relations, on personal development, on job satisfaction, on the necessity of having an alternative form of management in the business place that is not strictly linked to the demands of capitalist gain, etc. The difficulty faced by those who govern today is to find a balance between the law of the international market, which functions according to the principles of economism, and the legitimate demands of the citizen for personal living space and a certain guaranty at work (job security and retirement), which are "goods" that have traditionally been important to French society. The difficulty arises from the fact that in a certain manner these demands are inconsistent with the working rules of mighty international capitalism. There is for us Frenchmen or for us Europeans a contradiction between the acknowledgment, presently unavoidable, of the laws of this international capitalism and the preservation of that which is our specificity as a "*culture* of society." By this I call attention to the concern for social protection, to the job satisfaction of the individual, the harmonious development of the individual in society. All these elements of our culture of society find themselves largely in contradiction with a pure economism, inasmuch as that is a general theory about the running of society by the laws of economy.

ELC Well, what you say is reassuring. When I read the term economism in relation to literature, I immediately associated it with postmodernism. In recent years we have talked a great deal about postmodernism in the United States. You no doubt have done so as well, encouraged by the theories of Lyotard. According to one of Fredric Jameson's characterizations, postmodernism signifies an economic and philosophical tendency that concerns itself only with what "works best" at the moment. This means that a certain kind of generalized capitalism has been invading even the spiritual domain. The term economism in my mind thus conjures up the vision of a postmodern and certainly post-Marxist economy, which in its course worries little about authentic human needs and justifications and worries even less about ethical principles. To see the term economism appear at the MLA sessions, therefore, seemed rather disquieting.

JL Economism, indeed, implies the absence of any ethical preoccupation. About this I would say that in French society as I see it today and in the ongoing intellectual debate, all ethical considerations, to the contrary, seem extremely important. Moreover, there is in this debate a rather painful paradox, since Marxism had a fundamentally ethical dimension. As it turned out, the mishaps of history caused Marxism to suffer tragic deviations that occurred particularly in the countries under the sway of the communist regime. In the process we have lost the trace of what in Marx certainly had an ethical intention. Therefore, there is a certain paradox in the fact that the return of preoccupations with ethics, which had been promulgated by a movement that was quite heavily liberal (in the meaning that this word has in France and designates, contrary to its meaning in the United States, a rather right-wing idea) in the 1980s, developed essentially in opposition to Marxism.

ELC Would that be because of the fact that you have a socialist government? The situation you describe seems more apparent in France, seems to characterize France and possibly Germany more than the United States.

JL I don't think so, or then only partially. The rise of consciousness movements that could be characterized as ethical is a fundamental indicator of a political crisis. According to left thinking, politics is supposed to assume responsibility for many aspects of social life including happiness, to a certain extent. Again very generally, one could say that, on the contrary, a right-wing idea of government clearly separates public responsibilities (state administration, defense, law and order, etc.) from those of private life. We know from experience that such distinctions are very artificial; the domains of economy and education, not to speak of culture, could more or less enter the orbit of prerogatives the government claims for itself or that it is expected to claim for itself, even according to right-wing interpretations.

In the case of France, that's what is happening, since a large part of our right is at the same time liberal and Jacobin! On the other hand, it is certain that the socialist government—with respect to the reform of the law, to labor legislation, or to unemployment—was moved by "social" preoccupations that the right would not have acknowledged. Generally speaking I would say, therefore, that the left has a tendency to integrate ethics into politics, whereas the right leaves the responsibility for any commitment up to the private person. The political crisis has logically relaunched the debate on ethics.

ELC To come back to literature. Does this preoccupation with ethics appear in literature and literary analysis? For instance, is it noticeable in the dissertations that are being written, in publications, in novels?

JL Unfortunately, I cannot speak of the dissertations since I have no overview of what is being done today, but it is certain that problems such as genetic manipulation, discussions about the right to life, the right to housing, the right to the city, the problem of the suburbs, are political problems that are being recycled today under the name "ethics." But we also experience the reverse, such as the integration of the problem of the suburbs into politics; for six months now we have had a Secretary of the City (*un ministre de la Ville*), which is certainly a sign.

ELC A Secretary of the City of Paris?

JL No, a Secretary of the City—city being conceived as a social and cultural phenomenon that is specific to our contemporary civilization and that causes particular problems as a result of the fact that the suburbs have become poles of concentration for underprivileged populations. At first, the question was financial. People with the lowest income would go far from the urban centers to seek inexpensive housing. Then followed problems and politics of segregation, which affected primarily the immigrant population. Finally, we were running the risk of constituting ghettos. This provides a good example of the overlapping between politics and ethics. The exclusion, which has an economic origin, quickly turns into a fear of others, as well as among members of the same community, and finally it becomes racism. Today we speak of a right to the city, a right to urbanity as a right of the citizen. Yet, in the suburbs, not everyone benefits from this right.

ELC There you spoke as a sociologist rather than a humanist (*un homme de lettres*).

JL No, I speak as a citizen. This is the discourse of a citizen. One cannot speak of ethics as a specialist of literature; it makes no sense. Ethics touches all phenomena; it is, or should be—as I said before—the foundation of political thought instead of it being, as is often the case, the result of bad politics that make ethical questions emerge, as if there was a division of labor between the administrators of society and the "beautiful souls" (*les belles âmes*) who must not forget humanity.

ELC Okay. In order to reach some kind of a conclusion, if you allow me, I should like to summarize some of the impressions I received from the discussion we have just had. I think France is always less extreme, more restrained, more classical than the United States. For me, that is an established fact. Today, I came to ask you questions about Lukács, Marxism, the ethical and critical discourse in the aftermath of what happened in the East: Gorbachev's glasnost, the opening up of the East and Central Europe, the disintegration of communism, the bankruptcy, one could say, of the whole ideology that had served as a foundation to most of Lukács's mature works. From what you are telling me, there has been no rupture, there has practically not been any upheaval or even a significant intellectual response to this revolutionary political and social development. From what I understand, the event has in no way affected the critical and literary discourse, even less, one would say, than in the United States.

JL I cannot evaluate very well what happened in the United States, but I would certainly not speak, as far as France is concerned, of a revolution that could be linked to glasnost and perestroika. There have been revolutions in Central Europe, obviously. . . .

ELC This may be due precisely to the fact that today, in 1991, you already live in a socialist system, a softened communism. Your system corresponds ideologically a bit to the one that presently exists in the newly opened-up Eastern countries: a socialism fascinated by the advantages of a capitalism we have in the United States but that has not yet fully embraced capitalist practice. The difference between France and the newly democratized countries, obviously, is less extreme than with the United States, and this may be the reason why in France there have been fewer repercussions on the intellectual level and no major efforts to reject or even a need to reevaluate Marxist theories and consequently also those of Lukács.

JL I should like to point out that in France, including under the current "socialist" governments, we do not live at all in a system that one could, even slightly, compare to the former communist regimes in Eastern Europe. Our economic system is a capitalism just as it is in the United States. On the other hand, our social practice, similar to the one of many European countries, has assimilated into our political conscience a certain number of teachings derived from the social struggles in the last century. Should one say that we live in a social democracy? Maybe. Furthermore—and that is a specific feature of France—we have a tradition that we call "republican," to which is linked the idea of nation, and which defines the status of the citizen, his rights as well as the obligations of the State with regard to the equality of citizens. More particularly, that's the foundation of our idea of a secular republic which has had difficulties in establishing itself at the end of a battle that went from the French Revolution to the law of separation between Church and State (1905).

ELC The question, "What will happen after glasnost?" is not being asked in France?

JL The question is being asked by the whole world, of which it changes the former equilibrium, and by Europe, in an extremely dramatic fashion. But in France it has had only indirect effects. On the totality of the intellectual, philosophical, and political discussion in France, in my view, glasnost has had no fundamental impact. On the other hand, what does have an impact on cultural life is the fact that with the opening of the East, intellectual exchanges have resumed with Central European countries and the former Soviet Union. That's indeed what has allowed the development of a most important discussion with respect to the identity of Europe and the political and economic structure of Europe. In this, there are altogether fundamental questions concerning international politics that provide food for part of the political and cultural discussion for today and for tomorrow.

Translation by Eva L. Corredor

INTERVIEW WITH PETER BÜRGER

27 December 1991, Bremen

ELC You have dealt extensively with György Lukács's work, so I should like to ask you how you first came upon it, what impressed you most about Lukács's work and maybe about him, which works you read first, and how they may have influenced your own views.

PB When I studied in the fifties, nobody talked about Lukács, Benjamin, or Adorno. All these were just names, without any precise ideas attached to them.

ELC Did you study in France?

PB No, I studied in Hamburg and in Munich. During that time I did read Lukács's essay on the essay,* but it was horribly difficult for me, and I must say I did not get a full understanding of the text. We were only trained in analyzing texts, without a theoretical bias. The "immanente Literaturwissenschaft" was a kind of adaptation of New Criticism. Later, in the 1960s, "la Nouvelle Critique" (Goldmann, Barthes, Poulet), on the one hand, and Lukács and the authors of the Frankfurt School, on the other, opened up our narrow views. But interpretation remained a key practice for me.

ELC Once you began to read Lukács, what did you like about him? Was there anything that impressed you immediately or was he just difficult, obscure, and therefore a challenge?

PB I think what was immediately interesting in his approach was the relationship he established between literature and society. The other focus of interest was the concept of reification in *History and Class Consciousness.*** The chapter on reification also had an enormous impact on the Frankfurt School, although it is not often quoted by Horkheimer and Adorno. Today we know that it is this book which showed the young intellectuals of the twenties how to read Hegel in a leftist perspective.

ELC What is so interesting about *History and Class Consciousness* is that it does not speak of literature at all but has at the same time had

---

*Georg von Lukács, "Über Wesen und Form des Essays: Ein Brief an Leo Popper," *Die Seele und die Formen: Essays* (Berlin: Egon Fleischel, 1911). In English: Georg Lukács, *Soul and Form: Essays*, trans. Anna Bostock (Cambridge, Mass.: MIT Press, 1974).

**Georg Lukács, *Geschichte und Klassenbewusstsein* (Berlin: Malik Verlag, 1923). In English: Georg Lukács, *History and Class Consciousness: Studies in Marxist Dialectics*, trans. Rodney Livingstone (Cambridge, Mass.: MIT Press, 1968).

such an impact on literary analysis. Goldmann's theories are based on this book.

PB On this, and the essay on the metaphysics of tragedy in *Soul and Form*.

ELC Goldmann, in establishing his own Marxist theories, goes back to Lukács's early works but does not want to see the later Marxist ones.

PB It is the same thing for Adorno. It is *History and Class Consciousness* and the younger Lukács, but not the Lukács of the 1930s, that interest him.

ELC It is significant to see how different critics privilege one or the other Lukács, and how the Marxists often prefer the early, pre-Marxist works, while anti-Marxists find value in Lukács's later, Stalinist essays on realism and the historical novel. Of your works that take inspiration from Lukács, I have read mostly *Theory of the Avant-Garde* (Minneapolis: University of Minnesota Press, 1984) and *Prosa der Moderne* (Frankfurt: Suhrkamp, 1988). Has the latter been translated into English?

PB For the moment, there is no translation of *Prosa der Moderne*, but Polity Press just edited a book with essays on the sociology of literature under the title *The Decline of Modernism* (1992), and the University of Nebraska Press another one, *The Institutions of Art* (1992), which includes essays by Christa Bürger as well. With the *Theory of the Avant-Garde*, you now have a lot of Bürger in English translation.

ELC In reading your works that were available to me before the time of this interview, I found Lukács in them all, but at the same time also a confrontation with him. *Theory of the Avant-Garde* actually provoked me more, if I may say so, than *Prosa der Moderne*, maybe because by the time I read the second work I was more used to your thinking. You analyze modernist fiction, its form and function, and most of the time you posit your views between those of Lukács and Adorno.

PB Yes, in the *Theory of the Avant-Garde*.

ELC Do you think that your views had changed by the time you published *Prosa der Moderne*?

PB I think it is another way of approaching problems. The *Theory of the Avant-Garde* is a theoretical book. It proposes a theoretical frame for the study of avant-garde movements and emphasizes the importance of these movements for the history of art in bourgeois society. Critics often misunderstood this and regretted the lack of detailed analyses which I had done in a previous book on surrealism. *Prosa der Moderne* is quite different. Here I try to combine text analyses and aesthetic reflections. The theoretical grip is less rigorous; it grasps some of the results of the analyses, but not all of them. There are fragments of theory, but no totalizing view. My leading question in this book was whether the discourse on postmodernism affected our comprehension of modernism. So I went back to the canonized works of Baudelaire, Joyce, Kafka, and Beckett. But starting with Baudelaire, I was forced to go back to Heine (who is not a modern author for Adorno), and from Heine to the early romanticism of Friedrich Schlegel, where you find the concept of destabilized subjectivity, which seems postmodern today.

ELC The question is where to start. There are so many beginnings of modernism. The various theoreticians pick it up at different times, as you mentioned in your book. So you begin with romanticism?

PB It was not my idea to have romanticism as my starting point, but in a certain sense I was forced into this position. In the debate on postmodernism you have three possibilities. You can take the position of Adorno and stick to a narrow definition of modernism. Or you can abandon it totally and say "modernism is finished, anything goes." Or you can start from the assumption that, if there is this discussion about postmodernism, it might have happened because we have, or because we have had, this too narrow idea of modernism. In other words, I felt a certain drive to see whether it was possible to find a larger notion of modernism, englobing not only traditional modernism (roughly speaking: Proust, Joyce, Kafka, Beckett), but also romanticism and realism. Of course, that is a Hegelian view, romanticism and realism being the two sides of modern subjectivity: the one turned to the inner self, the other to the exterior world.

ELC Your critics say, and in particular Jochen Schulte-Sasse who introduced *Theory of the Avant-Garde*, that you are very precise in situating historically. I am particularly interested in this aspect of your work, because you are often critical of Lukács's historicism. I would appreciate your suggestions as to how Lukács's historicism could be improved, how it has to be changed in order to remain vital and useful. Lukács said in *History and Class Consciousness* that even if the immediate benefits and detailed results of Marxism are no longer valid, or if they are proven wrong, the one thing that will prevail is the Marxist methodology, historicism. This is quite important, particularly in the 1990s and in view of the recent downfall of communism in Russia and Eastern Europe. By making this statement, Lukács, very early in his career (1923), envisaged the possibility of an end to Marxism, while nevertheless maintaining faith in historicism and the Marxist methodology.

PB I think the problem with Lukács's historicism is that he tries to combine, on the one hand, a Marxist philosophy of history and, on the other hand, a normative aesthetic theory. For him there is a normative difference between modern literature, of which he is highly critical, and realism, of which he approves. As a philosopher of history, he shows that the evolution from realism to modernism was a necessary one, due to the withering impact of the bourgeois subject on history, but as a theoretician of art he condemns this evolution. That is inconsistent.

ELC In what sense are you different from Lukács? When you establish your model for the theory of the art-for-art's-sake period, the autonomy of art, and then describe art as becoming an institution for itself, are you not also looking at art and literature normatively?

PB Certainly not. Lukács is concerned with the social character of individual works, relating them to social reality; I tried to develop a theory of the function of art in society. One problem that is often coming up in the traditional sociology of literature is precisely how to explain the differences between works, since you have more differences on the level of works than you have in society. You need an intermediary category, which helps you to explain why the individual work is not totally determined by social forces. If you consider the concept of autonomous art as an institution, you get such an intermediate category.

ELC But you eliminate the intermediary function. The "nexus with life praxis,"* as you say, is not there. Art has lost its communication with society. It does not even *want* to communicate any more.

PB It is not me, but the institution that separates art from life praxis. The institution of autonomous art has a history which ends with Mallarmé. The historical avant-garde movements can be seen as an attempt to destroy the institution and to integrate art into life again.

ELC I can see this in Mallarmé, but not much beyond his time. How far do you go ahead historically in defining artistic form?

PB The *Theory of the Avant-Garde* is not a history of the avant-garde movements. It is not a picture of what had really happened, but a kind of construction which should help us make analyses of works in their social context.

ELC So it is a working model?

*Bürger uses terms such as "nexus with life praxis" [link with everyday life], particularly in *The Institutions of Art*, to signify his theory of the autonomy of art that he believes developed with the institution of bourgeois society. Since that time, and in particular with the advent of Romanticism, according to Bürger's historico-philosophical analysis, the work of art and literature no longer obeys any rules imposed from outside. It has lost its former link with "real life praxis" and demands to be judged according to rules it has set by itself.

PB Yes, it is a working model. In a sense I find very useful a concept of Max Weber—the "Idealtyp," the ideal type. And it is the same for Marx. He does not have this category, but when he is talking about capitalism, it is a model, a working concept he uses, but he does not give a description of the real situation.

ELC Lukács used many such working concepts, for instance, the concept of "imputed consciousness" (*zugerechnetes Bewusstsein*), or the concept of "realism." In reading your work, though, this was one of the problems I had. In recognizing the autonomy of art at a particular historical moment, you also observe an impossibility of communication between art and society, and with it, an impossibility of dialectics, I presume.

PB Yes, and I want to understand why this communication has collapsed in bourgeois society.

ELC Coming back to your model, if there is really no communication in bourgeois society between art and society, what will happen in the future? How can art be brought back to communicate? And do you really want this to happen?

PB I don't think it is important what *I* want, but whether the categories I propose can help us to explain why things happened and how they happened.

ELC You do not like to project. Do you have a utopia?

PB I know a student at Oxford who is doing a dissertation on aesthetics in Germany after Adorno. He finds two tendencies in the *Theory of the Avant-Garde*: on the one hand, some kind of nostalgic view of the avant-garde movement and the attempt to change society directly, and, on the other hand, a more resigned position.

ELC Resigned to what?

PB A resigned position of someone who has abandoned this idea of radical change, having recognized that it could not be put into practice.

ELC It is somehow comparable to the Goldmann-Lukácsean "tragic vision," is it not?

PB I should perhaps remind you that the book was written during the first years of the foundation of the University of Bremen. And in those days, the University of Bremen was a left university, *the* left university in the Federal Republic. (Today it is quite different.) You have in this book a reaction against a type of vulgar Marxism that explained everything from a point of view of class struggle but in a very simplistic way, which in those days dominated the seminars.

ELC Coming back to your own views of the avant-garde. Do you not, in many ways even in your models, follow the vision and criticism of Lukács?

PB No, no. I do not think so. I think it is quite different.

ELC You do not condemn it [the avant-garde], you do not call it decadent, as Lukács did.

PB It is not only a question of estimation, but a question of positing the avant-garde movements in the evolution of modern art. For Lukács, there is no difference between modernism and avant-garde, a difference that is crucial in my view. Modernism accepts the institution of art, avant-garde fights it.

ELC In your analysis of surrealism you frequently use the word "experience." You say that what the surrealists wanted was "free experience." Is this not comparable to Lukács's problematic hero, lost and alienated in established bourgeois society, who wants to regain his authenticity and freedom, the free experience of life, a home, warmth, and harmony?

PB No. Lukács is interested in the work of art, the great work of art, and in its mimetic force. The work of art is reflecting the conflicts in a given society. The problems with this kind of approach are: (1) The work tells you only what you know from history. (2) If artists abandon the idea of the work—and that is what the surrealists for instance do— you cannot think of it in the context of Lukácsean theories.

ELC You could say that they are journeying in order to find their utopia, their ideal experience, just as Lukács's problematic hero is journeying to find a home away from bourgeois society that did not allow him to be himself and have an authentic human life experience. Both are movements directed against bourgeois society, different forms of expression of an antibourgeois sentiment. The surrealists certainly do not engage in a formal search, a teleological journey to a final utopian place somewhere out there. The comparison is meant to be merely on the level of reaction to bourgeois society, the impulse to turn away from it.

PB It is important to specify: the activities of the surrealists are totally different from what art has been in bourgeois society, where a certain idea of the great work of art, its producer (the genius), and its reception (mainly contemplation) are institutionalized. The surrealists abandon this concept of art as a separate sphere and try to create something in reality—we can call it "experience." The place where that can happen is the surrealist group, which is different from the one surrounding Mallarmé on the famous "Tuesdays."

ELC You also state somewhere that Balzac was the last lucky one to have been able to grasp the world (cf. *Theory of the Avant-Garde*, p. xliv). That idea is very Lukácsean.

PB Yes, in a certain sense, it is. But you find the same idea in Sartre and Barthes. They also take the revolution of 1848 as a watershed (*Wasserscheide*), as a turning point in the history of bourgeois society and in the history of art. I think we have no reason to look at it in another way.

ELC Speaking of France and Germany, may I open a parenthesis here? I was wondering whether in the theory in which you state that art has no communication with society, whether you were not influenced by the fact that you were living in Germany, rather than, let us say, in France. In France, art has always maintained a close relationship with society and politics, whereas that has not been the case in Germany. Could that have been the reason why you went to such extremes in your views?

PB Maybe, yes. The theory of the autonomy of art is a theory that originated in German idealism, certainly, and was realized in the great neoclassical movement in Germany. Let us look at the French nineteenth century, though. Zola is an interesting example. If you look from the exterior, you can say that he is concerned with social reality, that is obvious. But if you have a closer look at the books, you can see, as Lukács did in his essay "Erzählen oder Beschreiben" (Narrate or Describe), which I always liked because there he is concerned with the form of writing and not only with its content, that Zola's technique of description is an aestheticist one. The various descriptions of the department store in *Au Bonheur des dames*, for example, are not really necessary in the context of the novel; they are impressionist miniatures. Lukács, on the one hand, observes very well this strange autonomization of the descriptions, which results in some kind of tableaux that can be isolated, but, on the other, he cannot accept this technique because he takes his standards of evaluation from the type of totalizing novel created by Balzac.

ELC Zola is experimental and in that sense more artificial. He produces one experiment after the other to make a point.

PB I do not think that is the point here. If you look again at the descriptions of the big department stores I mentioned, you can see that they are not realistic in the sense Zola thinks them to be. The young girl, who comes to Paris for the first time, will perhaps look at these department stores and be fascinated. But then comes the second description, the third, and the fourth, and the fifth, in the morning, in the afternoon, and so forth. There I think Lukács is right. You can see big parts of the text become separated from the whole, and this is exactly what can be called aestheticism in Zola. So, even in an author so obviously concerned with social reality, you have this tendency of autonomization of some parts, which are becoming pure works of art, and where the author seems interested mainly in the difference of the light in the morning, the afternoon, the difference of color, like an impressionist painter.

ELC Lukács said that Zola and his contemporaries had lost the right perspective of reality, and that Zola therefore did not really know what reality ought to be anymore. He was unable to write realist novels.

PB Lukács expresses two views on that topic. On the one hand, he says the autonomization of the descriptions is necessary because social reality cannot be grasped by a bourgeois writer after 1848 who, lacking a progressive historical perspective, can no longer comprehend society as a totality. On the other hand, Lukács condemns Zola's technique. You always have these two conflicting views in Lukács: a Marxist historicism and a normative aesthetic. But an ahistorical aesthetic is incompatible with radical historicism. It is impossible to combine them.

ELC I found very interesting what you wrote about realism, its already being a sign of modernism. You showed how Flaubert had the *need* to be scientific, which, according to you, was a sign that he no longer had confidence in his own vision. I think this is a significant insight into Flaubert and into realism as well.

PB We often have a narrow vision of realism. But realism is a modern concept, and we have to see it as such. That is why realism still comes up all the time. It has never really disappeared.

ELC You say that the concept of realism is modern. It nevertheless has been changing?

PB Certainly.

ELC If you say that Balzac is a realist, Flaubert already had trouble being a realist, and Zola did not succeed in being a realist anymore, so what has been happening to realism in the twentieth century?

PB I think you can have a look at Joyce and see that even in *Ulysses* he is interested in the detail of description. He is writing letters to friends asking whether a house is exactly at one particular place and its number is exactly that one. We are always fascinated by the monologue of Molly Bloom, but if you read the first chapter of *Ulysses*, you can find a very conscious kind of realism, which, however, is no longer interested in the total vision.

ELC Do you still adhere to the necessity of a concept of totality? It seemed to me that it was very important to you in *Theory of the Avant-Garde*. In your *Prosa der Moderne*, I am no longer sure. In reading you, I sometimes had the feeling that you were quite clearly moving away from Marxism and its concepts. There had been more confrontation and complication with Marxism for you in your previous work than there seems to be in the more recent one. I think you are drawn, whether you want it or not, toward postmodernism.

PB I think these are two questions. The concept of totality was important to the *Theory of the Avant-Garde*, but in a negative sense, in order to determine what the avant-garde work could no longer be. My question was: how could one conceptualize the type of work which no longer forms a symbolic totality? I found the answer to this question in Lukács's pamphlet against modernism, *Realism in Our Time* (*Wider den missverstandenen Realismus*),* where he points out the importance of Benjamin's concept of allegory as a model for thinking about modernist works of art. Totality there was an important notion for the confrontation between the organic work of art on the one hand and the allegorical one on the other.

ELC When I listen to your definitions of the form of modern art, I am still reminded of Lukács's characterizations and do not find much contradiction between the two. Lukács recognized *what* changed in art and in which direction it went, but he then gave it a political interpretation and added a value judgment that is different from yours.

PB Yes.

ELC What you say about Flaubert and Zola is not really shocking to someone who comes with a Lukácsean point of view. You just seem to be accepting their form of realism and their modernism more readily. The characterization of their works is not that different.

PB I agree with you when we talk about Zola, as we did. What you call political interpretation is in my view closely linked to Lukács's basic aesthetic values (the work of art as an organic totality, etc.). The question is whether or not we can treat these value judgments as contingent, without transforming Lukács's theory as a whole. I think we cannot. The same problem comes up with Adorno. If you take his confrontation between Schoenberg and Stravinsky, you have a very positive evaluation of Schoenberg as the modernist, and a negative one of Stravinsky as the traditionalist. But you can read the *Philosophy of the New Music* (*Philosophie der neuen Musik*) also in a different way, taking away all the value judgments he makes. But in doing that, you are no longer in line with Adorno's aesthetic theory; you transform it.

ELC I should like to quote you from your chapter on hermeneutics where you say that "what is socially relevant, depends on the interpretation's political stand." I think this may help us in our discussion

---

*Georg Lukács, *Realism in Our Time: Literature and the Class Struggle*, trans. John and Necke Mander, preface George Steiner (New York: Harper Torchbooks, 1971).

and also seems to be in line with your historicism. You are in fact saying that Lukács, when he reads something, must necessarily come to a very different conclusion or value judgment than you who are living fifty years after him.

PB Yes, but there is not just this difference. The two positions, the modernist and the realist one, existed already before the confrontations between Lukács and Adorno took place. The two philosophers belong more or less to the same generation. In the sixties you could look at them as being contemporaries. So I think these are different orientations, and there has always been this positive leftist interpretation of modernism, by Adorno, which is more the line I follow, and the critical interpretation of modernism, which is the line Lukács and the more orthodox Marxists have followed. There is a kind of political overdetermination of the whole aesthetic discussion of the period of the Second World War. Our modernist view, that realism is no longer a possible aesthetic, and that we have to abandon realism, was also a critical or polemical move against what happened in the socialist countries where realism was an official doctrine.

ELC Having been exposed to theoreticians in America who say that we are being swept away by postmodernism, that we cannot step out of postmodernism, I now turn to you who says that we cannot really establish a theory of modernism. After having completed your analyses of actual works of modernism, you attempted to establish a theory of modernism, you said, but found it to be extremely difficult because of the heterogeneous forms of the modernist works you had examined. Maybe this is a sign of postmodernism. Maybe it has caught up with you. So if we try to situate you, we must find a vision in your works that would be your own but would emerge from *within* postmodernism.

PB I think, but I do not know, whether there is an identity to characterize this person or that work, but I think one could look at this in different ways. I tried to situate the *Theory of the Avant-Garde* in the period of student movements, left uprisings in West Germany, a certain revolutionary rhetoric, and a certain reaction against all this. So I would say that it cannot be otherwise, it *must* be influenced by this situation. One must be open to whatever comes one's way at a particular historical moment. This is one thing, and then the other is that one must develop some force of resistance (*Widerstandskraft*) to it. Naturally, I do not know how far I succeeded in it. In *Prosa der Moderne* my first step was to get involved with some work, analyze it, and then observe how the individual analyses lead from one to the other without adhering to an a priori theoretical construct. I then questioned the analyses, and in doing that, fragments of Hegel's theory of modernity were very useful to me. Perhaps it was the postmodern situation, blurring the differences between categories, that led me back to Hegel.

ELC In *Prosa der Moderne* you say: "Kunst ist in der Moderne nicht einfach eine Sphäre *neben* den Sphären Wissenschaft und Moral, sondern sie ist eine aus dem Geiste der Moderne geborene Gegeninstitution" (Art in modernism is not simply a sphere *next to* the spheres of science and morality, but is a counterinstitution born from the very spirit of modernism, p. 17). What has happened there? You are suddenly calling art a "Gegeninstitution," a counterinstitution which, maybe, you would not have done in your *Theory of the Avant-Garde*.

PB Oh, yes, I would have. The use of the term results from a discussion, the origins of which may not be immediately apparent. Jürgen Habermas, in his *Theory of Communicative Action*, starts from the assumption that modernity can be characterized by the differentiation of three "value spheres," the scientific, the moral, and the aesthetic. And everything depends on the clear separation between these spheres.

ELC This is not a very Marxist idea!

PB No! Rather a Kantian or a Weberian one. Habermas's theory fits with the following reading of the *Theory of the Avant-Garde*: the attempt has been made by the avant-garde to negate the autonomy of the aesthetic sphere, integrating art into life praxis. This attempt failed. There is no reason to take it up again. My own reading of the book is another one: although the attempt to integrate art into life praxis failed, the problem raised by the avant-garde movements remains urgent. (Think of Joseph Beuys, for instance.) I am interested in looking at what happened to art and literature in bourgeois society. It contrasts with these other spheres, and I think the result is not only that there is somehow a clear distinction between the theoretical, the moral, and aesthetics, but that you have also an aggressive move from the side of the arts against morality and against theory. *Les Fleurs du mal* transforms some aggressive move against traditional moral thinking into an object of artistic value. And Rimbaud asks whether there can be another grasp of reality than with a normal theoretical instrument. Does there exist a kind of knowledge that is not the knowledge resulting from normal scientific processes but from magic or aesthetic experience.

ELC You believe in the force of magic?

PB The magical always comes up in the tradition of modernism, with Rimbaud, with the surrealists. That is one of the big forces.

ELC In the attempt to find the "original pure" form, the original truth?

PB Another truth and another *way* of finding truth.

ELC You have been preoccupied with the idea that everything is already mediated, that all we have is mediated forms. If this is so, unless you believe in some kind of revelation, some mysticism or what have you, what is the way out of this inauthenticity, this lack of immediacy? This is the first question. Second, what gives us the authority to make statements about these mediated forms. Are we not, and our judgments, mediated as well?

PB These are very difficult questions, and I am not sure whether I can give you adequate answers. Perhaps authenticity cannot be reached in transcending mediation but only in recognizing that the desire for immediacy, though necessarily unfulfilled, is a necessary one. Your second question asks whether we can make statements about society as a mediated totality, being ourselves part of this totality. I think the idea of total mediation is tinted with delusion. Take Hegel's *Phenomenology of Spirit*, which I like very much, but it is hard to conceive of the possibility of such a book, you cannot think it, unless it has been written by someone who believes he is really the spirit of the whole.

ELC Could you elaborate on this a bit further, please?

PB I am not a philosopher, you know. In the philosophical project of thinking totality, I suspect a bit of madness. My way of reading—for instance, the *Phenomenology of Spirit*—is different. I am not interested in the system but in forms of thinking that permit me to come to insights. And I am interested in the breaks which show that the system does not work. Perhaps this is precisely the truth of Hegel's book.

ELC Speaking of Hegel, truth, and spirit, I should like to come back to Lukács's realist writer and to irony. In your texts you seem to imply that for Lukács the great realist writer is identical with his character. In your chapter on the essay, "Essayismus und Ironie beim frühen Lukács," you say: "Der Author macht . . . sich selbst zum Objekt der Ironie" (*Prosa der Moderne*, p. 420), the author makes himself the object of irony. Do you mean of his own irony?

PB I think I said this at the beginning of my discussion of Lukács's *The Theory of the Novel*. There is a very important passage on irony. Lukács's idea is that irony is self-knowledge and thus the self-cancellation of subjectivity. The idea is that the author of the novel also has a position within the context or the totality of a certain society. How can he then say what he says—this is the problem we discussed with Hegel— how can he say what he says about society, if there is no philosophical or religious basis from which he can start? According to Lukács, he can do this with irony. The realist author can make up for his lacking objectivity, ironizing not only the characters in the novel but also his own superiority.

ELC Do you mean that he identifies with a character?

PB No, it is not a problem of identifying with a character at all. It is a certain attitude of the author vis-à-vis his own position toward the characters. He puts himself on the same level with his characters, but he does not identify with them.

ELC This leads to the question concerning the ethics of form. You say that literary form is like a gesture, that it is like an act. If acts express ethics, then you can also say that form is an ethical act. You continue saying, "der Essayist ist der problematische Mensch" (*Prosa der Moderne*, p. 414), who seeks his salvation from form.

PB All this is Lukács.

ELC Yes, and you add: "Er will keine Versöhnung mit diesem Leben" (p. 416). This is a problem, isn't it? If he desires no reconciliation with life, what does he want? Death?

PB What is fascinating with the first Lukács is that at that moment he has no philosophical system and he is looking forward to having one. This gives his writing a quite different aspect from his later work. He has no strict concept of what he wants to say, his writing thus becomes a way of thinking. The problem I pointed out in *Prosa der Moderne* is that in *Soul and Forms* you have a very harsh confrontation between life, taken as total chaos, and form as something that has to be forced upon life. It is intriguing that you find the same idea in the writing of right-wing German intellectuals of the twenties, such as Carl Schmitt. In the next step of his thinking, in *The Theory of the Novel*, Lukács no longer insists on this idea and develops a more Hegelian one, that societal life is always organized in forms, in institutions, what he calls "Gebilde" (structures). With the use of this term, he discusses the confrontation between the individual and society. That is the next step in the development of his thinking. But I agree, what is fascinating in the first Lukács is the concept of form as ethical act. That is interesting because it contradicts the idealistic aesthetics of reconciliation he later advocates.

ELC The difference between the two views of form may be more developmental than contradictory. In *The Theory of the Novel*, Hegel came into the picture. Before Hegel, in *Soul and Form*, Lukács saw what he believed to be a universal existential chaos because he had not yet come upon the idea that it might be socially conditioned and thus man-made. Suddenly, with the discovery of Hegel and then Marx, he found a possible solution to the problem.

Coming back to *Prosa der Moderne*, are you not doing there what Lukács did in *Soul and Form*: You write analyses, not theory. Maybe in your next book, you will come back to theory, you will establish the theory for what you did in your preceding work? Or, maybe in ten, fifteen years you will look back and establish the theory.

PB You never know what you will do in ten or fifteen years. What I am trying to do right now is to write essays *only*. The title of my next book will be *Das Denken des Herrn*, a hint at the Hegelian dialectic of the master and the slave. I detect behind the thinking of Bataille, Blanchot, Lacan, and Derrida some kind of going away from a tradition which has always associated bourgeois society with the figure of the Knecht, the slave. The crisis of modern society in the thirties, the crisis of the concepts of progress and emancipation forced these authors to look whether it was possible to adopt the perspective of Hegel's master, a figure Hegel and his French interpreter, Kojève, were not much interested in. This has come out as a guiding principle in the process of my writing. I had no previous idea to do a book on Hegel and postmodernism. You probably would find there another parallel with Lukács.

ELC You mean Lukács, the essayist, turned theoretician, and you, the theoretician, going back to essay writing? But in any case Lukács is still in the picture?

PB Oh yes. The first Lukács and Adorno.

ELC In the aftermath of 1989 have *you* yourself in any way changed toward Lukács and Marxism, and have you noticed how others have been affected by the so-called end of communism?

PB Certainly, certainly. But it is a difficult question for leftist people to deal with. It will take us years to know how to cope with these new problems. It would be too simple to say: "I was always critical of the socialist countries, and socialist politics in these countries, so it does not concern me." Even if it were true, it would be a defensive position, missing the point. Marxists in Western countries were always starting from the assumption that socialist economies could function, and maybe should function, in a better way than capitalist ones, but could function in *any* case. This idea has collapsed. I think the way to approach these problems is *not* to go directly to them, but to look at figures such as Lukács, to see what happened with intellectuals like him in the twentieth century. There are parallels between people as different as Lukács and Heidegger. In the *Metaphysik der Tragödie*, you find a lot of Heidegger, and when Lukács turns to Hegel and Marx it is his way of escaping from that philosophy of death. Today, with the crisis of the socialist project, a certain tragic thinking is coming back. Young intellectuals are fascinated by Bataille, Blanchot, and Lacan. Seeing no future for the modern Western societies, they turn to philosophies of death. One day they certainly will discover the young

Lukács, mainly the author of *Soul and Form*. That pessimism is on the agenda. You can see it also with Fredric Jameson's *Late Marxism: Adorno, or, The Persistence of the Dialectic* (London: Verso, 1990), where he, who was always critical of Adorno's pessimistic views, proposes a radically different and more positive reading of Adorno.

ELC Have you ever identified with Marxism? Have you described yourself as a Marxist critic?

PB I think I have not. But I was very near to Marxism in the sense that Hegel, Kant, and Marx were all very important to me. What fascinated me with Marx was, on the one hand, the concept of a theory having practical impact, the idea of a critical theory, and, on the other, the methodological insights of the *Grundrisse* (the idea that the history of man can explain the history of the monkey and not the other way around). Finally, I found and I still find extremely useful the dialectical model of an "ideological critique" (*Ideologiekritik*) that Marx developed in his early essay on religion ("Zur Kritik der Hegelschen Rechtsphilosophie") and that Lukács and Adorno have taken up in order to analyze works of art in bourgeois society, and Herbert Marcuse in order to grasp the functional contradictions of what he called "affirmative culture."

ELC What for you is the message that has to be derived from the end of communism in the East?

PB I do not know whether there is a message we can derive from the end of communism. Perhaps modesty in making theory, perhaps self-criticism. But I really do not know.

ELC Could you provide a few specifics about the possible role of Lukács in any such left intellectual self-criticism? Are there any aspects of Lukács's work, theories, or ideas that you think would be particularly useful to the process?

PB I do not think that we can take up some of Lukács's ideas and apply them to our situation. His thinking is a systematic one, and you cannot pick up some of the ideas and drop the rest, because they form a whole. But we can study Lukács as we study, for instance, Heidegger as a key intellectual figure of the twentieth century. We can thus point out the rigor of his thinking and the consequences into which he ran. The parallel is striking. Like Heidegger, Lukács is one of the great thinkers of our century, but, like Heidegger, he requires distant critical study, not identification.

INTERVIEW WITH GEORGE STEINER

30 December 1991, Churchill College, Cambridge

ELC The purpose of this interview is to map Lukács's presence today. I should like to ask you, for instance, whether Lukács could belong to your *Real Presences* today, how seminal you believe his theories have been, how important they have been for you personally, and where they stand today. In line with your recent work, "Heidegger in 1991," I should like to ask you for an assessment of "Lukács at the end of 1991." May I suggest that we begin with your first encounter with Lukács's work?

GS Yes, of course. Already at the University of Chicago, where I came very young, too young. Partially because this was a campus in the late forties with a strong Marxist and radical student presence, the name of Lukács began to become very familiar to me, and the first book I read, and which overwhelmed me, was *The Historical Novel.* I regard it as a masterpiece. I was myself very, very interested in the problem, particularly curious, very early, in the problem of crowd and power. No one, no one had ever taken Walter Scott seriously like Lukács did, and I shall never forget my shock of delight in the comparison between the great crowd rebellions in Scott, in *The Heart of Midlothian*, then Dickens, taking them up in *Barnaby Rudge*, the Gordon riots. A world opened for me of how you do comparative literature, of how you read. So I was probably much less able to see the Marxist element. That came later. It was the comparative approach to literary criticism, the enormous literacy, the range of reading, the range of awareness and of reference. It began naturally and then led successively to many other books.

In 1957 I was a Fulbright professor in Austria, and I went East. There were no tourists. You could only stop at three towns, etc., you know all about this. I had with me from Paris some personal letters from Lucien Goldmann to Lukács, and I had been asked to bring him certain books and magazines, and was young and stupid enough to think that would cause no danger. And it did not. I arrived at the bullet-riddled house beyond the Chain Bridge, at Belgrad Rackpart number 2. I went up, where a maid with a lace apron and lace hat, in the Vienna-Frankfurt-Berlin style of the great professors before Hitler, received me and said that the "Herr Professor" would see me. Of course, I had made an appointment. "Herr Professor" was sitting at the famous desk, very small, and "Herr Professor" liked, when he had a young idiot coming to take up his time, to see to embarrass him a little bit. Perfectly natural. Behind his head were forty–fifty volumes of the Aufbau edition, and he just looked at me and said nothing. In my fear, embarrassment, and shyness, stupidly, I said: "Herr Professor, how have you been able . . . ?" "Very easy, Steiner, Hausarrest, Hausarrest." And I fell in love with him at that moment because it was the most wonderful answer you could possibly give, an absolutely marvelous answer. Then I handed him the material from Paris, and he asked me what I was working on and what I had done, and I brought him my first book, the *Tolstoy or Dostoevski*, which I do think interested him. He was amused, he took it, he asked me whether I knew Merezhkovsky's work on the same thing, and within minutes we were talking shop. I saw him several times during that visit. The last time was particularly moving, at Christmas, dark, God it was difficult in Budapest at that time. I was staying at the Gellert, which was very privileged, but I do not need to tell you, it was a difficult winter. The ruins were everywhere from the Russian bombardment. Then, the last time I was leaving him, I was very moved and I said something again childish that I was worried about him or that we were worried about him in the West, a stupid remark. He smiled and said: "The chair you are now leaving, junger Herr, in half an hour Kádár will be here studying Hegel with me. So do not worry. Seien Sie nicht besorgt. In einer halben Stunde sitzt der Kádár hier." They were doing Hegel together, while he was on house arrest. He said it to make me feel reassured, to say "it is much more complicated than you think, and I am not in danger." Which he was not. So I was very relieved. We then corresponded from time to time. I met him again, I think in 1963. This time, he did not approve at all of my book on tragedy, which he felt to be dangerously idealistic, going in a direction which of course was not his at all, and he very deeply warned me against the enormous influence on me of Walter Benjamin. He said, "that is where you are going and das ist mystisch." There I was already older and more established internationally and had perhaps a little more courage, so we argued more.

Let me quickly tell you what is of truly seminal importance for me: The analysis of historicity entering nineteenth-century literature, the fact that the ancien régime is in another time, another category, post-French Revolution, post-1830, post-1848. To try to understand exactly how history enters the novel and poetry. In what way romanticism is also a form of historicism. That is the first and very large indebtedness since I began with him and it influenced me enormously. Secondly, I owe more than I can say to what I think is an insight of genius, his distinction between realism and naturalism. That has been central to my own thinking. Why, when Balzac lists 28 details, it matters and works, and why, when Zola lists 117, it is a fumble, it is dead. That profound insight, which has not been taken up in the West, barely understood, between classical realism and the analysis he does of the cap of Charles Bovary, which I have often spoken about, no one has rivaled. The analysis of the beginning of *Eugénie Grandet*, the turning against Zola, against Maupassant, and so on. This had a very funny footnote. The second time I saw him, Lukács pointed to a pile of paper on his desk, which was almost higher than his "little" nose, and said: "Ich schreibe die Aesthetik des Films, Steiner," he was writing the aesthetics of film. So I burst out, I could tease him, I was older, and said: "You have never been to a movie, Meister." So he said: "Wie können Sie das sagen? Ich habe einen Film gesehn, 'Der Blaue Engel' " ("How can you say that? I have seen a film, *The Blue Angel*"). That is a very important story, because I believe Aristotle only saw *one* Greek tragedy. He does not give a damn how many. If you are Lukács or Aristotle, *one* is enough. You got the point, the structural point. I say that half-seriously, but it was a wonderful story, because I understood something about Aristotle. You see, I have always suspected that he hated the theater, but the *Poetics* is our great book on the theater. I think Aristotle saw the *Oedipus*, and that is probably the only thing he saw. So Lukács had seen *Der Blaue Engel*, and—a wonderful parallel— that was enough. So the naturalism-realism thing also means a great deal to me.

ELC So what he said about Zola does not disturb you?

GS No. He is right. Absolutely. I love Zola, but I know why he is not Balzac, Stendhal, or Flaubert. The third time, and this has never been fully developed by him—but I judge whether men are men of genius or women of genius, not necessarily by the corpus, which is enormous, but by the kind of insight infinitely more intelligent than one ordinary person like myself can have . . . no I mean that!—so we went, and he was preparing his study of Zhivago, and I said to him: "Well?" And he said: "Totally dishonest." And he said, "I will now prove it to you." This is a very important story. This, I hope, you publish and expand. He said: "You remember the poems at the end of the novel?" I said: "Of course, very well!" He said: "We agree, they are perhaps since Pushkin the greatest Russian poetry, lyric poetry?" I said: "I cannot read Russian. I agree. Even in translation." He said: "There is the complete lie. No country doctor would write those poems. If Shakespeare had created a country doctor writing poetry, the poems would be those of a country doctor writing them." This is one of the greatest insights of genius, which changed everything for me. He said: "There is the lie, by

63

giving those poems to a doctor he makes the doctor's antirevolutionary view so overwhelmingly inspired, Shakespeare would never have cheated in that way." And I noted that, and this I can think about for years and years, it will continue. I am not sure it is right, but I keep having to wrestle with it, to think about it. That is one very great moment.

The other great moment was this. He had written a sentence, and we shall come to that book in a minute, *The Destruction of Reason*—that a man is "verantwortlich bis zum Ende der Zeit, responsible to the end of time for the *abuse*, Misbrauch, not the use, made of his work." So I said: "That cannot stand, that sentence." He said: "It does, and I can prove it." He loved to say: "Ich kann es beweisen, I can prove it." This is the Jewish Talmud teacher who says, "I can prove it." He was teaching me Talmud. He said: "You cannot abuse a single note of Wolfgang Amadeus Mozart. You cannot use it for a ceremony, for an evening, and so on." So I really worried about that. I came back to Princeton where my close friend was the great American composer Roger Sessions, who was also a philosopher and deep, deep thinker. I said, "Roger, for God's sake, help me with this answer." Because I had nothing to answer. I was defeated. Roger thought, sat down at the piano, and played the second aria of the Queen of the Night in *The Magic Flute.* He said, that one, you can. And then he smiled at me and said: "But Lukács is still right." It was a wonderful moment in my relation with Sessions. What he meant was that this was maybe the one aria which in a Nazi ceremony you could possibly have the band play. It is very dark and evil. But then he said: "But Lukács is right." And indeed it may be that nothing of Mozart or Schubert can be abused to the end of mankind on this planet. It is not a *fair* answer. It is a *wonderful* answer. Again it opened for me problems, problems, not answers. Our great teachers give us problems, not answers, and it opened that for me.

Now I should like to come to *The Destruction of Reason.* Every Tom, Dick, and Harry says: "Ha, what a dreadful book!" As it happens, they have not read it. It is a difficult book. It is a failure. And it asks the right questions. And it gives the wrong answers. *It asks the right questions.* The questions of the relationship between transcendental German metaphysics and what happened are very important questions. The answers he gives seem to me often vulgar; they seem to me to betray his own best insights. So I am saying, he asks the right questions and nobody else has. That book, which is perhaps his weakest, asks very strong questions. And there are questions that the Heidegger affair, the Paul de Man affair, have brought back to the fore: the relation between absolute, metaphysical thought and fascism.

ELC Do you believe in absolute thought?

GS That is why I am Heideggerian. Of course, I do. So did Lukács, and so does all Jewry. So, that is to give you an example of how even his weak work, and I reject that book, has been important for me. Trying to say what is wrong here? What has gone wrong? Only very major figures help you when they go wrong. This is one of the very good tests. Sartre's *Flaubert* is a mess, a very important one. It will take centuries to know why those four volumes, those four thousand pages, have gone so wrong. With little people like ourselves, when it goes wrong, it is ephemeral. Wastebasket. This is very important: With big people, when it goes wrong, it is very interesting.

ELC I am here, because everything I read by you on Lukács I thought was right.

GS This does not disprove what I am saying to you, not at all. Remember the essays I wrote as a very young man, the one on meta-Marxism, on the devil's pact, thirty years ago.

ELC Your sentence on Lukács's devil's pact with history is probably the most quoted critical sentence on Lukács's work.

GS Think of how early that was and how little I had read of him. So much was not even available in those days. In my opinion, critical works are only now beginning to appear. Three important books have appeared in the last few years on the early Lukács, for instance, the one by Lee Congdon.* It is only now that *Die Seele und die Formen*, the book on modern drama, and the very early essays are beginning to be available other than in the best of libraries.** I am still feeling my way into the early works. *Die Seele und die Formen* is an astounding book. The understanding, for instance, of Kierkegaard's break with Regina and Nietzsche's with Lou is now a cliché, known by every student. This comes from Lukács. The first time this was seen, it was seen by Lukács, a terribly young Lukács. Then, I knew Ernst Bloch well, until his death, and Adorno. So other "Lukácses" came into my life, the Lukácses they were fighting. Again, judge a man by his adversaries. When the adversaries are very big, he is important. Small men have small adversaries. Big men have big adversaries. So throughout my life, Lukács has been a very important influence. Perhaps I could put it

---

*Lee Congdon, *The Early Lukács* (Chapel Hill: University of North Carolina Press, 1983).

**Georg von Lukács, *Die Seele und die Formen: Essays* (Berlin: Egon Fleischel, 1911); in English: Georg Lukács, *Soul and Form: Essays*, trans. Anna Bostock (Cambridge, Mass.: MIT Press, 1974). Georg Lukács, *A modern dráma fejlödésének története* (Budapest: Franklin Társulat, 1911); in German: Georg Lukács, *Entwicklungsgeschichte des modernen Dramas*, trans. Dénes Zalán, vol. 15 of *Werke* (Neuwied: Luchterhand, 1981).

in a very simple way. The important thing when you write a sentence is to ask yourself: "Who will know that it is stupid?" And the loneliest thing in the world is when those whom you believe will know it are dead. I had in this country one or two men whom I used to send my stuff to before I published it, and they would say: "It is stupid." Koestler was one whose intelligence was prodigious. He hated Lukács for interesting reasons.* There were others, a scientist, a philosopher, a handful of people. And now I have one or two left to whom I know it would probably seem stupid. And that is perhaps the most important single, how should I say, catharsis or act of moral uprightness when you work—that is, to know that there is someone, like Lukács was for me when I published something, even when I did not send it. I would say, "Oh my God, what will he say when he reads it?" And I miss that terribly. I miss him deeply, deeply. There was someone whose reading would be so hostilely generous, so generously contemptuous. I say generously, because there can be a generous "no" which says you should do much better, or you have not thought this through. And I now know what is wrong with *The Death of Tragedy*, which has appeared in fourteen languages and is used throughout the schools of many parts of the world. I know what is wrong with it, and he has helped me see that. One's gratitude is endless to those who know better. So that is very roughly, but it is a lot, the extent to which I have been influenced by Lukács.

ELC You have not done as much work on the early as you have on the late Lukács.

GS No, because it is only recently that he has become accessible. And there are certain things which I am very bad about; for example, I can't yet stand Stefan George, who was very important for him. Now there has appeared finally a good Suhrkamp edition of Simmel on money. Very difficult.

ELC Simmel was very important to Lukács, particularly for his influence on *The Theory of the Novel*.

GS Terribly. I am trying to understand Simmel. My knowledge of Mannheim is very bad. And it is only very slowly with the letters, with the books on the early Lukács in Heidelberg, with everything that has happened since the discovery of the papers, with the Bloch letters

---

*George Steiner probably refers to the activities of Arthur Koestler at the time of the Stalinist terror (1934–39), when Koestler made himself the spokesman of the ex-communist, anti-Stalinist left in Western Europe, while Lukács managed—diplomatically—to survive in Soviet Russia. In his novel, *Darkness at Noon* (1941), Koestler denounced the Moscow show trials—and all those who did not actively oppose them—by describing the purge of an old Bolshevik for "deviationist" belief in the individual.

which I did review, that the background material which I badly need to understand that infinitely complicated theory is beginning to come through. And I have my own books, I do not have that much time left, but I have great joy in trying at least to approach some of the early material.

ELC I should like to ask you about Lucien Goldmann.

GS I knew him very little. *Le Dieu caché* was very important for me. That is my other side, the Racine side. I found *The Sociology of the Novel* unreadable, totally unreadable. No interest whatsoever.

ELC That was very Lukácsean, though.

GS Yes, but bad Lukácsean, in my opinion. And Lukács did not like it either.

ELC It was the theory in *History and Class Consciousness* applied to the theory of the novel.

GS Yes, but very artificially, in my opinion. Goldmann's little Heidegger study is interesting, nothing more. Goldmann is *Le Dieu caché* and is now, I think, totally forgotten. In France I know no one who reads it or touches on it.

ELC There are a few. There is his widow, Annie, of course, and Michael Löwy, who was one of his disciples but now works much more on Lukács, naturally. You did criticize Goldmann.

GS But only in passing. It is not anything I am very involved with.

ELC Goldmann was important to me. He asked the kind of questions you mentioned before which led me to Lukács. He asked me questions on my M.A. essay on Flaubert that no one else had asked me before and thus opened a new world for me.

GS I admired him personally. His early death was certainly a great loss, but it is not my field at all. If I have done detail work, it was in the Frankfurt School, with relation to Lukács, of course.

ELC You seem to admire Adorno very much? Are you interested in music as well, as he was?

GS Yes, of course. Without it we would not have our century. And there again, the quarrel between them, the "Misverstandene Realismus" and Adorno's jargon, that is a wonderfully important quarrel, as is the Bloch quarrel with Lukács on expressionism and on modernity, Lukács on modernity, his hate of modernity.

ELC What do you think of Lukács's rejection of modernism? You wrote a wonderful preface to *Realism in Our Time*, which is one of the first things I read by you, and which I found most helpful.

GS Look, my heart, my education are with Lukács. I was brought up in the Jewish Central European classical tradition, Greek and Latin from the start, at a French lycée, in the classical system. My father began teaching me Greek and Latin even before school. I am steeped in the classics. On the other hand, very modern music is indispensable to me.

ELC Pierre Boulez?

GS Whom I know, whom I worked with, whom I admire immensely, but more Ligeti, Nono, and especially Kurtag, who is to me now the most interesting composer out of Budapest. No, I do not share Lukács's rejection, but I do understand it, and I do not place it in Marxism. I place it in Central European Judaism, which was the culture which stops with Thomas Mann, which saw in Thomas Mann indeed its greatest hope and fulfillment. And as it happens, I suppose I would take *The Magic Mountain* and *Doctor Faustus* with me before *Finnegans Wake*. And I do not believe anybody has read *Finnegans Wake*. That is another great piece of bluff. And as it happens, three or four of the Beckett prose things seem to me supreme, supreme. The fiction *Molloy*, *Malone Dies*, and *The Unnamable* do add to the English language by subtracting from it, which is a paradox I would defend. *Waiting for Godot* and *Endgame*, yes, but much else, let time judge, I am not sure at all. And, of course, *very* much in modern art is cruel kitsch, sadistic kitsch. And Lukács was right when he saw in it relations to the Americanization of the planet, the industrialization, the *Kitscherei*. It is Disneyland, and he saw that danger clearly and early. In a sense he foretold, without wanting to, Zhivago and Solzhenitzyn. He foretold that out of that harem would come great classical acts of imagination.

ELC In reading you and listening to you, I find that you admire Lukács more for his mere intelligence than for what he has done, for instance, within Marxism.

GS Yes, much more. What I admire supremely is that he lived our century like few men on the planet. He lived it. Day and night. He lived in enormous danger.* There is this story about him and Becker, who was a real Stalinist swine—Becker is another story, a real swine but a very good poet—he and Becker were walking past the Kremlin one night in 1942, in the winter, when the Nazis were very near, and when every

---

*When the Nazis came to power, Lukács was vice president of the Berlin group of the German Writers' Association and a leading member of the League of Proletarian-Revolutionary Writers. When he learned that the Nazis were looking for him, he escaped to Moscow where he became a significant collaborator in the Institute of Philosophy of the Soviet Academy of Sciences. He wrote *The Young Hegel* and practiced self-critique of the views expressed in his early works, in particular *History and Class Consciousness*. During the period from 1933 until 1944, which Lukács spent in the Stalinist Soviet Union as a barely tolerated refugee, he tried to steer clear of politics and did not write about Russian literature. He continued the debate on expressionism and used his time to elaborate the concept of realism in various essays about predominantly nineteenth-century French and German fiction. Most of these works were published only much later, in the 1950s.

day German poets, writers, and critics were vanishing into the Gulag, and they knew it. You came to the house of the international press, and the office was empty, you did not have to be a genius—Lukács told me the story. You never talked in a house, never, not even with your wife in bed, because the bugs were there, the walls had ears. The wind was howling, it was so cold, they thought they would die just getting home. Becker says: "Georg, Georg, nur überleben, überleben, only survive, only survive." And again, walking near the river, "Nur überleben, nur überleben." Yes, correct, that is to me almost my favorite of the many stories he told me, and he told me hundreds of his life. "Nur über-leben." He did more than that. He bore witness to the century, by his errors, by his swineries, which were considerable, considerable.

ELC When? In 1918?

GS No, no, no. During the Stalinist time. With the son-in-law. You know how he was saved? That story is absolutely correct. It was at a bridge game with somebody and Beria,* at the end of Lukács's Russian period, when they had arrested Lukács's son-in-law and took him to the Gulag, when at the bridge game someone said to Beria: "Come on, do something for Lukács." Lukács denied what he knew about the camps. He is also the man who said: "The worst of socialism is preferable to the best of capitalism." He told me, I will die by that fact. He is the man who quoted to me and had on his wall written in letters of fire, not real letters, letters of fire: "Bertold Brecht: Always leave the good old for the bad new, verlasse immer das gute Alte für das schlechte Neue." He lived that—I do not, I do not agree—but he was not a parlor Marxist, he lived it in mortal danger. When he came out, feted, to the Rencontres Internationales in Geneva, with his wife, the world said: "Herr Pro-fessor, please, any chair you want . . ." But he said, "I am going back."**

---

*Lavrenti Pavlovich Beria, 1899–1953, was a Soviet Communist leader in Geor-gia, where he rose to prominence in the Cheka, the secret police. He became party secretary and later head of the secret police. As minister of internal affairs and, in 1946, member of the politburo, Beria wielded great power. After Stalin's death in 1953, Beria became first deputy premier under Premier Georgy Malenkov, but he was arrested on charges of conspiracy, tried secretly, and shot in December 1953.

**From 1946 until 1949 Lukács was highly active in discussions and philo-sophical confrontations, among them with Karl Jaspers at the "Rencontres interna-tionales de Genève." This was followed in 1947, at the height of Sartre's philo-sophical influence, by Lukács's major polemics with existentialism that led to the publication of *Existentialisme ou marxisme*, trans. E. Kelemen (Paris: Nagel, 1948). In 1949 Lukács took part in the Hegel conference in Paris, where he met Roger Garaudy, Henri Lefèvre, Lucien Goldmann, Jean Hyppolite, and Maurice Merleau-Ponty. But in the same year attacks on Lukács were renewed by Rudas, Révai, and Horváth for "revisionism," "right-wing deviationism," and objectively being a "ser-vant of imperialism." This induced Lukács to perform acts of recantation and to retire from active politics.

He knew the danger. He knew the danger, and he always went back. Oh no, oh no. He felt surrounded by people whose civil courage was minus, minus zero infinite and who, because they might lose a job during the McCarthy period—from 1947 until 1957—crawled, crawled, who would go around hysterically in fear of political correctness because they were afraid the Dean would call them in if they dared teach the truth. No, thank you. This was a man, who with a small physique, with frequent grave illnesses, a Jew, a Jew around whom everybody had been gassed or massacred, this man lived his convictions, with which one need not agree, to know that he is what the Greek word "martyros" originally means, which does not mean "martyr" but "witness." He has been witness to our time, one of the most important witnesses to the hellishness of our time.

ELC I like your metaphors, and you just mentioned again "flame" and "fire." Very often, describing the atmosphere in which you lived, you evoke the color "gray." You must dislike the color gray.

GS Yes.

ELC You also speak of Lukács's flame and fire.

GS Yes, in the gray, in the terrible gray, in the cold dust, he burned. He told me a magnificent story: You had to have your little suitcase, toothpaste, toilet paper, two razor blades, one for shaving, one to kill yourself if the torture is too bad. This is the real world, not America, not California. This is what the world is about. He said, he was all packed, in Moscow, ready for when the knock would come on the door, and it came. And he said to his wife, very calmly: "Es ist gekommen. It has come. Auf Wiedersehn." The car had drapes, a KGB car, and the airplane was blacked out, of course. He wondered to which camp they were taking him. He said to himself: "Interesting. They still treat me well enough to *fly* me to the Gador. It was still called Gador, not the Gulag. Then, enormous fences of barbed wire for miles and miles. He walks in, everyone salutes him, they say: "You are Professor Lukács. These are the captured German generals from Stalingrad, the staff of von Paulus. You have been appointed to teach them German history and literature." He said he almost fainted. He said proudly he was just able to hold on to the suitcase so as not to faint. An hour later he began with a lecture on Heine. In front of von Paulus and the two thousand captured German staff officers, his first lecture was on Heine.

ELC Did they provide him with books?

GS They asked him what he needed. He could do a Heine lecture, a Lessing lecture—I hope I can—without having books. That we do not need. But then the books came. But that story alone is so telling. He was so proud he did not faint.

ELC You are very forgiving, and forgiving in the sense that you seem to admire in Lukács something beyond good and evil that redeems him. I read somewhere that you were very critical of people who have no style, no class. Did this help Lukács? You say some pretty strong things about him, about his language, how forbidding it is, and that it is like a citadel that you have to penetrate, but once you are inside, you say, "Here is God's plenty."

GS Yes, of course. Look. I was saved in 1940. I could escape to New York. I was safely in bed during Auschwitz as a boy when I should have been dead. All my lycée comrades died, the Jews. I do not know how I would behave, so I accept nobody's opinion on these matters who does not know what he would have done. Do you understand me? [Discussion interrupted by a phone call.]

ELC It is difficult for anyone who has not lived and suffered through the same situation fully to comprehend or even to conceptualize it. Lukács says that there are men who better than others can understand reality and conceptualize or even fictionalize it, in particular his "great realist" writers. His criteria, though, seem arbitrary. While he tends to judge the novels of Balzac, Flaubert, and Zola according to the historical period that brought them forth, he includes among his realist novelists also writers of the twentieth-century such as Thomas Mann and Gorky. How do you view this problem? Is realism contingent upon a certain historical moment or can it, does it, exist at all times?

GS Realism is an eternal concept. Homer is a realist. Following on Hegel, Lukács gives a very famous analysis, as did Hegel, of the moment when Odysseus makes a raft upon leaving Calypso. Hegel said, when he read that passage, we know that it is somebody who knows how to make a raft. Realism is a relationship to the world, it is a relationship for these people of responsible commitment to that which you are invoking and describing. And that is not history bound. In certain periods, it becomes an aesthetic, in the mercantile-industrial era, and Lukács is not at all the only one to have said this. This analysis was already being made before Lukács, very much before Lukács. In French literacy, the preface to the *Comédie Humaine* makes many of these references and puns. Marx's letters make them with respect to Balzac and Shakespeare. I think realism is a constant possibility for him.

ELC So what happens to historicism? The question really is whether realism can exist today and whether it would not be anachronistic. For Adorno, the idea of realism today is ridiculous.

GS But that is utterly silly. Ninety-eight percent of all film, of all newspaper, of all television, is documentary. And in fact, the documentary has invaded fiction under the name of "fact-fiction" more powerfully than ever before, which Adorno never foresaw.

ELC So realism, according to you, does not necessarily have one form, one style?

GS No, it has many instruments. And there will always be room for that element and for contrary ones.

ELC This is what Lukács did not accept. He always criticized all the modern novelists, as he did, for instance, in the work to which you wrote a preface, *Realism in Our Time.*

GS For a much deeper reason. On much deeper Jewish utopian grounds. He felt that they were dwelling on defeat and on dirt. And this has nothing to do with literary theory whatsoever. This is an ethical prejudice. This is an ethical commitment to positive hope, to edification, a word we despise. But as it happens, *edificare* in Latin means "to nourish."

ELC You see Lukács very much as the Jew.

GS One thousand percent.

ELC It is only now that critics start speaking of this side of Lukács.

GS That does not worry me at all. I started speaking about it when I began.

ELC He himself also seemed to reject its importance, and he even says so in much of his correspondence.

GS Of course, as did the complications of Freud's attitude to Judaism, and Marx's anti-Semitism. So what. So what. Every reflex, every gesture of that wonderful head and hands, the whole life was under the shadow of the deaths of the Jewish people in Europe. He knew that Marxism was a Jewish heresy, one with Christianity, one of the great heresies out of orthodox Judaism. His whole commitment to a utopian possibility, a pessimistic utopia, was Judaic, through and through. The way he read, the way he commented, the way he taught, and in his later years, in terrible sadness, after the death of his wife, all those who visited him—I did not—all who saw him, who had personal contact with him, said that he had become almost the wandering Jew who did not wander any more, of course.

ELC That has not been written about until recently by his biographer Kadarkay.

GS Irma Seidler, Ernst Bloch, Mannheim, Simmel, there was nobody who was not Jewish. Lukács is one thousand percent Jude, Jude, Jude. Don't tell me that Adorno, Bloch, Benjamin, Horkheimer, that that is an accident. The whole Frankfurt School. These are branches of the parodistic, tragic heresies of the Talmudic in the time of the end of European Judaism.

ELC How do you see the continuation?

GS Difficult question. Very difficult question. You ask that question in the weeks of the "collapse of Marxism" . . . , quotes, quotes, quotes. That we may in a few years from now have a meta-Marxism out of Africa or Latin America of enormous dimensions, I do not know. But one would be a hopeless idiot not to know that it is conceivable. It is possible. We do not know. But let us assume . . . quotes, quotes, quotes "the collapse" of the classical central European Russian Marxism, there will be a horrid period of McDonald's, Disneyland, and Joan Collins will be read across the planet. Yes, of course, that is what they want. You have not been, you have not seen what is happening to East Berlin, have you? You should. You should see where the Goethe and Schiller books are gone. They are gone. There are porno videocassettes now.

ELC I have just heard in Bremen that the majority of young people graduating with the Abitur have not read Schiller and Goethe.

GS Of course. German, as you and I love it, is disappearing and becoming like franglais in France or the esperanto jargon of the new Californians. In these circumstances, I do not think anyone will read Lukács for quite a long time to come except a few small circles around Martin Jay and *Telos*, but then they are reading very little else. Why? (a) He is immensely old-fashioned in his form. (b) The field of reference, there are very few of us left who have read what he has read and recognize his references, which are the whole of classical European literature, which was the world that ends with Roman Jacobson, Thomas Mann, René Wellek, I do not need to name the obvious names. So the whole echo chamber of what he assumes you to recognize is gone, plus the Marxism that will for a foreseeable time presumably be recognized as a tiny academic interest, as other agnostic heresies when Christianity triumphs. All right? Time is a much more ironic, patient animal than we are. Time may have in its great eyes a vision we cannot even begin to see, horizons we know nothing about, what the place will be one day, what of the work will survive. I will not make an idiot of myself by trying to do a horoscope. On the other hand, it is striking that there are a number of people like yourself, who are working on him in one way or another in the West.

ELC Maybe I should like to end on something both you and Lukács have mentioned as very important, namely having touched upon Marxism, having read Marx. While you are criticizing Marxists and communists, you privilege those who have gone through it and have emerged from it, as if they had become better people. Lukács said a similar thing about Thomas Mann, a bourgeois writer, whom he nevertheless counted among his much admired realists because he had been touched by socialism. I can see the importance of such a learning process, but maybe even more so in the case of those who have read Hegel.

GS If one has not read *The Phenomenology of the Spirit*, one is not of our time. And really read it, not just little post-deconstructivist idiocies about it. I disagree respectfully, I think, with every comma and syllable in psychoanalysis, which is the Jewish version of Christian Science, a great Jewish vengeance on the Christians, in my opinion. But not to have read Freud, and not reading him often and carefully and seeing why I cannot accept him, would disqualify me from being an adult in our century. The same is true for others. Not to have read *The Eighteenth Brumaire*, *The Conditions of the Working Class in England* by Engels—very, very important—not to have read part of the *Grundrisse*, not to have read about the French Revolution, would deprive one of the masters of epic narrative and invectives, which is to have missed the turning point of modern history even while disagreeing totally. For heaven's sake, it seems to me, before a guest comes, you wash your hands. Before one aspires to minimal literacy, one tries to justify that hope. Lukács has knowledge of the whole history of utopian, proto-messianic, radical philosophy. His knowledge of Kautsky, of Plekhanov, etc., give to his readings a formidable density. I read few men where you know that, before the page that you are reading, an enormous homework has been done. He is a man who, differently from so much that now is in fashion, did not bluff. Now, what came out was often intolerable, unacceptable, anything that you want. But one knows what one is wrestling with, one knows of the intensity of the raw material, where he comes from. He puts his cards on the table, yes, but not always, not always. And of course to have survived the Stalinist period, and then to have survived when I saw him in 1957 to 1959, and so on, and so on. It was a *salto mortale* over the abyss, but he managed.

ELC I was surprised that you had not included Lukács among the authors you discussed in *Real Presences*.

GS No, I could not. Those seven giant books I mentioned, I do not see anything of Lukács in those years. If he had written the one he was planning, before Irma Seidler's suicide, when he was planning a huge book on the meaning of truth and beauty, that would be in this list. We do not have it. But we have much. An enormous legacy.

INTERVIEW WITH FREDRIC JAMESON

11 March 1992, Duke University

ELC You have been writing about Lukács for more than twenty years now. I am thinking of your first work, "The Case of Georg Lukács," in *Marxism and Form* (Princeton: Princeton University Press, 1971), and your article, "*History and Class Consciousness* as an Unfinished Project" (*Rethinking Marxism* 1, no. 1 [Spring 1988]: 49–72). Amazingly, in this last text, which you wrote in 1988, you seem to have anticipated the events which followed soon thereafter, in 1989, with the downfall of the Berlin Wall and the bankruptcy of communism in Eastern Europe and Soviet Russia. You were among the first and are one of the most recent critics in this country to have addressed Lukács's work. It would be very interesting to know how and when you encountered Lukács for the first time, which of his works you read, and whether you actually recognize any Lukácsean influence on your work and thought.

FJ It was actually my first contact with Marxist criticism in the 1950s when I went to college. I read somewhere about what was described as a preposterous piece of Marxist criticism in which Thomas Mann's *Death in Venice* was interpreted as an allegory of the breakdown of Prussia and of the authoritarian Junker personality. I found that a strange but fascinating idea and later on came to associate the name of Lukács with it. The second, more formal intimation of Lukács's existence came through *The Magic Mountain* itself in the character of Naphta, about whom everyone said that it was a terribly disguised portrait of Lukács.

ELC Lukács disputes this allegation.

FJ I believe that Lukács has claimed that Thomas Mann made him at least much better dressed than he actually was when they met. Interestingly, at least from my own point of view, my approach to the Frankfurt School and Adorno also came through Thomas Mann, so it is a matter of a very central modernist classic of those days leading me, at least, on into other and new directions. Then, when I studied in Berlin in 1956 I began to have a much better idea of who Lukács was. Indeed, part of my education in those years was going across into the East—the Wall did not exist yet, of course—and bringing back those big blue volumes of Lukács's literary and philosophical essays, without having any idea of the kind of debates that were to rage around them in the German Democratic Republic in those days, and without, of course, the benefit of *History and Class Consciousness*, which remained unpublished in English and even more legendary for me until much later. In fact, my first contact with *History and Class Consciousness* was by way of the French translation in the late sixties.*

ELC Do you prefer the early Lukács or the later one?

FJ Well, I actually find that the fin de siècle, the very early Budapest Lukács, with his "Circle" and the theater and so forth is for me relatively and temperamentally repellent. There is a whole obsession with idealistic, Kierkegaardian motives, a whole period of weltschmerz, that I am not terribly interested in. Although I recognize the philosophical interest of those days, that side of Lukács is not the one that I feel closest to. On the other hand, in the early period, there are works that I think are very important, the *Modern Drama* book, for example, which will be increasingly recognized as crucial in many ways, as well as the two newly discovered Heidelberg aesthetics, the *Heidelberger Philosophie der Kunst* and the *Heidelberger Aesthetik*, which, although unfinished, are very remarkable anticipations not of anything of Lukács's own, although he clearly draws on them in his final *Aesthetics*, but of a true modernist position that he may be more expressive and symptomatic of than most of the people of that time. I plan to work further on those volumes. But I should add that I am much less interested again when Lukács returns to traditional, more Aristotelian aesthetics in his later years, although, given his importance, everything he wrote is bound to be of interest to us now.

ELC You seem to like *The Historical Novel* (London: Merlin Press, 1962), to judge from the prefaces you have written to it.

FJ I think it is a very good example of what Lukács was able to do in his realist period. I have reasons for placing a value on that maybe a little bit different from the standard evaluation, but I am also interested because I think the subject remains enormously relevant; namely, the question of whether historical representation is possible in any given period, and what its constraints are. It seems to me that in the postmodern age in which there is again a great plethora of historical representations, in particular in film—I paradoxically call them "nostalgia films," even though they are deeply ahistorical—and where there is also a return of interest to history in general, of an almost unorganized, visceral kind, which has to break with earlier historical forms and has not really found its own mode of expression. This is true, I think, both in documentary work, in historiography itself, and things like the New

---

*Georg Lukács, *History and Class Consciousness: Studies in Marxist Dialectics*, trans. Rodney Livingstone (Cambridge, Mass.: MIT Press, 1971); in French: *Histoire et conscience de classe*, trans. Kostas Axelos (Paris: Les Editions de Minuit, 1960).

Historicism. For this situation, Lukács's analysis, which obviously bears on very different objects from ours, that we could not think of reviving still has much to say and maybe much *new* to say.

ELC You were not disturbed by the Stalinist slogans in *The Historical Novel*?

FJ No. It is a text written in Moscow in the 1930s and published there, and this is simply part of the conventions of the period and the regime comparable in that respect to the various obligatory references to the monarch or the sovereign in seventeenth-century classical literature. It's probably dishonest to remove these things, as it has often been done in English translations, and not only of Lukács.

ELC A monumental biography of Lukács by Arpad Kadarkay* has just appeared, from which Lukács emerges as a personally very unattractive human being who, as he says of himself, is incapable of goodness, who cannot love, does not love his parents, and politically is quite a fierce Stalinist at times. Does it disturb you to learn about such negative human qualities of the man Lukács?

FJ Well, I think that biographical representations should never be taken at face value. These are always possible representations among others, and I can imagine that this might have been done in a very different way by another writer using much the same information. I have already said that the psychological features of the early Lukács I find rather unattractive. He himself in effect produces that picture of himself by analyzing himself in those terms. Even there, one need not take that particularly at face value. I think that under those circumstances one can admire his movement from subjectivity to a certain objectivity. It is something one could stage in a different way: that is, rather than assuming that his political commitments come out of a failure of the subjective or a bankruptcy of interpersonal relations, one can imagine a very different biographical representation in which that turn to the political is precisely a fighting through to social commitment out of certain kinds of personal deficiencies. As for the Stalinist polemics, I think that the atmosphere of the Third International in those days, particularly in Hungarian circles, was very violent and polemic. I imagine you could show that some of Lukács's attacks are in reality counterattacks, because he had many enemies. The problem is to decide—and then that is a moral decision which is really not up to anyone to make it, at least in my view—*who* started it, *which* comes first: Did Lukács persecute Brecht because of his attacks on realist art or is he simply responding to the attacks of the earliest left-wing mod-

* *Georg Lukács: Life, Thought, and Politics* (Cambridge, Mass.: Basil Blackwell, 1991).

ernists on his own positions in Hungary? As far as this goes, already back in the Béla Kun period, I think, it is very hard to decide that. I am not fond of the overly shrill polemical tone, but the intellectual milieu, I would think, in all cases determines the tone that is ceremonial, and we could certainly go back into other kinds of philosophy and find the same stand.

ELC Kadarkay says that Lukács's Stalinism appears only in his official publications and never in his private writings, and that he never defended Stalin privately, so he may have done it just for survival purposes.

FJ The point that I am trying to make is that it is not just for personal survival but was required for the public participation in the debates of party intellectuals in those days, particularly if you wanted to modify the party line, and that was essentially what Lukács was secretly trying to do. He had to take public positions which necessarily had to be violent, given the force of the official positions that he was trying to resist. So the tone is set by the public sphere itself in this case and in many others. Intellectuals cannot really choose the mode in which they argue, but it is determined by the nature of the medium, so to speak, and the nature of the public sphere.

ELC Lukács has been criticized for his eclecticism. In his choices of "true realist writers," for instance, he includes not only Balzac and Walter Scott but also Gorky next to figures such as Thomas Mann. In his definition of realist writers, the criteria that seems very important to him is that all his realist writers, and this includes Thomas Mann, had at one point or another to have been exposed to socialist thinking. The controversy appears, though, in the case of Zola. Lukács persistently criticizes and condemns Zola, even though Zola was one of the most outspoken socialist writers of his time. How can one reconcile these views?

FJ I think that there is a higher expediency here at work. In other words, Zola was not only a writer with certain political positions who might demand to be judged on their basis, or evaluated on their basis, but he was also the inventor of a mode of writing, naturalism, which was current in Lukács's day and which Lukács indeed identified with socialist realism. It is important to read the attacks on naturalism as coded attacks on socialist realism. That means that if you are going to use Zola symbolically in that way, as the disguise for your attack on what is publicly impossible to attack as such, then there will be a certain deformation in the way Zola is seen. But there may also be a larger doctrinal issue here, which has to do with Zola's politics, which are essentially liberal. Perhaps one wants to say that even after the

Commune, political positions were not yet sufficiently well defined to make these kinds of judgments. I think there is an instructive paradox in the way in which Lukács wants to use Balzac positively, a writer notoriously far more reactionary than Zola, but is suspicious of a liberal, centrist, or even social democratic position like that of Zola. This is all part of the ambiguities of political judgment of that period. I would also want to say that in this ranking of the great writers of the past it seems that it is like the issue of "noble pagans" for medieval Christianity, where there is also a moment in history when a certain kind of revelation is made: the people who write before that cannot have had the benefit of that revelation, therefore you do not judge them in the same way as you judge those who come after this unique break in time. Obviously, the moment in Lukács's rather schematic history writing of the period, particularly in the history of German literature, is the *Communist Manifesto* of 1848. Since Zola falls after that divide, he tends to be more harshly judged as someone who ought to have known about the dispensation but did not take the full consequences of it, than Balzac who could never have known of it but did indeed anticipate features of it in his own work.

ELC Lukács is very critical not only of Zola but also of Flaubert and Stendhal. In his words they had "lost the right perspective."

FJ Oh, yes, but I do not think that is right in the case of Stendhal, is it? I think Lukács is always very positive about Stendhal.

ELC He is, about one or two characters in Stendhal's *The Scarlet and the Black*, for instance, about Mathilde, who according to him is a truly positive, realist character, but he is critical of most others and the romanticism of the whole novel itself.

FJ Well, that is not altogether wrong. I think Stendhal is critical of romanticism himself, but surely Lukács understood that *The Charterhouse of Parma* included one of the great representations of popular insurrection as well as giving the classical picture of the dark reaction of the Restoration years. These are the historical features Lukács saluted. I think that there were also reasons why Stendhal's own intellectual passions were necessarily far more ambivalent; but in any case, Stendhal died before 1848. In the case of Flaubert, I do not think that there is any problem about that. One can document Flaubert's attitudes; his letters about the Commune are notoriously bloodthirsty, and *Salammbô* is something of a blueprint of a counterrevolution. In *A Sentimental Education*, obviously, one gets a somewhat more balanced picture of revolution. I think one could talk about, and people have evoked, a rather different Flaubert, one who was youthfully progressive but disillusioned by the failure of the revolution of 1848

(David Gross has done some interesting work in this spirit on Flaubert's early papers). The cynicism of this particular Flaubert comes precisely from a kind of youthful idealism, the sort that you find incarnated in the figure of Dussardier in *A Sentimental Education.* One need not have quite exactly Lukács's view on that, but on the whole, I think, that he is not wrong. In the case of Zola, you have also to add that literary history itself has always been very ambivalent about Zola. It is not just the Marxists who hesitate and who are uncertain as to what to do with this work, but it is bourgeois literary criticism from Zola's own period on up. It has been seemingly the naturalists in particular (I think Dreiser and Norris would be a case in point in the United States) and naturalism in general that have been very difficult to domesticate and to canonize. So, if we have problems with Lukács's evaluations, we ought to consider them in the context of this larger problematic of naturalism.

ELC In reading *Modern Drama** you see that Lukács is already very critical of Zola in his first major publication, which was certainly pre-Marxist. The Zola criticism was very much in the air in the early century when Lukács began to write. In speaking of this context, I should like to bring up one of your own critical terms, "the logic of capitalism," and ask you whether one could recognize in Zola's writing the phenomenon you evoke by this notion, "the logic of capitalism," or whether it seems to have appeared later in history?

FJ I did not mean the term to be stylistic, and I think if one wanted to look at Zola from that point of view, one would have to talk, as I believe Lukács indeed does, about the way in which Zola's style tends to produce these larger-than-life symbols and this vitalist rhetoric, which, I think, dialectically could be seen as a result of reification and alienation in the very style itself. It would be a very indirect and mediated case to link Zola's style and his novelistic procedures with this "logic of capitalism." Rather, one might evoke a "logic of capitalism" at an earlier stage, one in which the triumph of modernization is secured but in which language is still trying to replace the loss of value by a certain kind of rhetorical overemphasis; it seems to me that something like that is what is going on in Zola, along with another feature that the resolutely antipsychoanalytical Lukács would of course be very insensitive to, which is the peculiar libidinal charge of naturalist language and description. There Deleuze has written very well on the relationship between naturalism in film and in literature and on certain aberrant psychological impulses.

---

*Georg Lukács, *A modern dráma fejlödésének története* (Budapest: Franklin Társulat, 1911); in German: *Entwicklungsgeschichte des Modernen Dramas*, trans. Dénes Zalán, vol. 15 of *Werke* (Neuwied: Luchterhand, 1981).

ELC So, to use again one of your own terms, when you say that "narrative failure becomes reified" in the modernist text, this would not be the case, not yet, in Zola?

FJ Yes, I think so, but it would mean something different in him, namely, that "narrative failure" leaves its mark in this symbolism, in this rhetoric, in this vitalism, in the way in which it is reified into a certain number of rhetorical devices in Zola, and into a certain temporality, and a certain repetitive rhythm, and so forth. So in that sense, I suppose that one could approach Lukács's dialectic that way, who in effect sets naturalism and symbolism (or nascent modernism) back-to-back as it were, and identifies them as being two faces of the same thing. I would rather myself say that in modernism, narrative failure becomes the occasion for a kind of new reflexivity about representation itself that I do not think one finds in Zola. But the initial situation, that is, the difficulty of forging narrative as such in a new situation of modernization, *that* I think Zola may share with modernism.

ELC I should like to turn to realism, which is Lukács's positive term. In your article, "Beyond the Cave,"* you confess that you find both positions, "the defense of realism just as much as the denunciation of it equally convincing, equally persuasive, equally true." So, you seem to feel somewhat uneasy with the concept of realism proposed by Lukács?

FJ Well, I think the problem is this, that one has to separate the "transcendental" meaning of realism from its immediate historical representatives in nineteenth-century fiction, and it is a very tricky operation. It seems to me that there is a way in which one could say, as Brecht did, that it is intolerable to hold up these old-fashioned models of realistic narrative in the twentieth century; it would be futile and sterile to go back to those. They spring from historical periods that are over and done with, their procedures and styles are outmoded, and, surely everyone largely agrees with this estimate in practice, no one would want to read a novel written in the style of the early nineteenth century unless it were specifically marked as a pastiche of that historical style. On the other hand, you can also say that Lukács is using *that* nineteenth-century moment to construct a model of a more general historical situation in which an opening to the social totality is possible and a kind of narration is possible which solves some of the problems of the modernist crisis of representation. I think someone like Brecht would surely have been much happier with that kind of reading, although I

*Fredric Jameson, *The Ideologies of Theory: Essays 1971–1986, Volume 2, Syntax of History* (Minneapolis: University of Minnesota Press, 1988), p. 121.

take it that he also felt that Lukács was the very quintessence of the academic critic who lays down rules for this and that and constantly attacks aesthetic innovation and experimentation as such. And again, there too, one could have much sympathy for that (but remember that we earlier spoke of resituating Lukács's hostility toward experimentation in his earlier Budapest situation in which he was himself the object of attack by the Bolshevik futurists). But if this reading of Lukács is adopted, then we are talking about the way in which a certain kind of narrative might have as its vocation what I would call a "cognitive mapping" of the social totality; and in that case, if one wants to go on using that word, one has a notion of realism which is much broader and that might include a lot of Third World writing today or "magic realism" and would not limit us to the older, very estimable realist models of the classic nineteenth-century novel, which pretty clearly are not suitable for postcontemporary conditions.

ELC You say in your reflections on the "Brecht-Lukács Debate" that the "originality of the concept of realism lies in its claim to cognitive as well as aesthetic status," but you also say that the "cognitive" was overemphasized, which then really turned against it. This leads me into my next question. You yourself speak of the "ideology of realism" somewhat critically. In general, today there is a lot of criticism of realism. Critics speak of the "seductions" of realism, its dogmatism. They say it is a "mirage." Is it a "seduction"? Is it naive?

FJ I guess I have several reactions to that. I have a question whether we want to go on using the word, whether the word is not too strongly identified either with Dickens and Balzac or with Lukács himself, either one now being thought of as old-fashioned and taking us back to a period that is over and done with. On the other hand, I continue to think that the problem raised by this realist discussion remains a very interesting one, and it would be a pity to lose that, to lose the problem, which is a rich one and turns on cognitive mapping, whereas we might very well wish to lose all the solutions that were proposed in that particular period. I think it is worth pursuing the debate in this sense, even if one has to mark this word and ask oneself questions about it. I do return to it in my film book, *Signatures of the Visible* (New York: Routledge, 1990), where I talk again about realism and modernism. The other thing one wants to say is that there is a more general return to storytelling in the postmodern period. There is also, I think, a tendency, a movement away from the subjective, the introspective, or the psychological, and those were things that tended to mark the modernist swerve away from realism toward the dreamlike or the unconscious, or experiments of that kind. So it may be that the atmosphere today, if it is not hospitable to old-fashioned three-decker nineteenth-century novels, which pretty clearly reflected bourgeois culture, may nonetheless be more hospitable to a certain kind of storytelling realism quite different in spirit from the great modernist classics. Thus, perhaps realism is back today on some other agenda than that of Lukács. It would also be important to try to look at realistic narrative on a world scale and think about the practice of narrative in non-Western countries as well as by internally marginalized groups and cultures in late capitalism itself. It seems to me that in this media culture we have absorbed a whole set of modernist techniques which we no longer think of as being nonrealistic or antirealistic, so that future realism could include those without having the kind of de-realizing value they had in the modernist period. If you look at the way people are trained by advertisements, I mean one assumes that there is a basic realism to television advertising, because it wants to sell products, it wants to identify products, it wants to give some very specific social signals, it is very important that there not be much ambiguity about television advertising. But would one call that a realist aesthetic anymore? I do not think so in some older sense, but in a situation in which young people grow up on this form of image and in which their readings and consumer tastes are trained by such images, in a world like that, maybe realism might present features that Lukács would never have dreamed of.

ELC The criticism addressed to the concept is that realism is really dogmatic in the sense that it makes a truth claim based on this "zugerechnete Bewusstsein," the anticipation or comprehension, the imputed consciousness of a situation or condition that "ought to be." And if you go away from that definition, saying that it was wrong, what is the framework of realism, what replaces it? How do you know what is real and is not only your own personal, individual perception?

FJ I don't agree with your use of the phrase "zugerechnete Bewusstsein," which I think has to do with the perspective a given class can logically take on social reality, but I do agree that it's very dangerous for critics to try to dictate to writers, and it seems to me that it was one of the least admirable features of Lukács to have seemed to lay down the law to realistic writers in our century and tell them what to do. But on the part of the writers, surely you cannot have a relativism unless you have multiple reality positions, and one would think that an individual writer would want to stake out one of those and represent a certain kind of reality, running the risk of having it negated or relativized by someone else's reality. In any case, I guess, that is how I think of this stigmatized word "totality," and "totalization," namely, that there is a framework of contemporary reality that is late capitalism itself, which cannot really be relativized even if it is not always present in the same way in all of our existential and group experiences. I think one incapacitates oneself in advance when one assumes that it is oppressive to suggest the interest in tracking this presence of this structure of domination and establishing it; I would have thought that any form of resistance to it would depend on mapping out the form that that structure of domination and control takes. So I am of two minds about the relativists' position here.

ELC In your own approach to realism—I remember your calling it at a conference in Kansas "global cognitive mapping"—what is it that is guiding you? You said that you ask philosophical questions, you establish the relationship between characters and situations, you try to grasp the positioning of the individual and the collective subject. Could you give an example of what you do in your practice of "cognitive mapping"?

FJ Yes, but you see I do not want to propose any single model for that. It seems to me that the most interesting artists would be those who suggest lines of flight that open up beyond the individual on the existential situation and even beyond the national situation of this new world system that we are in. This doesn't mean that such opening lines of flight are accessible to everyone. In an older period, people had much clearer if no doubt more ideological and erroneous representations and visions of what the nation was and how individual lives fit into that. It seems to me that now people feel in a much more obscure and confused way the presence of a whole multinational reality in their individual lives. You can imagine this coming through both in the form of tourism and in the form of inflation, loss of jobs, and so on and so forth. The question would be, what traces that obscure or unconscious feeling leaves on the form itself. I would say the interest in cognitive mapping is not to propose it but to claim that we are doing it already and then find out how in the various national situations this dim awareness of the shaping presence of larger work-systemic forces is registered. That would be the most auspicious beginning for any project of cognitive mapping.

ELC The danger I see in all this, and the critique one could address to the concepts of realism, totality, and even the concept of history is that all these terms could actually be seen as reifications which the critique would like to avoid.

FJ Well, but it may be unavoidable. I mean Adorno has pointed out in his aesthetics over and over again that art, at least, depends on reification. You cannot imagine a work of art that does not try to use reification in some way, otherwise you would be faced with a completely disembodied, transitory project that has no stability or objective existence. And I suppose that critical terminology also reifies as does philosophical terminology. The point would rather be to mark these reifications as such and to be aware of them and to know with a certain resignation that there always comes a moment when this kind of necessary reification exacts its negative price, at which point the established terminology or the established model or the established mode of representation then becomes pernicious.

ELC You just mentioned television and commercials and their "realism." Is this not rather a "pragmatic realism," though, or does it offend you to see it that way? Do the implications of the term "pragmatic" in this context disturb you?

FJ You have to explain what you mean.

ELC They are pragmatic in the sense that they are supposed to sell. Their aim is real, but it is also goal-, or more specifically, money-oriented.

FJ I see, but the whole point of the postmodern is that we are in a situation in which the pragmatic is no longer enough. I think you can see in all these commercials—some of them very expertly and artistically done, by the way, and by very talented people—that there is now necessarily a surplus of culture as opposed to the pragmatic aim, and indeed that the pragmatic aim in many of these cases, in order to fulfill itself, practically must remain a mere pretext. It seems to me that today an ad which abandoned the frills and decided simply to sell its product would be a complete failure. These ads are successful only if they make fun of the project of selling things. So I think that the role of the pragmatic is certainly there, but it has been minimized, and there is a whole expansion of the cultural sphere that has taken place in which these allegedly pragmatic aims are positioned in a new way. And no doubt something of that sort could be said about literature and the pragmatic things it once tried to do. I think it has been pointed out that postmodernism, for example, tolerates the didactic to a much higher degree than modernism ever did. Modernism wished to get rid of the didactic. Many more kinds of facts and documentary discourse can be housed in the atmosphere of postmodernism and in postmodern works than was ever the case in the modern. So one can imagine the return to a certain kind of *content* in literature and art in a relatively new way, and that opens up this possibility which has to be taken into account. I do not think we can foreclose the possibility of a kind of left or radical postmodernism.

ELC In all your criticism, you always insist on the importance of history, and very often you criticize a movement because it did not work with the notion of history. I am thinking of your critique of structuralism, for instance. But then you also say that Lukács himself is "ahistorical." Would you like to comment on this?

FJ Yes, yes. I think what I meant by the ahistorical component in Lukács was the moralism and the ethical component, as in the case of Thomas Mann. Lukács uses Thomas Mann as an example of a fellow traveler who has much of the modernist culture without surrendering to what Lukács thought was modernist reification, and suggests then, that this is a new form of critical realism, and that it is available to other artists by way of an essentially ethical decision. It is at that point that the genuinely historical is turned off. That is to say, when Lukács deals with earlier forms, he is very aware of the ways in which the historical period imposes limits on the form and on the formal practices of these writers, imposes limits or opens up opportunities, as the case may be. There is a sentence in Hegel's *Aesthetics* that puts Lukács's formal approach very well: "Formal defects are always to be attributed to defects in content." And by "content" Hegel means, obviously, not just thought but the whole mode of existence of the society and the kinds of psychological experiences that go on in it, the kinds of thoughts that are thought, and the kinds of values, the types of events that people experience in their daily lives, and so on and so forth. It seems to me that that was Lukács's great insight; and from *The Theory of the Novel* (1916) on into the realist period, it was the greatness of Lukács to insist that problems in narrative are always related to limits in social experience. So when he then looks out on the modern world, the Weimar and the 1920s, the bourgeois Europe of the 1930s, and suggests to writers that it is an option of theirs to return to a realist form of writing simply by adopting the proper political attitude, whether that means joining the Communist Party as such or finding it in themselves to have the kind of sympathy that Thomas Mann from time to time had for the left, then I think we have passed the line in the boundary over into some sort of voluntarism in which it is no longer the social situation that sets the boundaries and exercises a certain determination over the writer's formal practice. That is what I mean by Lukács's "ethical moment," and one finds it when he comes to deal with contemporary writing, something which he is notoriously not able to do. So I would restrict that critique of Lukács's ahistoricism to that. Obviously, one can have arguments with his interpretation of history, too, but that is not what you meant, I think.

ELC No, well, Lukács obviously did not appreciate modernism and modernist writing.

FJ Let me interrupt just for a moment. The new biographical evidence seems to suggest that this [distaste for modernism] is a very old feeling in Lukács. That is not Stalinist dogmatism or anything like that. He seems to have been sensitive to a certain symbolist moment in the modern period, the Maeterlinck in his early theater work. He seems always to have been hostile to the new, more machine-oriented, futurist moment in modernism, in the very early years of the century. Presumably, this hostility to this more full-blown form-breaking modernism was only intensified and enhanced by the attacks on him of the communist left in Hungary, the younger generation of left-wing modernist communists, who were exceedingly suspicious of Lukács in the first place and opposed his entry into the party in 1918. So I think one has to take those things into account. One is tempted to see this as a form of old-fogyism, and he himself was only too happy to identify with Goethe and Hegel and their dislike of their younger contemporaries, the romantics. So there is much truth in what you say, but I think this earlier history of his antipathy to a certain modernism has to be taken into account as well.

ELC Well, you do say somewhere that in a way we now may have lived long enough to have caught up with some of Lukács's rejections of a certain literature, and as a result can understand and accept his views, such as the criticism of certain modernist writers, better today. We have moved on, since the 1960s, to what you have called the postmodernist mode so that we can judge modernism maybe somewhat similarly to the way Lukács judged it half a century before us.

FJ Well, yes, maybe not the same way Lukács judged it, but let us say that we are far enough from modernism so that his own distance from modernism does not bother us in the same way as it did the interested parties; that is, we are no longer fully invested in that debate. In the older days, one would always have said, in one's enthusiasm for Joyce or Kafka or surrealism or whatever, that Lukács was simply obscurantist and old-fashioned and so on. Now I think maybe we are distant enough that we can be a little less passionate about those judgments and to entertain a suspension of disbelief in weighing some of Lukács's thoughts on the matter.

ELC To bring in another quote here, you say that "postmodernism is a theoretical discourse that is not philosophical." Does this mean that modernism was still philosophical and that we, the postmoderns, are no longer philosophically inclined today?

FJ What I meant was that what we call "theory" today, theoretical discourse, is a postmodern thing and that it happens after the traditional discourses of philosophy have in one way or the other been exhausted. So what I would say is not necessarily that modernism was philosophical in general, but that there were still philosophical modernisms and that there may not be *philosophical* postmodernisms but rather theoretical postmodernisms. So I would consider, for example, that Heidegger is one of the last of the philosophical modernists, whereas the uses of Heidegger in the contemporary period become theoretical and postphilosophical.

ELC Could one say, then, with Lukács in a way, that the modernists were philosophical in the sense that they struggled, for instance, with irrationalism, to use again one of Lukács's terms?

FJ Yes, I think one could say that, but I would give it a twist that I think you probably do not mean to imply, namely, that one of the things that has disappeared for the postmodern is precisely this antithesis between the rational and the irrational, despite Habermas. It seems to me that those are sets of categories that are not altogether appropriate today. I am not sure that we have the same notions about the irrational any more. I do think, though, that one would want to add something else to the matter, namely, that in some of these writers, including Lukács himself, the hold of an old-fashioned philosophizing is clearest in the project of a philosophical aesthetics itself. There is a way in which perhaps all aesthetics are posthumous from Kant on; Hegel's aesthetics notoriously theorize the very end of art itself; and in Adorno aesthetics is literally posthumous, while he meanwhile posits something like the death of modernism. But the return of Lukács to a traditional aesthetics of that kind marks his own limits, marks his own commitment as a philosopher to philosophy as such, as well as the limits implied precisely by that commitment in a period at which philosophy is ended.

ELC I mentioned somewhere else that I much appreciated the definition of postmodernism which you provided at a conference in Kansas. You said at that time, if I remember well, that "modernism *died* and that postmodernism *happened*." Again, coming back to my question, does this mean that modernism died, no questions are asked anymore, that postmodernism accepts the legacy, what there is? Is there less questioning in postmodernism? Is postmodernism institutionalized to that point?

FJ Well, I would not put it quite that simply. I think that one of the reasons why modernism died, one of the signs of its death was *its* institutionalization, that is, the institutionalization of modernism, the creation of the great modern museums, the creation of a modern canon, and so forth, whereas postmodernism wants to resist that kind of canonization and institutionalization. What the formula you quoted meant was that when the whole modernist impulse slowed down and dried up, then, at that point, a number of new things began to happen which only gradually became identified as a general postmodernist ethos or atmosphere. I do not think one could talk about a postmodern movement in the same way one could talk about a modern movement or a modernist movement. Postmodernism did not coalesce in a movement, although it got media recognition and identification and it was eventually named. But since it is resolutely anti-avant-garde, one does not find the same mode of emergence as one does in modernism, when one has the great manifestos and the great moments in which a whole new modernist wave declares itself.

ELC Do you call yourself a "critic *of* postmodernism" or a "postmodernist critic?"

FJ I think that depends on what meaning the slogan has. If postmodern today is meant as a certain number of philosophical propositions about relativism and so on, then I guess I would rather avoid that label for myself. But I do not consider myself a critic of postmodernism in the way that Lukács surely must have thought of himself as a critic of modernism, that is, as someone who denounces this trend in ethical and political terms. I do not feel that that is the right stance to take.

ELC So you are not opposed to what is happening today?

FJ Well, my objection is to words such as "opposed," "criticize," "judge," and so forth, because I do not think that those are the choices we have in this kind of cultural system.

ELC I liked very much one of your sentences, one of these wonderful sentences one finds in all your texts. This one, I believe is on the very last page of your *Postmodernism, or, The Cultural Logic of Late Capitalism* (Durham: Duke University Press, 1991), where you admit your occasional frustration with the slogan of "postmodernism." At the same time, you wish to retain it as "still the most effective and useful in dramatizing the issues." Do you often feel this way?

FJ Yes, but I think one could say the same thing—returning to our discussion of realism—about that word, that is to say, these terms are useful when they open up fields of conflict and polemic and discussion, when they make differentiations possible, when they open up problems. I think they are much less useful when they are used as badges of positions or as labels. Then I would get very uncomfortable with them, but if they are properly marked, as a new discursive field, which obligates one to raise certain kinds of issues and problems and confront new kinds of issues and problems, then I think it is perfectly proper to launch or to use the term either realism or postmodernism as such a declaration of intent. Now, as I said for realism, there may come a time when even the word is no longer useful in that way. Then, I guess, we move elsewhere, but by that time history has moved on, too.

ELC You say somewhere that we have to "reinvent" realism, so maybe it will be just quite different, without any dogmatism attached to it.

FJ That is right. And maybe, then, the word would not be desirable.

ELC May we go on to something else? The topic of this book is more specifically "Lukács After Communism." Looking at the bankruptcy of communism, how do you see, how do you interpret what happened in Russia and Eastern Europe? Does it affect your belief in Marxism?

FJ Okay. Let me begin an answer by sticking to the Lukács part of it. I think that one of the ways that one has to look at Lukács's life work is as a contribution to socialist pedagogy, that is, he was not merely making critical judgments or writing literary history, but he was thinking about what in Ernst Bloch's rather different terms one talks about as the use of the heritage, *das Erbe*, and the role that that should play in socialist formation, socialist education. I do not know whether I publicly discussed this wonderful preparatory school in Cuba before, which had a two- or three-year humanities course which is greatly enlarged from what Lukács foresaw. They had semesters on the classics, on the history of poetry, on Lukács's great realists, on their own national revolutionary literature, on contemporary writing. There was a way of imagining the connection between a certain formation in world culture for teenagers and the whole elaboration of a more general socialist pedagogy. Surely, when properly used, Lukács's work would have been very important in that. Now, was he ever so used? Or was Marxism not often in the state party systems misused in alleged philosophy courses that were not more than a teaching of snippets of Marx and Engels by rote. It is certainly clear that there is now a tremendous hangover of Marx, Marxism, and Marxist terminology in the East, that it will take many generations to overcome—a visceral dislike of Marxist language as such, along with a feeling among many of the intellectuals that that is old stuff and that they want new Western terms and codes and concepts and that all this is to be relegated to ancient history. So, clearly, some of Lukács's immediate fate in the East will be dependent on such feelings (but at the same time he will surely become a research industry). There would be three countries in which I think he might play a more immediate role: One is Germany, but it is difficult to see what the new Germany will look like intellectually. It will surely not finally be a prolongation of the old West Germany but something rather different. It will be interesting to see what eventual part Lukács will play in that. But I think this postmodern period is also a period of intense nationalism and pretty obviously, and whatever happens to the great East German writers and however they are reassimilated into a unified German canon, a foreigner like Lukács, however deeply imbued he was in German culture, may find it more difficult to exert an influence. Then there is also Austria. I really do not know to what degree the Austrians might be willing to think of Lukács as having something to do with them; but clearly the Hungarians will have their own specific way of appropriating Lukács's heritage as a national classic, and I think that will probably be the expression of a kind of ambivalence or mixed feelings in which pride, national pride, and political distaste play an indeterminable role.

ELC Today, you do not even find Lukács's books in the bookstores of Budapest.

FJ Today presumably not, but later on it will surely be of the greatest importance to the Hungarians that they produced a massive figure of this kind. So it is hard to know. Now, that sort of opens up the answer, the more general answer to the matter of Marxism in the East. I guess, from what one hears, the disaster is so enormous that it is very hard to see what kind of stable form this is going to take. I would assume that if a mixed economy finally subsists, then certain forms of social thought are going to have to subsist along with it, and the kind of things that Gorbachev was proposing, new kinds of social democratic theories, which necessarily will draw on Marx, will inevitably have to be developed. If these countries become market economies entirely, then I think that politics will begin to express itself by way of what we call dependency theory: that is to say, under those circumstances the form that radical thought will take—and there will always be radical thought even in the second world—will not be the Marxist language of internal commodity production and the exploitation of workers, but rather the language of imperialism and the analysis of the way in which weaker states are manipulated by the world system as a whole. But that some form of radicalism will gradually reemerge does not seem to be in doubt.

ELC Is it perceived as a letdown, a disappointment, by left-wing critics to witness the bankruptcy of communism? What is the lesson for the left-wing intellectuals to be drawn from this experience?

FJ Well, I think there are many lessons about the kinds of socialist culture that were achieved and that have presumably left their traces in people's way of thinking. I still find it difficult to think that people who grew up in the Soviet Union in those structures of socialism, however one wants to nuance that general term, would have quite the same habits as those of us on the outside, and, indeed, I think they do not understand very well the kinds of habits of consumption and values and attitudes of the West and in particular of Americans. That is to say, they do not understand consumerism any better than they grasp our lack of social services and the ruthlessness of market structures over here. On the other hand, maybe the development of market and consumer mentalities goes very fast indeed and then in that case that will be our great cultural problem and political problem over the next years, diagnosing the rapidity of that change. My position on the collapse is that the party state, whatever its relationship to one's own ideal of socialism, was a very successful instrument of modernization. In the modernist period, to use our language in a little larger socioeconomic way, the communist states and the Soviet Union and China were successful achievements. It is when we pass over into the intensified force fields of a third moment of capitalism, of a late, global-information, multinational capitalism, and when these states are submitted to the tremendous cultural and economic intensity of that system, that they are no longer viable. So I would not by any means want to talk about simply the failure of communism. It seems to me that it was successful at a certain moment in constructing heavy industry, but at the point when the whole capitalist system itself expanded into its third stage, it is at that moment that those states became unproductive. When they deliberately opened themselves to the pressures of the world system, they were clearly unable to withstand its intensity. But you can say this in another way. You can say that their collapse is cultural, that it had to do with feelings about consumers' goods, consumption, information, and so forth, reached by populations who had achieved a level of literacy and technological know-how, who had achieved modernization, in other words, who had arrived at a certain level of what we otherwise would call bourgeois culture, and who then were exposed to the kinds of lifestyle and cultural influence coming from the West for which the socialist culture proved to have no adequate response. So one could just as easily speak of a failure of socialist culture in this respect.

ELC In our earlier talk you mentioned that you did see a continuation and validity of Lukács's work, for instance, in present feminist and black liberationist theories.

FJ This is so-called standpoint theory, as that is outlined in *History and Class Consciousness*. It really comes out of Marx, of the first published work of Marx, the *Introduction to the Contribution to the Critique of Hegel's Philosophy of Right*, the theory of radical chains. It is not original with me but was dominant in particular in the sixties, particularly in the black movement, and has since then, much more recently, been adopted by socialist feminists. Yes, I think it is very important. There one can be as pluralistic as you like, but it seems to me that standpoint theory opens up possibilities for difference and diversity which do not completely abandon the matter of collective action, of collective mentalities and their respective epistemological possibilities in the social totality.

ELC You mention in your article on *History and Class Consciousness* an interview with Lukács, from which you quote Lukács as saying that the most important thing is that there should always be a new beginning. In your "Reflections on the Brecht-Lukács Debate" you have another one of these disarming sentences which I should like to quote in this connection. You say that "attempts to go beyond Marxism typically end by reinventing old pre-Marxist positions." Are you going that way? As you know I have been talking to several Lukácsean critics who seem to follow similar paths, beginning again with Lukács's beginnings, his early works, which are his roads to Marxism. You mentioned to me the other day that you were presently very interested in the *Heidelberger Aesthetik* (1916–1918). Are you, too, going back to Lukács's pre-Marxist positions to emerge, in a sense, anew from there?

FJ Well, I think one should resist doing that. I also had in mind the return of many contemporary philosophers back over Hegel, to Kant and pre-Hegelian positions. Kant is very interesting indeed and interesting in new ways for us today, but I would not want to return to Kantianism. No, if I am doing any of that it is returning for more sustenance to Hegel himself. It seems to me that there is an enormous richness in Hegel provided we imagine a Hegel who follows the *Grundrisse*, so to speak, rather than a Hegel who precedes Marx altogether. It seems to me that this is a time when people no longer understand what dialectical thinking is or why the dialectic came into being in the first place, when they have abandoned the dialectical for less rewarding Nietzschean positions. So there is certainly a need today for a revitalized vision of the dialectic. There I would certainly not abandon Marx, but I would want to go back to Hegel for an enlargement of the way we have normally understood Marx. This is not any particularly new idea with me. Lenin already said that no one could understand *Das Kapital* who had not already worked his way through Hegel's logic. There is some provocation in this statement, to be sure, but it might again be suggestive for us, and I would also add that I find things happening in psychoanalysis and particularly in Lacanianism which are far more dialectical than most of the other poststructuralisms. I think the coming years will show an unconscious need for the dialectic which some of us on the left ought to have the mission to satisfy.

ELC Would Lukács be in that picture?

FJ Surely. Yes, yes. You see my operation in dealing with Lukács was always to suggest that the writings on realism, the most familiar and even banal, the most seemingly dogmatic looked much richer when they were reinterpreted as later chapters or versions of *The Theory of the Novel.* And I think that then much of the rest of Lukács could be revitalized in that way, if we looked at some of the earlier things, *Heidelberg Aesthetics* among others, the drama book, and so forth, who knows, maybe even some of the last works. It seems to me that a picture of Lukács that is considerably less Stalinist, dogmatic, and one-dimensional can emerge from that, for he is clearly one of the great twentieth-century dialectic philosophers. After all, Marx never wrote his philosophy of Marxism, one may doubt if that is at all possible in the terms of Marxism or the dialectic itself, whether there could be a philosophy of that traditional sort, a philosophical defense of Marxism as such. There have been attempts, Sidney Hook's early one is still very important, but, surely, if there was to have been imagined a philosophical underpinning of Marxism, *History and Class Consciousness* was one of the most dramatic attempts to produce one, and that, I think, is a very great philosophical act in the history of modern philosophy. It was a very great and creative conceptual leap on Lukács's part, whatever one thinks of the results. So, that must be, I think, registered to his enormous credit.

ELC You did call it an "unfinished project."

FJ And that is always, I think, a healthy way of dealing with the past.

INTERVIEW WITH CORNEL WEST

25 March 1992, Princeton University

ELC Thank you very much for agreeing to talk to me about Lukács. What I particularly appreciated in your book *The Ethical Dimensions of Marxist Thought** was that your approach to and interpretation of Lukács's work seemed to have an urgency and a relevance to your current preoccupations that I had not found in most other academic critics. I felt that Lukács really "spoke" to you and said something vital to you. In the introduction, which is very interesting and which is also one of your most recent texts, you mentioned that you felt "seduced" by Lukács and the Frankfurt School, and that it actually happened here at Princeton. So I should like to ask you how it happened, how you encountered Lukács, and which books you read.

CW We had a study group here in the early seventies with a number of graduate students in philosophy, political theory, and social theory. Mainly, people were studying with Sheldon Wolin. I also was close to Richard Rorty at the time, but Sheldon Wolin was the catalyst for a number of us who came together and began to read Lukács, Foucault, Derrida, Deleuze, Lyotard, and a host of others. We read the Frankfurt School as well, Adorno and Horkheimer. We had some real tensions in that group, and a tension primarily between those of us who thought that Hegelian versions of Marxist theory were the most interesting, and then the anti-Hegelians, mainly linked to the Parisian intellectuals, especially Foucault and Derrida, Foucault probably more than Derrida. Derrida I think is much closer to Hegel than Foucault. We had some wonderful knock-'em-out, drag-'em-out fights. I was always convinced that Lukács's essay on reification was the most powerful text that I had read that fused philosophical reflection with an analysis of capitalist society as well as a sense of urgency as to how to change and transform it. So that essay for me remains one of the great essays in contemporary thought, not just in Marxist tradition, not just in Hegelian philosophy.

ELC So it was *History and Class Consciousness* that you read first? Had you read much of his other works, his literary analyses?

CW No, not at all. In fact I began with the 1923 collection, *History and*

---

* *The Ethical Dimensions of Marxist Thought* (New York: Monthly Review Press, 1991). Chapter 6 of the book is called "The Hegelian Marxist Position: Lukács's Ontological Quest." All references to the book can be found within the present text as *EDMT*, followed by the page number.

Class Consciousness, and then worked backward and read *Soul and Form* and *The Theory of the Novel*, and so on. It was primarily the philosophical Lukács, because I actually did not become preoccupied with literary criticism until the mid to late 1970s. Early on, it was primarily the history of philosophy. Actually, it was Lukács who led me back to Hegel's *Phenomenology of Spirit*. I had read parts of it, but I had read it in a very different way. Lukács sent me back. That was partly because Kojève was an interlocutor. We were reading Kojève's lectures on Hegel at that time.

ELC Was that here or in Paris?

CW No, that was here in Princeton. Not in class, just among ourselves.

ELC I am trying to find out how Lukács might have influenced you in your thinking and what you might have in common. I know that you describe yourself as a "prophetic, Christian, pragmatist freedom fighter," and that you are also conservative in some ways.

CW I guess so, like somebody who wants to preserve something. I would make a distinction between somebody who is in a *preservative* mode, who wants to preserve certain elements, and a *conservative*, that has the thicker ideological connotation.

ELC Based on Lukács's biography that was just published and some books I brought back from Hungary on Lukács's alleged messianism, one could establish a parallel between you and Lukács in the sense that Lukács can be described as a "messianic, Jewish, Marxist, social critic" and also a conservative. There is the parallel with your religious side. You are a prophetic Christian, and he is said to have been very interested in messianism, especially at the beginning of his career. I am wondering whether you feel that you share a prophetic-messianic religious interest or sentiment with him, or is this something that you would rather not discuss.

CW That is a very good and complex question. First, I think, in Lukács's case, here is someone who, of course early on in his career, starting with existential angst, those very early essays, let us say 1910 to 1917, it is Dostoevski, it is the problems of life, it is the meaning of life, it is the emptiness of life, it is the spiritual sterility of life that he is grappling with, around the Stefan George circle, an esoteric but fascinating group. There is always in Lukács an attempt to link quest for meaning with quest for freedom. And the quest for freedom is a kind of quest for deliverance, because it has quasi-religious residues in the quest for meaning. The quest for freedom has primarily a social and political character, but the individual dimension of that quest for freedom is also very important for Lukács. I think in Lukács the quest for meaning and the quest for freedom are inseparable, and that describes part of my own quest. I myself am certainly deeply influenced by Kierkegaard, deeply influenced by Dostoevski, by a host of persons preoccupied with the meaning of life and the absurdity of the human condition. At the same time, I am also preoccupied with the struggle against injustice, institutional and personal forms of evil, and I see that as similar to Lukács's quest for freedom. So the quest for meaning in the Kierkegaardian tradition and the quest for freedom that comes out of a Marxist tradition do establish some parallels between my own pilgrimage and that of Lukács.

ELC In listening to you, I find a difference in your terminology and the one used by Lukács. Lukács, I believe, thought of himself as a social critic, whereas you describe yourself as a freedom fighter.

CW You are actually right, even though the meaning of an intellectual freedom fighter for me, this fusion of intellectual engagement, political transformation, and existential struggle, is so tight that my first identity would primarily be that of a freedom fighter who engages in the fight for intellectual, political, social, and existential freedom.

ELC You turn to Marxism but you also affirm that Marxism is not a religion. And again, there is a similarity between you and Lukács that I found in your writings which I should like to quote. You speak of your own "leaps of faith" and that you are embracing "the absurdity of the human condition" (*EDMT*, p. xxvii). In Lukács's biography, which I mentioned to you earlier, the author Kadarkay says that Lukács, and in particular the young Lukács, could "arbitrarily leap from doubt into belief and find relief from the torment of doubt by affirming the absurdity of the human condition."* I think the parallel is quite striking.

CW Very, very interesting. But I tell you one fundamental divergence between my own view and that of Lukács. For me there is always a dialectic of doubt and faith, of skepticism and leap of faith, so that I am much more influenced by Pascal or Montaigne, who is part of a particular tradition of faith but who understands that the doubt is inscribed within that faith. I am thinking of an introduction by T. S. Eliot to Pascal's *Pensées*, where he talks of how doubt and faith are intertwined, whereas with Lukács, I think, you do get a quest for certainty that would hold doubt at arm's length, and I am quite critical of something like this.

ELC Yes, I will have questions on this a bit later, if I may. In reading you, I felt that you described yourself primarily as a prophetic man, as

---

* Arpad Kadarkay, *Georg Lukács: Life, Thought, and Politics* (Cambridge, Mass.: Basil Blackwell, 1991), p. 103.

a theologian. You are a believer, but you do not speak often of metaphysical things. You remain down here. In that sense, you are more a social critic than a prophet.

CW Yes. If I am in any way prophetic—but a prophet without metaphysics—what I mean by that is that I am fairly historicist in my own formulations about how we go about understanding the Real and the Truth, and hence I am talking more in terms of tradition and community than I do simply of truths and facts. So you are absolutely right, I have a *very* strong antimetaphysical bent. And again, it is very different in Lukács. Lukács would talk not only to make some implicit metaphysical claims but rather explicit ontological claims. He is much more with those who do believe that metaphysical grounding ought to be in place for claims much more than someone like Dewey or Rorty.

ELC Another question I have relates again to both you and Lukács: You say somewhere that we have a "need for a Simmelian moment." Simmel spoke of "sinful" modern times, which Lukács picked up, in particular in his early work, *The Theory of the Novel.* You yourself have written about "Nihilism in Black America: A Danger That Corrodes from Within" (*New York Times Magazine*, 15 September 1992, p. 45). You say that "America is in the midst of a mess of social breakdown . . . cultural decay is pervasive" (*EDMT*, p. xi). Cynicism and nihilism today return very often in your accusations of modern times. The question is whether "modernism" is really sinful again? It was "sinful" for Simmel, it was sinful for Lukács in the early century and, listening to you, it is sinful again or still a century later. Is the modern age really more sinful than the previous ones?

CW No. I do not think so. I think that we have to understand modernism as a very complex, heterogeneous development with a variety of different streams and strains. The kind of attacks on modernism that Lukács puts forward, I would be quite critical of. That would be too narrow, too truncated in its reading. I think there are some insights there, there is no doubt about it, but we certainly cannot replace history with myths and turn away, internally, from the social and political and attempt to create some kind of fetish of art before which one could pay homage, as in fact the social and political struggles were held at arm's length. I think that Lukács's insights there are quite useful, but I do believe that modernism as a very complex development is not one that could be usefully described as "sinful." It has the connotation of blindness, but not sinful. We are talking about the crisis of a civilization. We are talking about the challenges of the people of color. We are talking about the inability of the elite to envision a democratic expansion. We are talking about the rise of the Soviet Union and its attempt to find an alternative to what seems to be a Western crisis in the 1920s. This was a very fascinating moment, but a moment at which it is quite understandable that someone wanted to turn away from history as some arena from which betterment could be procured. Now for me, when I talk about nihilism and cynicism or what have you, especially among the working poor and very poor in the United States, I am talking in fact about the various ways in which commodification and reification completely shattered the institutional buffers for an already devalued, despised, and oppressed people, and where therefore the levels of destruction and self-destruction escalate among these people. Levels of destruction and self-destruction that call into question any sense of meaning, struggle, and any sense of hope for the future, and especially for any oppressed people in the United States of African descent. The only thing we have really had is some sense of meaning and some sense of hope, and once that is gone, then we are in a living hell, in a Dantesque and most profound hell, and that is actually what we have in some parts of our country.

ELC I should like to come back to this a bit later and ask you here about the importance you attach to history. You say that "Rorty's historicist turn was like music to my ears" (*EDMT*, p. xx). George Steiner was jestingly criticizing Lukács when he said that Lukács had sold his soul, that he had made a "devil's pact with History" because the devil had promised him the truth. Again, there is in both you and Lukács this strong belief in the function of history. What do you see today as major historical "conditioners"? You say that you strongly believe in historical "conditionedness" of human existence. So what is conditioning us negatively today, and what in particular is conditioning the poor? Is it capitalism, the government, the drug lords, the Mafia? What do we have today that causes this nihilistic outlook and desperation?

CW Two points. One is, that I do not believe in History, capital "H." I am much closer here to Antonio Gramsci, I believe in histories, with a small "h," and therefore History with a capital "H," associated with questions of certainty, must go. That's what Steiner means, and that is fine. But histories, with a small "h," with all the specific ways in which over time and space human practices and social practices, both structured and unstructured, go in shaping and molding who we are, that is for me the terrain which we are talking about, either progress or regress, betterment or disempowerment. Now when we look at the historical conditions of the present, again I would say one major factor is what I call, loosely, commodification. What I mean by that is simply the degree to which market forces now hold sway in every sphere of our society and in a crucial kind of a way echoing Lukács's notion of reification. What happened to a society when in fact market forces saturate a society.

ELC So you think that the drug world is in a way reifying the young people today and making them into a commodity for capitalist exploiters?

CW They become a commodity. It generates gangster mentalities, because of the question of getting over, as they would put it, instead of getting better, and that gangster mentality promotes a war against all. And it is market-driven because it is a matter of buying and selling, in that case drugs or bodies, primarily women's bodies, but it is market-driven. Now I do not want to argue that commodification is the sole force at work today. Not at all. We have got political lethargy, in terms of the political electoral system. We have got a competition between nations that imposes constraints upon our economy and nation-state to create a public sphere in which there is some vitality rather than squalor. And, of course, we have this massive, unprecedented redistribution of wealth from the working people to the well-to-do in the last twenty years. The withdrawal of public provisions has to do with the level of impoverishment, material impoverishment of poor people, which is a very crucial element as well, in addition to cultural consumption. There are a number of forces that act as historical conditioners, but one of the highlights I would still call the force of commodification. Again, Lukács influenced me in this as well.

ELC I found very interesting your periodization of history. As you know, Lukács established the periodization of literary genres, for instance in his *Theory of the Novel.*

CW I liked that about Lukács, even though we know that it could be slightly arbitrary. But we need periodization.

ELC You have proposed two of them which I found interesting, what you call "The Age of Europe," from 1492 to 1945, and then "The American Century," from then on (*EDMT*, p. xvi).

CW To 1973, yes.

ELC At the same time, I found interesting that, in speaking of the "American Century," you also attempted to show the influence of Afro-American culture, for instance, on American music and in general on American style. I mentioned this to some of my colleagues who said that they had never looked at it this way. To Europeans this might be more obvious because of the clearly non-European characteristics of American music, dance, etc., particularly in dance, jazz, and the blues. But at the same time, and again, you are very critical of this American century and the modern period (I know, you told me earlier, that you are not *more* critical of this century than of previous ones). You also state that the "Age of Europe" had a negative influence on what is happening right now, being maybe at the root of it.

cw It does have an ambiguous legacy. The great contribution is the institutionalizing of the critiques of arbitrary power, of the illegitimate forms of authority, which are *democratic* institutions, but, of course, there are significant racial, sexual, and class constraints on those democratic practices, and this is very important in this Age of Europe where it had been overlooked. So it is an ambiguous legacy. You got white supremacy, vicious male supremacy, you got class exploitation, on the one hand, and you have the hammering out on the ground of democratic practices, on the other, which are basic for the acceptability of social democracy.

ELC You deplore that there is no strong leadership in this world. Isn't it that in order to be a great leader you have to have a dream or vision? If you look back in history, great leaders usually had some vision, good or bad, to offer to the young by which to inspire them. Martin Luther King had a dream. How do you envisage the future? Do you have a dream or vision for the twenty-first century? In your writings, you actually seem to refuse to voice such a dream or utopia.

cw Oh, yes. I know that is true. But I am not really a dreamer. I have strong anti-utopian elements given my link to the skeptical tradition. What I do have, though, is a deep, deep commitment to moral convictions and that these moral convictions can be linked to amelioration, can be linked to social betterment, but that amelioration and social betterment are regulated more by moral ideas than a social dream, a dream of a new society and so forth. Of course, much of this has to do with my own peculiar brand of Christianity. In Christianity, you have a strong anti-utopian element in terms of talking about human history. If any dreaming is going on at all, it has to do with the coming kingdom. This coming kingdom is such a radical disruption with the present that it is difficult to talk about the kingdom within the realm of human history. So it kind of dangles like some sort of a Kantian regulative ideal.

ELC Let us go back to Marx. You speak critically of people who are "trashing Marxist thought" and of contemporary critics who practice "faddish ironic skepticism" (*EDMT*, p. xxii).

cw Yes, yes, and they tend to be the same people oftentimes.

ELC Wait, wait, one moment please, since I find that you yourself are sometimes a bit critical of people as well—and I am often sharing your criticism, especially in the case of Derrida and Foucault. In speaking of poststructuralist critics, you say that "they talk about their subtle relations of rhetoric, knowledge, power, yet they remain silent about *con-*

crete ways by which people are empowered to resist" (*EDMT*, p. xxii). With regard to the New Historicists, you say that they are "preoccupied with thick descriptions"—I love your terms!—"of the relativity of cultural products while thoroughly distrustful of social explanatory accounts of cultural practice" (p. xxii). Then you also speak of Foucault in relation to power. You say that you can learn from Foucault about power. As I remember reading Foucault, he is usually *critical* of power, he wants to undo it and show how the power of discourse, for instance, has been used to control individuals.

cw He recognizes no escape. His relational concept of power means that we are always inscribed within some matrix of power, and so we can be critical of the various forms that it takes and the manifestations that it has, but he recognizes that we are always already within a certain matrix of power relations. I think he is absolutely right about that.

ELC At the same time, reading you, you do not see power only as a negative, you want to empower, give power. Are you, in that sense, different from Foucault?

cw Yes and no. On the one hand, I want to talk explicitly about empowerment. Foucault would say, of course, he wants gay comrades to be empowered, if I may say so. On the other hand, though, I am like Foucault skeptical of any concentration of power. This is where my democratic sensibility comes in, because I do believe in fact that a concentration of power does tend to corrupt. I do believe that absolute power corrupts absolutely and hence needs the democratic mechanism for the accountability of power. But the fact that my starting point is among a relatively powerless people, I have got to be able to talk about power in a positive way, not simply in political terms, but also in existential terms. We are dealing with African people whose humanity has been radically called into question. Therefore, you have to talk about empowerment in terms of taking one's humanity for granted or affirming one's humanity or being able to accentuate one's humanity in conditions in which humanity has been so radically called into question.

ELC I should like to ask you about "engagement." In reading you, I felt that in some of your views you seem actually closer to Sartre than to Marx. In the *New York Times Magazine* interview that was published a few months ago (15 September 1991), the interviewer called you a "young hip Black man in an old white Academy." Did this shock you?

cw Yes, one never knows what one's friends would talk about.

ELC I am picking this up because both Lukács and Sartre were criticized for being social critics but also and maybe foremost for being intellectuals and privileged people who did not get their hands dirty.

Sartre, in particular, in his ivory tower wrote volume after volume about the bourgeois critic Gustave Flaubert while inciting others to engage in revolutionary action. How do *you* show your engagement beyond your teaching here at this beautiful university?

cw Right, right. I think part of it has to do with my being one of the honorary chairpersons of the Democratic Socialists of America, being part of a great legacy, of Norman Thomas and especially Michael Harrington. As honorary chairperson it forces me to be engaged with issues of labor, feminist issues, antihomophobic issues, antiracist issues. It is the leading left organization in the country, maybe the only one, and its numbers doubled in the last few years. In addition, of course, there is also my work in black churches, where I am in touch with ordinary black people.

ELC Do you talk about God at that church?

cw Oh, yes, very much so. I preach on Sundays, so I do talk about God, about social issues, and there is a long tradition of prophetic speaking in this church, the linking of the question of freedom with rich spirituality. We talk about faith and hope and service, so that I am nothing but an extension of a very long prophetic. That is another reason why there is a certain concern I have for tradition, why T. S. Eliot and others mean much to me, even though the tradition that he is talking about is very different from the tradition that I am talking about. But the very *concern* with tradition, also in the work of an Edward Shils, for example, means very much to me. I am deeply concerned about the dynamic character of tradition, except that for me the tradition that I am talking about comes from below and sometimes beneath modernity. It is a tradition of struggling and resisting, black peoples' tradition, whereas the tradition they are talking about tends to be from above. But there is still so much to learn about the heroic tradition in a market society. We need more subversive memory. I think subversive memory is one of the most precious heritages that those people had.

ELC This kind of thinking and feeling maybe dictates the amazing sentences you compose, of which I should like to quote a few. About Marxism, you say that "one of the major ironies of our time is that Marxist thought becomes even more relevant after the collapse of Communism in the Soviet Union and Eastern Europe than it was before." You do see the relevance of Marxism today? You are convinced that Marxist thought is an "indispensable tradition for freedom fighters" (*EDMT*, p. xiv)?

cw Oh, yes. Very much so. And the reason why that is so is that Marx was fundamentally concerned about the interlocking relation between corporate financial and political elites who had access to a disproportionate amount of resources, power, prestige, and status in society. Certainly, that is a starting point for understanding any society that we know of today, especially the United States. Once we lose sight of the very complex relations between those three sets of elites, corporate, financial-banking, and political elites, and the reasons why the working people, the working poor, and the very poor find themselves with very little access to resources, once we lose sight of that, which the Marxist tradition, which was not the only but the primary tradition which would analyze this, once we lose sight of this, then we have little or no analytical tools in our freedom fight. That is why I think that Marxism today becomes even more important, and this is especially so now that Eastern Europe is going to undergo a kind of Latin Americanization in which market forces become even more important. We see that in Latin America, where corporate America circumscribes local capital, and where the state elites go about carving up and digging up those resources among the masses that remain so tragically impoverished. I think we are going to see a certain kind of Latin Americanization sweeping across Eastern Europe as the corporate elites and transnational corporations hungrily go searching for markets.

ELC You defend Marxism and the relevance of Marxist thought, including "its ethical dimension after the cold war as an indispensable weapon" (*EDMT*, p. xxxiii) in this freedom fight. You stress Marxist ethics. Could you explain what you understand by "Marxist ethics"?

CW Sure. First, I want to make a historical point. Marx is fundamentally a product of romanticism, one of the great, very complex movements in modern Europe in response to the promise and tragedy of the French Revolution, or as Hazlitt put it, the dawn of the morning star, the springtime of the world. That sense of hope and expectation of social transformation, which so much of Europe felt, was lost of course after the reign of terror. The second wave of romanticism in which the fundamental values consisted of the many-sided development of individuals, the values of a harmonious personality that was able to flower and flourish in its own unique and singular way. . . .

ELC This is very Lukácsean. . . .

CW Oh, yes, and it comes right out of the *Letters of Aesthetic Education* by the great Schiller. Marx was deeply, deeply influenced by this. But secondly, democracy. This is why I spend so much time trying to show that when Marx, in the *Communist Manifesto*, defines communism as a struggle for democracy, what he means is in fact that these ordinary people, workers, ought to have some control over the conditions of their existence, especially the conditions of their workplace. This is a profoundly democratic idea. Once you link the values of flourishing individuality, a profoundly romantic notion, with the expansion of democratic operations and practices, I argue that you are at the ethical core of the Marxist project. As we know, Marxist-Communists, Marxist-Leninists, and so forth have subverted, bastardized, violated, undermined such ethical claims. But when we look at Marx himself as a thinker in nineteenth-century Europe, driven deeply by these ethical values, although never wanting to be viewed as a moralist—he is concerned about being scientific—we know that these ethical values are deeply inscribed within his own project, and then it seems to me that we recognize that those values have much to say to us.

ELC Some people are opposed to the very idea of ethics, saying that ethics establish something that has to be obeyed or followed. People do not want to be told how to behave.

CW We have to make a distinction between ethical dimension and ethics per se, because *every* social issue has an ethical dimension. What I mean by this is that there is some value judgment built into every issue, some moral vantage point from which the world is viewed. This is not solely a moral vantage point, but there is a moral dimension to the vantage point from which the world is viewed. Unfortunately, there has been a reluctance and sometimes downright refusal of Marxists to talk about ethics. I think that has been a major problem. They have tended to displace that ethical discourse with a teleological-historical discourse that is completely unconvincing, catechistic, and just raw material for managerial elites to come in like Leninists and then command, regiment, and repress the masses. So it seems to me that we have to talk about an ethical dimension but also be critical of an ethics that is imposed from on high. I do agree with that kind of critique that one ought not simply impose from on high. As radical democrats, we engage in discourse in which we acknowledge the ethical dimension of what we do and try to persuade persons: first, that the values we hold are convincing, and second, that the ways in which we go about conceiving of what these values lead to regarding our politics, how society ought to be organized, are possible.

ELC Are your own ethics compatible with both Christian and Marxist ethics, or do you find incompatibilities with them?

CW If you believe as I do that Marxism is a particular species of second-wave romanticism, and if you believe that romanticism is in many ways a naturalization of much of the Christian narrative about the past and present. . . .

ELC Are you treating it as a religion?

CW Well, there are religious residues; I would not say it is a religion per se, because religion for me does have something to do with God talk or has something to do with ways of life in which the divine and the sacred are accented, whereas with the naturalization of Christianity and the romantic movement you do often get the elimination of God talk and you do get a displacement of the divine and sacred with the imaginative and the creative. So I would not call it a religion in that sense, but there are religious residues.

ELC Another approach to Marxism that I found very refreshing in your works was your use of "difference" in naming the areas in which Marxism still would have much to do. This is naturally very different from Derrida's "différance," one of the central terms in his deconstructivism. I found your use refreshing because you are coming back to the literal sense of the word in the real world after twenty years of Derrida playing with the letter "a." So, would you say that race, gender, sexual orientation, age—all these possible differences—have assumed the place of the proletariat in Marxist theory? When you look at them, all these people, all these groups, are not the masses, they are rather marginal, they are outside, they are minorities, not the masses.

CW That is true. First of all, we have to disabuse ourselves of the notion that there ever was this proletariat as logos. The proletariat itself is a construct that is shot through with all kinds of divisions, cleavages, and heterogeneities, and so on, so that there is the sense that there never is any centering in a group or in the masses, even though the modes of production do create the possibility for such centering, but the notion of proletariat as center and the others as marginal we have to be suspicious of. On the other hand, certainly, we talk about gender, race, and sexual orientation, which have *always* been there, therefore it upsets me when people are talking about movements among these people as *new* movements. They are *new* relative to a Marxist discourse, a working-class movement. But, my God, the struggle against patriarchy predates 1789.

ELC There have been revolutionary women at the time of the French Revolution, like Olympe de Gouge.

CW Exactly. You take for instance David Walker's *Appeal to Colored Citizens of the World*, which is one of the most powerful critiques ever launched of white supremacy, in 1829! The young Marx is eleven years old. So the struggle has been going on, so they are not really new social movements but they are significant social movements. I do think that we have to talk about alliance and coalition because none of these movements in and of themselves or by themselves have the power to deal with the rule of capital, that is, the rule of those interlocking elites I was talking about. Oftentimes some versions of these social movements based on race, gender, and sexual orientation do not even talk about the role of corporate power, which is as limiting and limited as one can imagine.

ELC Are you optimistic enough to believe that this will change eventually?

CW Oh, sure; oh, sure! Well, it is going to be a long process. I think Raymond Williams's "long revolution" is an apt metaphor. But there are many of us who will go down fighting, trying to ensure that linkages are made, so that we can target the role of these elites not in any vulgar or immoral way but simply acknowledge the degree to which they have had this disproportionate amount of power and resources that ought to be shared and distributed with constitutional constraints.

ELC You are very laudatory about sophisticated Marxist theory, you say that it is indispensable, but then you also feel that it is inadequate. It is not complete. It is not enough. Where do you see its shortcomings? What else is necessary? Where do you find or get what is necessary?

CW The Marxist tradition has no serious or subtle conception of culture, and by culture I mean the sphere of desire and pleasure, the various quests for identities, e.g., nationalism—Eric Hobsbawm's book on nationalism is a good example of this, a good example because it shows some of the insights of Marxism on nationalism. We know that nationalism is primarily about elites' carving up territories in order to control markets and control populations. That is true for any kind of bourgeoisie that casts itself on a nationalist mode. We also know about nationalists' desire for association, recognition, and protection, which all has to do with desire, with how you bestow meaning upon yourself, with notions of mortality and notions of monumentality that still have hold on men's imagination. So nationalism must be understood as a psychocultural phenomenon as well as an institutional phenomenon among elites. You see Marxism simply does not speak to the levels of psychocultural realities. You need Freud, and you need novels, you need the blues and spirituals, a whole host of other insights.

ELC I teach future officers, future leaders, among them there are some minorities, blacks, women. I was wondering what you would tell them. What would you tell them to read?

CW Well, one, they should read a lot of history. They could begin with Paul Kennedy's book on *The Rise and Fall of Great Powers*, so that they would have a sense of where America is now, so that as future leaders they have a sense of the general sweep of the last seventy-five or a hundred years. Secondly, they should read histories that help give an account of how they now have opportunities in places, whereas they had those opportunities denied before, and what the nature of those struggles were that made them gain access to such privileged spaces in

American society, how difficult, protracted and how sacrificial those struggles were, and then try to situate themselves in relation to that tradition of struggle. But that is a tough one because, you know, there are always "betwixt and betweens" being at the Naval Academy and that deep conservatism, deep suspicion of any radical critique both for intellectual as well as personal and career reasons. They have to struggle with that. They have got to wrestle with that.

ELC I am teaching a course in French civilization in which I sometimes speak of contemporary criticism, and I have noticed that in particular my black students are usually very interested in contemporary criticism, even in theories such as Derrida's deconstruction, when I bring in some examples as to how it could be used in social criticism concerning blacks or women in the deconstruction of established discourse. My black students are usually much more interested in this than the average white midshipman to whom it is not of great urgency. I am thinking of one of my students in particular to whom I sometimes talk about such theories and who seems to have questions concerning them.

CW Racism is everywhere in these days, sexism is everywhere in society, so they experience themselves as *other*, as you can imagine, in some way even degraded at the Naval Academy or Princeton or any other elite place. These are theories that speak to that condition, I would imagine.

ELC If I may ask you a few more questions, I should like to come back to something which I think is characteristic of the methodology you use in your essays on Marxist ethics. You seem to support very strongly the idea of "radical historicism" and be critical, almost in a purist fashion, of those who do not adhere to it, including Engels. In your analyses of Feuerbach, again, it is interesting to note *what* you single out for your discussion and *how* you define radical historicism. You virtually do away with the Marxist utopia. You see radical historicism as a process of which you approve, which you love, if I may say so, and which you embrace. This is, in your view, what historicism should be.

CW Yes, this is a very, very significant point. Actually, I do the same thing in my essay on Jameson. I think that is just a built-in bias, and in the end it may be unjustified. That is a built-in bias against utopianism, and yet for so much of any quest for freedom the utopian dimension is crucial. I want to make a distinction between human hope and a utopian quest, because human hope for me is always being able to keep going, to sustain struggle, with ideals, but that is very different from a utopian impulse where you try to project a whole different and better society that could be realized and actualized. I am suspicious of the latter in trying to promote or preserve a form.

ELC You like process, praxis, and continuation. I have written down at least ten notions that you reject. Here are a few: rational necessity, universal obligation, philosophical certainty, eternal truth. How can you reconcile this with your prophetic approach?

CW That's right. It is a peculiar, peculiar kind of prophetic, because my conception of the prophetic is not one in which one speaks from on top, which is continuous with the great and grand Jewish and Christian traditions of the prophetic that I know of, in which "Thus says the Lord," or "Eternal truth speaks from on top." My notion of the prophetic is a democratic one in which, in the midst of the quotidian, the commonplace, in the midst of the messy struggle in which one's hands are dirty, that one is holding on to moral convictions and tries to convince others that they ought to be accepted, even though these moral convictions themselves can still be subject to criticism and change in vision and what have you.

ELC You are really preaching *hope*, I think.

CW That's it. That's right. But it is a hope that is grounded in a particular messy struggle, and it is tarnished by any kind of naive projections of a better future, *so that it is hope on the tightrope* rather than a utopian projection that looks over and beyond the present and oftentimes loses sight of the present.

ELC In many ways, you are quite Pascalian. The Pascalian wager is there and also Pascal's "Essayons donc de bien penser." Is this really what you are preaching?

CW Exactly. You hit the nail on the head, in the sense that my Pascalian sensibility is probably my central sensibility.

ELC Again, it is a stress on the process, the thinking, the being process. But I think, to come back to Lukács, that you credit Lukács too much for being a process theoretician. For Lukács it is very important that "what there is" today is bad, and he seems to have a definite idea of "what there ought to be." There is in him at least this teleological drive toward what there ought to be. I like your interpretation, because I think you are "updating" Lukács; in this sense, you are going beyond his limitations. I have often felt that Lukács's theories were too closed, that he used too many norms—for instance, for "realism." You emphasize the importance of process. Is it a dialectic process?

CW Again, for me the dialectic is understood in a heuristic way rather than an ontological way, and what I mean by that is that it is a dialectic that is positive in order to keep the process going rather than a dialectic that is somehow inherent in and implanted within the real. And so I want to keep the process going, and I see dialectic as a very crucial means of doing that, both practically and theoretically. And, of course, what we mean by dialectic, and this is what I love about Lukács, is his concern with protracted struggle.

ELC In trying to identify your values, locating them in your texts, I was amazed by some of your statements that seemed almost metaphysical, for instance, when you speak of "sacrificial love," and. . . .

CW There is nothing metaphysical about it. It is just almost sublime, you know, because the thing about sacrificial love is that it has no metaphysical foundation for it. It is simply a leap that we make in our short lives that gives it so much meaning and infuses it with so much significance. It is a dangling experience. You take a tremendous risk, you become tremendously vulnerable, but there is no metaphysical ground. No security, nothing guaranteed, no surety whatsoever.

ELC There are no truths that you are clinging to. The quest for truth and philosophical certainty are anathema to the kind of radical historicism which you admire. Again, you are maybe Pascalian in the sense that you recognize an end to what humans can do and can understand, and simply subscribe to the process of life and its own limits. You affirm life and have hope and maybe faith in life.

CW Well, in addition to the Pascalian sensibility, I have a deep Chekhovian strain. What is so great about Chekhov? I think he understood this better than others, that we are able to love, care, and serve others— and this is so true of his life and his art—but we are able to do that with there being no deep faith in life or human nature or history or what have you. And then it does not mean that we are antilife, it does not mean that we are cynical toward it, it is simply there, and we do these things because, given our tradition that has shaped us, we do in fact feel that it does give life so much meaning and richness and so forth. Now, as a Christian, I do this against the backdrop of certain narratives, the Gospel, the synoptic Gospel narratives, but again there is no metaphysical underbearing.

ELC In reading such ideas in your text, it made me think of Camus. Camus says that the only thing we can do is give affection, joy, and share in it. I am thinking of *The Plague*, in which the doctor continues to treat his plague-stricken patients in the midst of all hopelessness. This gives his life essence, quality. And it is not metaphysical in Camus either.

CW There are lots of parallels between him and Chekhov. I still think that Chekhov had the highest expression of this deep sense of love, and care, and struggle, and service. It is just that for him, it is not against the Christian backdrop as it is for me.

ELC I am coming to the end of my questions. In that article in the *New York Times*, they described you as a great "synthesizer," and I see that in you as well. You bring together contradictions, you are a black star at a white academy, you are a believing Christian in a secular society, you are a progressive socialist in the age of capitalism, a cosmopolitan, public intellectual among academic specialists, a radical traditionalist. Do you see yourself in those descriptions? Do you have a calling to bring together seeming contradictions?

CW It certainly is to build on the best of Lukács, which promotes synthetic and synoptic views and visions of the past and present. In fact, one of the things I said before, one of the things I *love* about Lukács is this synodical mode of thinking in which you always try to relate parts to a whole, with notions of totality, even for me heuristically posited, that are very important in that they highlight interrelations and dependencies.

ELC Is the notion of totality important to your thinking?

CW Oh, yes. Very important.

ELC How can you reconcile this with your admiration for Deleuze?

CW No, I think Deleuze is wrong about this. I think poststructuralists are wrong about this. I think they are right to trash certain conceptions of totality that elide and elude difference and diversity, heterogeneity and alterity, and so forth. But I think they are wrong to think that by trashing those particular conceptions of totality, that they have done away with totalities per se. I think we need to posit totalities with all the openness and flexibility that one can muster, but we must posit totalities in order to look at the dynamic relation between parts.

ELC I am coming to my final question. In your present prophetic pragmatism, is there a Lukács, and where is he? What is his future there?

CW Of course, politically, there is no Lukács at all in terms of his links to Stalinism. I actually believed that there was a Luxemburgist moment in the early Lukács that has been overlooked, but the general association of Lukács with Stalinism is in fact quite empirically verifiable and therefore there are no political links for me in this regard. Philosophically and intellectually, there are strong links, because my vantage point from looking at modern society, especially American society, remains the processes of reification and commodification. That is where I begin. So there is always a Lukácsean beginning. Methodologically, I begin with synecdochal ways of looking at the world, the relation of parts to a totality. So, again, I believe that is deeply Lukácsean, even though he has no monopoly on it, because there is the Christian view about relations of parts and whole, and there is the Hegelian one, but I mean Lukács is part of this Hegelian-Marxist sweep in terms of the relationship between the parts and the whole. The Lukácsean moment for me would be on two levels, on the methodological and the philosophical.

The irony is, here I am, as a black Christian, deeply indebted to the Marxist tradition, to Pascal, Chekhov, the blues, spirituals, the black church, and what have you, defending certain distinctive elements in Lukács's project and yet, at the same time, recognizing that Marxist theory and Marxist secular sensibility are both indispensable *and* inadequate, something to build on but also something to bring serious critique to bear on. The same values of individuality and democracy that I see in Marx, in Schiller, and the democratic tradition, now also filter through the best of the black church, lead me to this radically secular Budapest-born Marxist, even though I come from "the hood." In this sense, the struggle for human freedom is indivisible.

ELC Would you like to add a final note to our discussion?

CW No, not really. I think this is one of the best interviews I have had. What you have actually led me to see in myself I rarely get a chance to think about. I am on the run all the time and do not really get a chance to think about especially this Pascalian-Chekhov stuff. Thank you very much.

INTERVIEW WITH ETIENNE BALIBAR

14 November 1992, University of Massachusetts, Amherst

ELC Let me tell you about this project. It will consist of a series of interviews on "Lukács after Glasnost." I am talking to scholars who at the beginning of their career may have been influenced by Lukács's work or thinking and took him, so to speak, as a point of departure for their own work and theories.

EB What I can tell you is that I represent almost the exact opposite pattern. I might therefore have a very marginal place in your inquiry, but maybe that is interesting nevertheless. As I said, I am almost an opposite pattern in the sense that at the beginning of my career was my collaboration with Louis Althusser in the sixties. I was then a young student, a member of the communist youth organization, and very quickly also a member of the communist party, which I joined in 1961, as did other young intellectuals of my generation. Of course, we were all on the left, which was a result of the memories of the *Résistance* and the colonial war, and there were also cultural and intellectual reasons. Of course, we were divided as it is often the case in life, we were split in different groups and had different ways of understanding Marxism. I myself was studying under Louis Althusser who at that time was beginning his public career. He was starting to publish his first essays and very quickly associated some of us with his work. He had a very collective conception of intellectual and political work, which of course for us was very interesting and exciting. I mention this only to say that Althusser himself was not very Lukácsean, as you know, to say the least.

ELC I was wondering whether at the same time you also encountered Lucien Goldmann?

EB Yes, that is a very good question. Lucien Goldmann was a very prominent figure at that time in the French discussion, and not only on the left, because a few years earlier he had published his most famous *Le Dieu caché*, in which he proposed a very innovative interpretation of Racine's tragedies and Pascal's thought. This had made him enormously influential among the young generation and also the target of very violent attacks from the conservative, traditional critics. I personally had read and had a great interest in *Le Dieu caché* when I was preparing my exams at the Ecole Normale. I had admired it very much. But I must confess that I adopted very quickly Althusser's view that the Lukácsean tradition belonged to the humanist interpretation of Marxism, and we were favoring the structuralist interpretation of Marxism.

That constituted a very, very deep split. We took part in the debate as disciples, and you know that disciples are always more sectarian than their own masters, but at the same time I knew that Althusser had a very good personal relationship with Goldmann—at least I thought so.

ELC Goldmann was interested in structuralism. After all, he did develop a "genetic structuralism."

EB Yes, that is true. I think we had a distorted view, I confess this now, of some of his positions, but that was due to the controversies of the moment. The result of it was that Lukács to many of us at that time, at least to me, was a symbolic figure in the history of Western communism more than an object of proper study. Lukács and Korsch were twin figures which appeared as those who as early as 1923 tried to develop an internal critique of Marxist orthodoxy. That is how we saw them.

ELC Lukács tried to develop it more than criticize it, I think.

EB To us this was at the same time a significant historical event and a blind alley, if you like.

ELC Why blind alley?

EB Because we were very opposed to any form of what we called a Hegelian interpretation of history, and we would see that as a form of return of Hegelianism into Marxism itself. Our idea, right or wrong, was that we should develop a critique or a new foundation of Marxism, not in that direction, but almost exactly in the opposite direction. So our great names were not Lukács and Korsch but Brecht, Lévi-Strauss to some extent, and Freud above all. Now to come to the other end of what you called my career, I will give you an example. A few years ago a conference was organized at the State University of New York at Stony Brook, not far from here, by a group of American Marxists or at least people on the left, on what they called "Althusser's Legacy." To me, that was very interesting and at the same time puzzling and disturbing because at that time Althusser was still alive, although he was completely out of the public life. I had to say something, and for the first time try to appreciate not only the value but more precisely the place that he had occupied in the history of Marxism. Yet at that time I was concerned with a more historical, an almost philological question, which was the question of when and why the notion of a "subject of history" had been coined. It was one of Goldmann's last writings, a series of lectures which were published posthumously by his pupil Ishaghpour, on Heidegger and Lukács, which took me in that direction and brought me to my conclusion. I had become quite convinced that Goldmann was right in claiming that the confrontation with Lukács had had a decisive, very direct influence on the writing of Heidegger's

Sein und Zeit and that you could trace and even recognize direct allusions to some precise Lukácsean formulations on reification, etc., in the final paragraphs of Heidegger's work. This took me one step further. I wanted to determine exactly who for the first time had spoken of a "subject of history." And after having looked for that in all possible places, from Hegel himself to Marx, and also later writers, I came to the conclusion that this formulation had been invented by nobody else but Lukács himself in *Geschichte und Klassenbewusstsein* (*History and Class Consciousness*).

ELC Maybe even before, in the *Heidelberger Philosophie der Kunst* and the *Heidelberger Aesthetik*?

EB You are now bringing me to something very important. Which were these writings?

ELC Some of Lukács's correspondence and early writings were discovered in a suitcase at the Deutsche Bank in Heidelberg as late as the 1970s. Among them the works that have since been published as *Heidelberger Philosophie der Kunst* and *Heidelberger Aesthetik*.* The latter contains the important essay on "Die Subjekt-Objekt Beziehung in der Aesthetik."

EB Yes, that is exactly the point, and I will certainly look at these volumes. But from what I have read until now, I have the impression that in "Reification and the Consciousness of the Proletariat," the central essay in *Geschichte und Klassenbewusstsein*, which I reread very, very carefully at that time, that is, only a few years ago, you could almost follow the intellectual process which leads Lukács from the discussion—it was an epistemological discussion on the subject-object—to the invention or the creation, which is at the same time intellectual and stylistic (it is a matter of writing), of this expression—the "subject of history."

ELC Do you mean the proletariat?

EB No, no. The fact that it is identified with the proletariat is of course crucial, but what I am concerned with here has an even wider significance in the history of Western philosophy. It is directly or indirectly the result of Lukács's intervention and his influence on Heidegger and other twentieth-century philosophers, even when they do not know that they owe it to Lukács. We all read now the whole history of the great German idealistic tradition, starting with Kant and continuing with Fichte, Hegel, and Marx himself—who of course is a typical German idealist in that respect—as a history of the successive elaborations

---

*Georg Lukács, *Heidelberger Philosophie der Kunst (1912–1914)*, vol. 16 of *Werke* (Neuwied: Luchterhand, 1974); Lukács, *Heidelberger Aesthetik (1916–1918)*, vol. 17 of *Werke* (Neuwied: Luchterhand, 1974).

of the "subject of history," which becomes identified with "mankind" in the philosophy of Kant, with the "*Weltgeist*" in the philosophy of Hegel, with the "proletariat" in Marx, etc. But, in fact, that is a retrospective projection. I do not say that there is nothing in these philosophies that has anything to do with the concept, but the expression, the formula, I think, was coined by Lukács. *Words* are decisive in philosophy, because philosophy is a practice of writing.

I am sorry, I wanted to be brief, but I am not. Why did I refer to that Althusser conference (published as *The Althusserian Legacy*, ed. E. A. Kaplan and M. Sprinker [London: Verso, 1993])? What I wanted to tell you was the following: In the sixties I would not read Lukács very much, mainly because of the influence of Althusser. In the late eighties I became aware that the whole trajectory of twentieth-century Marxism—I mean creative and critical Marxism in the twentieth century—in some sense is limited. It has a starting point and an arrival, and the circle has been closed. The starting point is Lukács's *History and Class Consciousness*, and that is where the notion of the "subject of history" is coined, and then the whole twentieth-century history of relationships between Marxist thought and philosophy is concerned with that problem. You find it everywhere, in France, of course, in Sartre and Merleau-Ponty, but you find it in the Frankfurter Schule, where it is also crucial. Why is Althusser important? I do not say that he is as important as Lukács, but his book *For Marx*, which has very striking stylistic similarities with *Geschichte und Klassenbewusstsein*, is exactly the same sort of collection of essays with a deep philosophical commitment and at the same time a direct connection with current political events as well as a very important aesthetic dimension. They are not treatises, they constitute a different way of doing philosophy. What Althusser does in *For Marx*, however, is put an end to the discussion of the "subject of history" by introducing a concept of ideology which transforms the very notion of subject into a typical feature of bourgeois ideology. So that is the cycle I have had in mind. I became aware of the fact that, when I started thinking in Marxist terms about philosophy under the influence of Althusser—whether Althusser had directly read Lukács or simply heard of him indirectly and through various intermediaries, for example, Merleau-Ponty—Lukács had played a crucial role, without my knowing it, in the background of the positions I was taking together with others. Now I do not want to choose, I do not want to say that Lukács is right or Althusser is right, but I think that this is an absolutely decisive comparison and confrontation in the history of twentieth-century Marxism.

ELC Are you saying that Lukács's Marxism has come to an end?

EB Yes, I am saying that, yes.

ELC How about Althusser?

EB Oh, well, he might have come to an end at exactly the same moment and for the same reasons. This is a very good point. I am not totally at ease in speaking English, but nevertheless, let me say that the very notion of an end is an ambiguous notion.

ELC I noticed in the discussion this morning that you do not like ideas of a "telos." Do you have a utopia?

EB Me? Another good question. Of course, I have utopias, but I do not think my utopias are personal utopias. I think that utopias are really transindividual realities. You cannot have a personal utopia. Utopia is a mixture of prospects, critical analyses, and hopes, which you share with others.

ELC Do you believe in a *Weltanschauung*? Is your utopia connected to or derived from a *Weltanschauung*? Is it something that is "in the air"? Do you at all work with the concept?

EB It is not really a working concept in my case. It also brings us back to the whole Hegelian discussion. By introducing *Weltanschauung*, you are referring to what Hegel would have called the *Zeitgeist*.

ELC You have no use for such concepts?

EB I am still very Althusserian in the sense that I do not believe in the unity of the *Zeitgeist*.

ELC You mean that you do not believe in any sort of *Aufhebung* or synthesis?

EB I do not think that there are successive stages which are global and which succeed one another in a linear way, but that might very well be a simplification of what somebody like Lukács would have in mind. Besides, I am not so sure that Lukács was so fond of *Weltanschauung*.

ELC He worked with the concept, but it was Goldmann who really developed it.

EB Probably borrowing from Mannheim and even the Diltheyan tradition as much as from Lukács himself. Well, you are shifting the discussion from one type of questioning, of how I would explain the processes of the twentieth century, to another kind of questioning, concerning my own beliefs.

ELC Let us go back to the first questions.

EB What I was going to say, in very simple terms, is that undoubtedly I am now and have for some time been in a process of reevaluating the importance of Lukács in the intellectual history of the twentieth century. To my own surprise, possibly because I was too ignorant, too naive, or too sectarian, I have now become aware of the fact that he is a very central figure, to say the least. You might say that this is a very limited point of view, and that I should be more appreciative of his writing, but because of that particular and very famous book, *History and Class Consciousness*, I very much believe in conjunctures in intellectual history. This is not to say that Lukács did not write other things, but something that had played such a crucial role at the crossroads of politics and philosophy and, therefore, also for Marxism with its own tradition and difficulties, and finally for philosophy in general (not only Marxist philosophy), there are very few books which have produced the same effect. I would say now that Lukács's book, the one precisely which he later, in very ambiguous, successive moves rejected and only half-heartedly recognized, is such an event.

ELC In listening to you, with surprise and interest, I still find a major incompatibility remaining between you and Lukács, which is the question of methodology. I do not think you can get close to Lukács without reconciling yourself at least a little bit with history and time.

EB Do I give you the impression that I am not interested in history?

ELC Well, I was going to ask you to place it, because it has not become that clear to me from your talks at this conference.

EB Hmm, hmm. Well, a conference is not always the best place.

ELC This morning, I also reread your chapter on "class" (Etienne Balibar and Immanuel Wallerstein, *Race, Nation, Class: Ambiguous Identities* [London: Verso, 1991], pp. 153–184).

EB Oh, yes, oh, yes, that is not Lukácsean at all.

ELC No, and I think that it shows very well the differences between your method and the one of Lukács.

EB Certainly, certainly. To make a comparison between what you call *my* method and Lukács's method is too imbalanced; I mean, I am not claiming the same kind of originality. It is true that I belong to a certain tradition in Western Marxism, and together with others I try to keep working along certain lines. That is to say, there is a structuralist background in the way I discuss classes, for example, or the relationship between class and institutions in general, including party institutions. I think what I write now is much more historical than what I had written together with Althusser at the time of *Reading Capital*, but it certainly has not narrowed itself or become closer to the historicist tradition to which, rightly or wrongly, I would assign Lukács's vision of the emancipation of the proletariat.

ELC Lukács is very much a dialectician. He works with notions of duality, whereas what I find in you is the idea of plurality. I was very surprised yesterday when you spoke of a "triadic" approach, a triangular approach, which is dynamic, but I see you more pluralistic than just triadic.

EB That is true. You know this was a very partial and to some extent, what we call in French "ludic" ...

ELC Yes, "ludic," playful, exploratory. ...

EB A "ludic" discourse. I would not present it as a framework for a historical explanation.

ELC On the other hand, I was very intrigued, as a Lukácsean, and personally very interested, in your use of "metaphor." Your notion of metaphor is clearly influenced by the current linguistic discourse and the insistence on the signifiers, or rather the multiplicity of signifiers, that can be used to designate, for instance, a crisis.

EB Yes, that is true. But let me take a detour to add something to this discussion. Let me mention the question of fetishism. That is a crucial point, I think. What is extraordinary in the case of Lukács is that he was one of the very few philosophers, including Marxist philosophers, who, starting from Marx's very significant but also very short chapter on "The Fetishism of Commodity," really added something to Marx's views. First of all, he invented this notion of *Verdinglichung*, reification, which you cannot find directly in Marx. The word *Ding* does play a very important role in the Marxist presentation of fetishism, but there is nothing like *Verdinglichung*, reification. So that is again a creation of Lukács, and this creation, which I very often discuss with my students, some of whom are very Lukácsean (I like that enormously!), was absolutely necessary in order to transform what in Marx, however important it was, nevertheless remained a partial or a limited moment in the description of capitalism into a global instrument of explanation of bourgeois society. To Lukács, this was absolutely necessary in order to generalize the elements provided by Marx and apply the same kind of critical discourse, not only to theoretical relationships between the buyer and seller of goods, but also to the cultural sphere, the epistemological sphere, in order to give an explanation of a complete totality. That is why it made such an impression on Heidegger and had such an effect on his concept of "being in the world" and the lived experience of the bourgeois world, which is a consequence of capitalism.

ELC But you are opposed to the idea of reification, are you not?

EB Well, wait a minute. You told me that I was still, or more than ever working in a direction that is influenced by linguistics, and I accept that, because I have a different reading of Marx's chapter on fetishism, or better said, I think that for that same reason the confrontation with Lukács is so fascinating, because the Marxist concept of fetishism is really crucial and can be developed in different directions. I think that Lukács chose, in a very powerful manner, one of the possible directions, but there is another direction which you can take, which is the direction of symbolic structures. That is an alternative to Lukács, so to speak.

ELC You structuralize it, whereas Lukács put it into a progress, into a time-frame, history.

EB Yes, for Lukács history is a continuous progress of alienation and emancipation of the subject. But I do not think that you can simply repeat Marx, the very crucial philosophical elements in Marx. Marx is not simply a historian, not simply an economist, he is a philosopher. His way of being a philosopher does not rely upon a separation between the different disciplines; they are totally intertwined with his empirical investigation and conceptualization of social structures, but he is absolutely as important in the history of philosophy as Kant, Descartes, or Hegel. Now what to do with that? There are always academicians . . . this is not to say anything against them . . . scholars, teachers, who simply want to repeat Marxist philosophy. A creative attitude, though, means that you read it, you interpret it, and you eventually transform it. I think that Lukács did not simply repeat Marx. Neither did he simply repeat Hegel. And that is why I find his way of generalizing and applying the notion of fetishism to an interpretation of modern history so exciting and challenging. Although I do not agree with it or adopt it myself.

ELC You are obviously most interested in *History and Class Consciousness*, which, as you know, was written in 1923. Amazingly enough, in that book Lukács, similar to you today, envisages the end of Marxism. He says that if all the results of Marxism should come to an end and become invalid, there is one thing that will continue and that is the Marxist methodology. It was fascinating to me, in listening to the papers at this conference, that what they seemed to have in common was the Marxist methodology, the historico-political approach to analysis, which, however, would not be in line with your interest. How do you feel about this? What I am leading to is the question as to what, according to you, is still valid of Marxism today, what continues. If Marxism has come to an end, then why are all these people here, why this conference?

EB This will surprise you, but this time I shall make use of *Aufhebung*,* at least in the sense that Marxism has come to an end.

*In using the Hegelian term of *Aufhebung*, Balibar distances himself from the strictly anti-Hegelian, structuralist Marxism of Althusser, with whom he co-authored *Reading Capital* in 1985. *Aufhebung* is a principal and complex notion in Hegelian idealist philosophy that signifies a utopian moment in History at which, according to various critical interpretations of Hegel, the "world soul" or "world spirit" (zeitgeist) realizes itself. The zeitgeist reaches a moment of sublimation when it overcomes, annuls, but at the same time preserves, opposition in a peaceful unity.

ELC In your article on class, you do speak of *dépassement.*

EB Yes, this is the classical translation. *Aufhebung* has never been translated into French in a satisfactory manner. This is one of these typical German terms which German philosophy claims absolutely, so *dépassement* is not very satisfactory. It is too mechanistic. *Dépassement* means that you are ahead of something, you are overcoming something and look at it retrospectively as something which has been left behind, whereas, of course, the idea would rather be that Marxism can and possibly should be transformed, possibly—this is very dialectical—by means of reintroducing its very opposite. Althusser used to say that Marxism is a "finite" theory, and in French there is a play on words in this, because "fini" can be understood as "finished" but also, of course, as "finite." Let us take "finite," which means that Marxism was never able to explain everything. In the current conjuncture, for instance, when we are discussing what exactly happened in the Soviet Union or what kind of processes led to the collapse of the Soviet regime, etc., we are precisely dealing with historical events which I think people will never understand if they limit themselves to "Marxist" concepts. That is what I objected, in principle, to some of my friends this morning. Even if they are very clever and very right in their use of Marxist notions of exploitation and domination, there is something which they might never understand in that history, which is not yet completely passed, if they do not add to the Marxist concepts something crucial which was repressed in Marxism. I think that this has to do with ideology, not in the sense of "superstructure," but rather, and this is even more provocative, *with ideology as an infrastructure*, a deep level of the human and the social, human interaction and social life, which is not a result or a superstructure of the relationships of production, but much more something which underlies relationships of production.

ELC Here comes the Freudian influence on your thinking!

EB Yes, no doubt, provided you do not understand it as something archaic and mythical or as something purely individual, but precisely as the imaginary web, so to speak, of interindividual relationships, which has to do with establishing, connecting the individual with the community. This is something which you cannot explain in purely Marxist terms. In some sense it is something which Marxism, not only for bad reasons, wanted to exclude. But what was the result? The result was an enormous, complete inability of Marxist theories, even the most critical and most sophisticated of them, to deal with certain dramatic and very violent social events which occurred in the twentieth century. And that began with Nazism and fascism. And my position is that Marxism, even the best Marxism, was proven unable to really understand what had happened. I mean there were some very interesting attempts, the Frankfurter Schule, Wilhelm Reich, Gramsci, all these people to some extent had the feeling that there was something enigmatic in the efficiency of Nazism and fascism, what Reich would call the "omnipotence of ideology," a very strange formulation, a very dangerous formulation because it can very easily produce some sort of fascination with the discourse of Nazism itself. But that was the turning point. I think if the crisis—something like a crisis of Marxism and therefore the necessity of acknowledging a finite character of Marxism and an end of Marxism in some sense—has to be located, it is not in recent years, but as far away as the 1920s and the 1930s, immediately after Lukács had written *History and Class Consciousness.* Something emerged which the Marxists never conceptually acknowledged.

ELC I think you are right there, because maybe Lukács's weakest book is *The Destruction of Reason.*

EB Absolutely, because that was a desperate attempt, facing the enemy and opposing its doctrine. For that reason, he became at that time something which he was never before that, namely, almost a positivist.

ELC I am not sure we see this the same way. You seem to be coming to this problem from Deleuze, even though you said this morning that you did not quite agree with the Deleuzian approach, his rhizomatic *réseau.* What you just said seems to relate to a Deleuzian infrastructure, a network, his *réseau.* You say that Marxism could not account for all that happened. I am not yet convinced, but find your objections interesting. One of my major problems with this kind of vision still is, particularly when you talk about the plurality of metaphors to describe crises, that you seem to oppose duality, the dual structure, which I still recognize in most crisis situations.

EB I would say that there are different sorts of crises. I remember Marx's book, *The Eighteenth Brumaire of Louis Bonaparte*, which I think is a very important and beautiful book. That book was retrospectively "sanctified," so to speak, and Engels, of course, was largely responsible for that. In this sense he played a negative role.

ELC Not for Lukács. Engels was important to Lukács, particularly for his development of the concept of realism.

EB You are right. Engels was a fantastic mind. What Engels is responsible for is having presented the *Eighteenth Brumaire of Louis Bonaparte* as the typical example of historical materialism in the way he was defining it and codifying it, namely, a book in which the derivation of ideological phenomena and forms of consciousness from the economic process would be presented in full clarity and detail. But when you read the book, it is a book written in the middle of a revolutionary crisis and immediately after a bloody and horrible defeat of the proletariat. Now, I think that what Marx tried to show is that a crisis like this, beginning with an economic collapse and becoming a political crisis, then a revolutionary confrontation, and then a counterrevolutionary issue of this revolutionary process, is at the same time a process in which existing social unities, class unities, or camps, if you want to call them that, are decomposed. They are split. The beautiful unity and stability of the social category is dissolved, and at the same time there is, of course (and you observe this even in contemporary events), there is a tremendous tendency and pressure to impose dualistic structures on the complexity of the social phenomena. So, I would not say that dualistic structures or patterns do not exist, I would say that dualistic patterns are characteristic not of the long-term processes but of explosive and very short-term critical conjunctures. There is undoubtedly in Lukács, especially again in his 1923 book, and also in his biography of Lenin which was written in the same year as occurred the influence of Rosa Luxemburg, there is this dramatic and even catastrophic or cataclysmic move and orientation that sees the whole process of history as a process in which the conflict, the inevitable conflict, progressively matures and leads to an acute opposition between two camps. Of course, that is probably how people would live the revolutionary events in Germany and marginally in Central Europe in 1918–19. But this is not proper to Lukács. I would not say that it does not belong to the Marxist tradition. It belongs to the Marxist tradition undoubtedly and probably also to some other political traditions from the nineteenth century. It is a very romantic vision of history.

ELC I agree with what you call the romantic aspect of the vision of history in many Marxists and, I believe, also in Lukács. If I was fascinated by your theory of metaphors, it was precisely because I am trying to find ways to update Lukács, rescuing him from the lingering visions and influences of the nineteenth century. As someone said in one of the sessions today about Freud: Freud was fine for his time, but times have changed. It could have been you saying that what existed in the mid-nineteenth century with regard to the proletariat and the bourgeois society was valid then, but today we need new metaphors for the modern crises.

EB I was more cautious than that.

ELC I actually thought that the idea was fascinating except that your metaphors to me still seemed to be metaphors for various kinds of dualities.

EB Well, what you are saying gives me intellectual pleasure, but I was more cautious than that. My point was simply that we must become aware, especially when we speak about such "objects," dialectical objects in the Kantian sense, as "the world" or "world history," that our concepts are completely intertwined with metaphors. The classical positivist thought would recognize that we are using metaphors and conclude that we must get rid of them and stick to the "pure" concept. But that is not my position. I think that it is an absolute illusion to imagine that we can "eliminate" metaphors. The way in which we can gain some degree of freedom, and therefore also creativity concerning metaphors, is not to imagine that we can get rid of them, but it is rather to understand that we can play on them. As Mao used to say in a different context, revolutionaries should learn to play the piano. It is something like that. Not one single tune but different possibilities.

ELC The way I envisaged it is that the metaphors change in history.

EB That is true.

ELC And, as such, this idea is very acceptable to me.

EB And as a way of challenging these commonplaces about "modernity," which to me is again a very unsatisfying category, I want to suggest that a number of propositions which are supposed to be characteristic of modernity, of the modern way of thinking about politics, in fact have very ancient if not archaic roots. But I certainly do not want to suggest that the range of possible metaphors is limited and consists only of intellectual and symbolic structures that we inherited from a very remote past. That is why I am so happy Frank Cunningham posed the question* of whether there can be, whether there can exist, *new metaphors* for political and social thinking.

ELC There must be new metaphors, it seems to me.

EB I would agree.

ELC You are not a dialectician, but in many ways you are very much a transformationalist, and in that sense I think you have inherited a lot from the eighteenth century.

EB The eighteenth century?

ELC Yes, yes. Don't you see that? The Diderot of the Letter on the Blind . . . ?

EB Oh, yes, in that sense, certainly. That is one tradition, not in his-

---

*This interview with Etienne Balibar was recorded at the time of a conference, "Marxism in the New World Order: Crises and Possibilities," University of Massachusetts, Amherst, 12–14 November 1992. Frank Cunningham (University of Toronto) chaired a session on "Revisiting Utopian Socialism: Charles Fourier and the Gotha Program" and read a paper, "The Critique of the Gotha Program Revisited: Socialism and Equality Post-1989." He intervened in the discussion after Balibar's paper, "Has 'The World' Changed," which allowed Balibar to acknowledge the inspiration provided by Deleuze's metaphor of the "rhizome."

torical materialism, but in materialism, that I think is a very important one. You may not know that, and I am not very fond of commenting on my own intellectual trajectory, but even more than Diderot, of course, I have been busy reading Spinoza. He is an interesting case in the history of philosophy and also as a philosopher who has something to tell us and give us, provide us with some intellectual tools for the present. This is again largely the effect of the teaching of Althusser, who himself always claimed to be a Spinozist, but Althusser was referring to certain very specific propositions in Spinoza, especially those which had to do with the critique of imagination and the critique of the notion of epistemological criteria, the "guaranty" of truth and things like that. Probably because of this influence and new circumstances I, with others, started to reread the theological and political treatises and the *Ethics*, and I wrote an essay called "Spinoza: The Anti-Orwell." That is what I found fascinating in Spinoza, and that is not so different from what you described in relation to Diderot, this materialistic way of investigating the plasticity or the transformation of structures.

ELC Coming back to the topic of this interview and also close to a conclusion, I should like to ask one more question, if I may. What do you think is the most important aspect of Marxism? You are telling me that Lukács's Marxism has come to an end, even though, at the same time, you seem to appreciate his concept of the "subject of history." You somehow have closed the books on him. I hope you will open them up again for our next discussion, maybe in Paris.

EB No, no, I have not closed the books. On the contrary—and I am giving you a more personal answer here since it seems the best thing to do—what I am doing right now is reopening the question of philosophical anthropology, and I understand it as an investigation of the relationship between processes of subjection and processes of subjectivation, the passive and the active side of the same question, to borrow words from Foucault. Lukács and his notion of the subject of history is important here, because you have to investigate present-day processes and discuss burning issues of the present, be it racism, nationalism, or other things, and, at the same time, to reread the history of modern philosophy as a history of a debate around the notion of the subject. So, even if none of us will ever again believe in the existence of one "subject of history," be it called Mankind or *Weltgeist* or Proletariat, or Revolution, this is not to say that you can have a mere negative attitude toward that philosophical elaboration. It is part of philosophical history.

ELC It would take you away from Althusser. Would you feel bad about that?

EB Well, yes, certainly. Althusser himself started several things, but did not finish them all. So I find it a bit ridiculous to ask a question, as somebody did yesterday, a good friend, as to what Althusser would think of our present way of continuing the discussion.

ELC Well, I did not like the question either, because it implied that Althusser would have remained stagnant. But besides that, besides the notion of the subject of history which presently interest you, do you see anything else of Lukács's theories continuing . . . ?

EB Many friends of mine say that his *Ontology* is an important work.

ELC It was heavily criticized by his disciples Agnes Heller and Ferenc Fehér.

EB Yes, but that might be for reasons that are not only theoretical. The immediate disciples are not always the best-placed persons to make use of somebody's intellectual legacy. So I ask for your permission to postpone an answer until I have read the *Ontologie de l'être social*. It has been translated into Italian.

ELC I just saw at the book exhibit that Humanities Press has begun to translate it into English.

EB Good, thank you.

ELC I thank you very much for this interview! I do not know yet exactly . . .

EB . . . what you will do with it, but that is your problem!

INTERVIEW WITH TERRY EAGLETON

9 March 1993, St. Catherine's College, Oxford

ELC Let me first thank you for agreeing to this interview and tell you a little bit about my project. As you see from the list of the previous interviews, I have talked to several major scholars who, I think, may have been touched by Lukács's theories. What I am trying to assess is Lukács's significance today, what he has meant and still means to the twentieth-century critical and philosophical discourse.

In most of your books I have found references to Lukács's work, in some just one or two brief notations, but in *Ideology* (London: Verso, 1991) you have an entire chapter devoted to Lukács and Gramsci ("From Lukács to Gramsci," pp. 93–123). In this chapter you call Lukács's *History and Class Consciousness* a "great work" (94) but then proceed to quite heavy criticism that could serve as the basis for our discussion today. Some of my questions, I hope, will allow you to establish or reaffirm your difference.

To begin with, if I may, I should like to ask you how you came upon Lukács, when you first read him, and what impact the initial encounter had upon you.

TE I think I first heard the name of Lukács from Raymond Williams. When I was an undergraduate at Cambridge, a few of us asked him if he would run a special class on the novel, and I remember that in the very first session of that class, Williams spoke about *The Historical Novel* and referred to this person I had never heard of before, György Lukács. He also read a little bit out of Lukács's *Historical Novel*. I then read some of Lukács and soon moved here to Oxford where I began to run a seminar on Marxist criticism, but Lukács at that point—this was in 1969–1970—was really the only Marxist critic we knew. He began it all. We then explored others. We read Goldmann, Caudwell, and so on, but Lukács was very much for me the source, he was my first introduction to Marxist criticism. I could see certain parallels between Lukács and Williams, but Williams at that point did not know a great deal about Lukács. I think his work had, almost unconsciously, followed certain Lukácsean patterns.

ELC But then you turned away from him.

TE Well, I think what happened was this: no sooner did we begin to explore Lukács and so-called Hegelian Marxism than the whole of the late 1960s and 1970s started happening. New theories were bombarding us from all points of the compass.

ELC Althusserian?

TE Althusserian very much so, but some others, too, I think. I came under the influence of Althusser, I wrote *Criticism and Ideology* (London: Verso, 1976) in that context. But in fact, I was never—for the record!—as devoted and uncritical an Althusserian as it sometimes has been suggested. Put it this way: when I think, and when I thought then, about Althusser, there was not a single one of his major doctrines that I didn't have serious reservations about. He provided a kind of language, a kind of ethos, a set of concerns, a range of concepts, that I found very fruitful to work with. Since then, people have sometimes asked me what I think of Althusser. In my preface to my collection of essays, *Against the Grain* (London: Verso, 1986) I try, in a very few pages, to draw up a kind of balance sheet on Althusser. Unfortunately, not many people seem to have read it, which is why they keep asking me!

ELC I have read it, but I still would like to ask you a few questions.

TE Sure.

ELC One of the things that I think distinguishes you from Lukács is the relatively greater importance you attribute to the subject. I thought that this probably came from Althusser or also from others, maybe Lacan, psychocriticism.

TE Yes, that's right. I think there has, however, been some overemphasis on how far Althusser was really useful in this respect. He was useful for subjectivity insofar as he offered you the category, but I think he only took you to a strictly limited distance on that. So there is perhaps something of that in what I derived from Althusser, but the worst effect of that period was that people then began behaving as though they had read Lukács and had confidently gone beyond him. The situation rapidly got to the point, at least on the British left, where really they hadn't explored Lukács but it was exactly as though they had. It was as though they could take all that for granted and then go off somewhere else. So I have been very pleased that a serious turn back to Lukács has been increasingly on the agenda.

ELC When, where?

TE Jameson's work has always stood as a reminder to me that that tradition has not just evaporated. And then there have been one or two interesting and serious attempts to look at Lukács again, like his biography.

I do not want to overemphasize the nature of that turn: I do not mean to say that there has been a global rehabilitation of György Lukács, but as the structuralist Marxism of the 1970s receded somewhat, partly under its own problems and pressures, then the way was open for at least a more open-minded approach to Lukács.

ELC I have not noticed this in your own work too much yet. On the contrary, what seems to prompt people to put you closer to Althusser rather than, for instance, to Lukács, is your anti-Hegelianism, your antihistoricism and the nonhumanistic approach to interpretation.

TE Yes, although as far as antihistoricism goes, I derived my suspicion of historicism at least as much from Walter Benjamin as I did from Althusser. When I wrote works like *Criticism and Ideology* (London: Verso, 1976), and *Marxism and Literary Criticism* (Berkeley: University of California Press, 1976), I was very influenced by Althusser, but quite rapidly, by the time of the early eighties, when I wrote things like *The Rape of Clarissa: Writing, Sexuality, and Class Struggle in Samuel Richardson* (Minneapolis: University of Minnesota Press, 1982), *Walter Benjamin, or Toward a Revolutionary Criticism* (London: Verso, 1981), *Literary Theory: An Introduction* (Minneapolis: University of Minnesota Press, 1983), and so on, Althusser was still there, but there were now many other influences. In other words, what I would call the card-carrying period of Althusserianism was over.

ELC I found interesting that in your book, *Literary Theory: An Introduction*, there is only *one* reference to Lukács (p. 65). There are many references in your previous shorter book on *Marxism and Literary Criticism*. Then, there was a period, when you did not speak of Lukács very much at all. More recently, in *Ideology: An Introduction* (London: Verso, 1991), you seem to come back to a confrontation with Lukács. In speaking of *History and Class Consciousness*, for instance, you rank it among the "richest, most original documents of twentieth-century Marxism" (p. 99); you speak of its "breathtaking central section" (p. 104), but you also voice major objections to it, claiming, for instance, that it is "marred by a typically idealist overestimation of 'consciousness' itself" (p. 103). In praising Althusser's insistence on the materiality of ideology, you criticize Lukács's "disembodied class consciousness" (p. 149). You speak of Lukács's "anti-scientism" (p. 104), his "elegiac nostalgia typical of Romantic conservative thought" (p. 104). You repeatedly attack Lukács's belief in a "pure proletarian consciousness" (p. 104), "a pure class subject" (p. 102), which, according to you, leads to a mechanistic approach to class. In your own views, a class is less pure, less homogenous, more "contaminated" (p. 102). In all this, you tend to view class and ideology as two very different notions, which brings me to my next question. In *Marxism and Literary Criticism* you propose a definition of ideology to which I could subscribe more easily than to some others. Ideology is seen as "the ideas, values, and feelings by which men experience their societies" (p. viii). Isn't the same true of class, and couldn't class and ideology therefore be brought together and be criticized in the same way?

TE Well, there are two issues. The first issue is my stance toward Lukács. Let me say this: I think that Lukács is a very great Marxist philosopher, and I don't think I would have said that so unreservedly in the 1970s. I would certainly want to say that I feel I have not done justice to him in that respect in my work. On the other hand, that does not save him, of course, from being criticized. I still think that I would make those central points of criticism of him. Put it this way: I would now have to do the kind of loss and gains balance sheet on Lukács that I tried to do on Althusser. Certainly, I have severe criticisms of Althusser, too.

As far as the criticism of class and ideology goes, I would say this: one of the gains of Althusserianism, I think, on that issue was that it avoided a crude reduction of all ideology to class ideology; in other words, it avoided a kind of expressive or direct relation between social class and ideology. And that helped one to see the complexity of ideology, the relative autonomy of it and also the ways in which all kinds of ideology are *not* directly associated with class. On the other hand, the loss of that was the loss of the concept of the class subject. I think that disappeared really in Althusser. The gain of Lukács, I think, is that this is a very central concept in his work. The loss in Lukács, I still think, is that he does tend to assume sometimes a too directly expressive relation between social class and a particular ideology. But a social class—to respond to your point—is certainly not reducible to a set of ideas and values.

ELC You sometimes speak of a "class subject." I'm not sure that is a term Lukács would use. Lukács also refers to "class consciousness" where you tend to speak of "self-knowledge" and "self-consciousness," which is rather interesting since you seem to wish to modernize Lukács and also bring him closer to your own purposes. You read into Lukács a bit what you would like to find there.

TE That may be so, but I don't think it's necessarily detrimental to Lukács. To talk of a class subject, the good side of that talk is to talk of agency. That is precisely what Althusserianism is not very capable of providing. I think Althusser has a theory of subjectivity, but I don't really think he has a theory of agency. Whereas if one speaks in a more Lukácsean way of the class subject, whether or not Lukács himself would use this concept, I think that leaves room for such an agency in a way Althusser does not. On the other hand, and there is always another hand, I also think that it won't do simply to transfer onto a social class the properties and characteristics associated with an individual subject. And I think that Hegelian Marxism sometimes makes that mistake.

ELC You do criticize Lukács's concept of the proletariat as a class and you say that he simplifies it, idealizes it. This is one of your criticisms in *Ideology*. You object to the "purity" of class that can be taken mechanically and exchanged, one class against another class.

TE It is rather homogenous. There is a sort of ultraleftism associated with that "purity."

ELC At the beginning of your book *Ideology*, you speak of Lukács's treatment of process. Lukács is frequently criticized, and I believe excessively so, for his so-called reflection theory. You have softened that impression, even without referring to a concept Lukács uses very frequently in that context, which is the concept of mediation and the mediating process. You attempt to show that Lukács's is not just a pure reflection theory but rather a more complex transformation theory.

TE Yes, that's what I have tried to do. I think that surely there are different epistemologies in Lukács at different points. I think that sometimes in his talk on realism you can see a kind of reflectionist or correspondence epistemology at work, but I don't think that is adequate to the complexities of *History and Class Consciousness*, where a much more active, interventionist notion of consciousness is at stake, which can't really be accommodated on the reflectionist model. So I would see a kind of unevenness or difference within Lukács on that subject.

ELC You mentioned realism. What is your attitude toward Lukács's concept of realism? You sometimes feel that it is fetishized by Lukács, and you are particularly critical not so much of Lukács himself as of those who have used the Lukácsean concept.

TE Yes, I would put it this way: I think that I was influenced in the 1970s by the semiotic and poststructuralist critique of realism, which, I think, is intellectually very interesting—not very original—but I was never convinced by it. That is to say, I learned a great deal from it about the limits of realist representation, but I was never convinced by the idea that the whole of realism from Defoe to Dostoevski had just been a ghastly mistake and somehow should never have happened. It seemed to me grossly implausible and very unhistorical to argue that realism was an inherently reactionary or conservative form, which was really the kind of argument that the film theorists in Britain and some of the Parisian theorists were running. I never accepted that. I always had a much more conjunctural estimation of literary forms. I have always argued against the claim that there is a one-to-one correlation between a literary form and a political fact. And it is a good Brechtian position to argue that that depends on the conjuncture. If one now tries in an act of historical imagination to return to the early eighteenth century or whenever the rise of realism occurred, then it is hard for us to reimagine the revolutionary effect that realism must have had in the sense of taking humdrum social life very seriously. The impact of that must have been extraordinary. We have really naturalized that now. Realism was their avant-gardism; it had the same disruptive and estranging effect. So I am very suspicious of general doctrines of realism, either in the Lukácsean sense, if I am reading Lukács right, that there is something inherently progressive about it, or in the anti-Lukácsean sense that there is something inherently reactionary about it.

ELC So you don't find realism today. You think that realism belongs to one particular historical moment, that it is not something that continues, is transformed, and takes new forms.

TE *Realism* is a bedeviled term, isn't it, because it can mean a number of things. It can mean a particular epistemology, it can mean a particular historical period, it can mean a literary genre. I think the danger of the argument that realism continues today is perhaps the widening of the term of realism so far that it ceases to have very much aesthetic bite to it. In other words, there is a sense of the term *realism*, let's say a convincing sort of text, which any writer would lay claim to. In a normative sense of the word, the most avant-garde writer would want to say that his or her text had a certain realistic effect.

ELC Maurice Roche, whom I interviewed about ten years ago, claimed that his work was realistic, even though it is as different from Balzac as it could be.

TE Or you could have a Brechtian notion of realism, which is really the political relation between the play and the audience, which is different again, a reception notion of realism. So I think the term is very fraught, and it sometimes therefore helps, I think, to confine it simply to representational art. And as far as that goes, one cannot be politically dogmatic about that. Sometimes that can be politically effective and sometimes not.

ELC One important question I have concerns your dialectics. Are you a dialectician? If I may quote you a bit from *Ideology*, you do speak of the "material participation of ideas" and ideas "in active struggle" (p. 93). One term you use very often, in particular also in relation to feminism, is "you have to go right through it" . . .

TE Oh, yes, all the way through it and out the other side.

ELC You also say that art itself is a "material reality" (*Against the Grain*, p. 21). I do not quite see how your dialectics really work.

TE I have been somewhat quiet on the issue of dialectics because I am a little wary of a certain sort of full-blooded, dialectical philosophy, you know, shades of Engels's dialectics of nature, and also wary of the way it has become rather sloppy. It comes in so many forms that it becomes almost a kind of hurrah word, it carries its own positive impulse. However, having said that—and I am particularly nervous about the reifying term "the dialectic," which seems to me to be extremely questionable—I value dialectical thought in the sense of trying to salvage what is valuable and usable about an essentially negative phenomenon, trying to rescue from the great bourgeois tradition, as Lukács himself so marvelously did, what is positive and productive about it. This has really to be cherished today in the face of a postmodernism that is in my view drastically undialectical, looks at complex, many-sided historical developments such as the Enlightenment and just takes a negative attitude toward that.

ELC I think Fredric Jameson tries to maintain dialectics in his many postmodern interrogations of other theories.

TE I think Jameson's dialectical thought springs from his Marxism. Jameson has said that capitalism is at once the best and the worst thing that has ever happened. That might be a bit hyperbolic, but that is a style of thinking that is profoundly alien to the postmodernist mind. I think the postmodernist mind, for all its supposed pluralism, really does work in terms of sharp antitheses: centered subject–decentered subject, identity–difference, and so on. And dialectics is able to interrogate that. I still think that the *Communist Manifesto*, which, as one has to remind critics of modernism, is full of praise for the bourgeoisie, for the great bourgeois revolutions, is a scandalous way of thinking to those who like their politics much more simple.

ELC Your critic, James Rolleston (*Diacritics* 21 [Winter 1991]: 87–100), says many things about you that I cannot agree with.

TE Me, too.

ELC Okay. He sees you very much in the Hegelian-Marxist tradition. He calls you teleological, which I do not see in you at all. I think that you actually oppose telos as I think you do utopia. He brings you, I believe, excessively into the Hegel-Marx, telos-utopia camp. Do you see yourself as teleological?

TE If you get shot at from both sides, it probably proves that you are roughly at the right place. Do I believe in a telos? Well, as the man said, it all depends on what you mean by telos. Do I believe in a certain Hegelian sense that some kind of end point is even now imminent in reality as part of its unfolding dynamic? Would I actually believe that? No, and I don't know anybody who does. But that is hardly the only meaning of teleology.

ELC You say somewhere that Marx in the *Eighteenth Brumaire* was not really utopian either but had some kind of a "poetry of the future," if I quote you correctly.

TE Well, that is a utopian gesture. I have often returned to that passage in the *Eighteenth Brumaire* and much of what I have to say in *The Ideology of the Aesthetic* (Oxford: Basil Blackwell, 1990) is about how the aesthetic is at once ideology and utopia. I am not at all as opposed to ideas of progress and movement and imagining utopia as I have been sometimes said to be. If teleology means some inexorable historical progress, I do not know anybody who believes that. This therefore is a straw target and is a distraction from the true argument, I think. The argument is whether one believes that in certain historical conditions genuine transformation and improvement can feasibly be made (and I certainly believe that), or whether, like the antiteleologists, you set up such a straw target of teleology in a full-blown metaphysical sort of way that the argument against it proves itself automatically. If that's the way one defines teleology, nobody will believe it. But if one has a more reasonable understanding of purposive, collective political action toward certain goals, and of indispensable causal conditions, then, sure, if that is what teleology means, I am a teleologist. It all depends on how you define the term.

ELC All this is very interesting. You say somewhere that Lukács is not a metaphysician, that he is much more a materialist. When I talked to George Steiner, he said that Lukács was definitely a metaphysician, that all Jews are. From your books I thought that you described yourself as a Marxist but did not identify with the Marxist utopia of egalitarianism. How would you characterize your Marxism? How are you a Marxist?

TE I have never said that I do not believe in a classless society. Of course I do. I am a Marxist. Of course I believe in the Marxist utopia of a classless society. But then again, it depends on what one means by utopia. Once again the typical move there is caricaturing, is to advance a notion of utopia like the notion of telos that is so idealistic, unreal, perfectionist, conflict-free that nobody will believe it. Again, the device is that those kinds of concepts are set up so as to write themselves obediently off. So the argument is, are you a utopianist or not a utopianist? Of course, you are not a utopianist if one has already predefined the concept of utopia in a non-acceptable way. However, the question is, why should one do that? Why not have a more realistic sense of, let's say, a society that is feasibly but radically transformed from what it is at the moment? If that's what utopia means, among its many possible meanings, of course I believe in utopia. I wouldn't be a Marxist if I didn't. Nothing to do with perfection, which bores me as it bores everyone else.

ELC I should like to explore this a bit further. Why are you, how are you a Marxist? Are you still a Marxist?

TE Yes. Not only am I still a Marxist, but I would see myself as a shamelessly unreconstructed Marxist. I am a shamelessly unreconstructed one, not because I have not been very much influenced by contemporary post-Marxist thought—I have, and I believe Marxism should always be open to that—but because I am a traditionalist, as I think all good Marxists are traditionalists. I find it alarming that in the United States in particular, in a perhaps rather traditionless society, tradition is automatically seen as conservative and reactionary. But as Trotsky once said, we Marxists have always lived in tradition, we have our own traditions to which we must be faithful. Not uncritically faithful. I am a traditional Marxist in very boring and banal ways. I am a Marxist because I believe that it is feasible by transforming the social relations of production so to reorganize production on a global scale as to bring a much happier life to the vast majority of people. I stress the word "feasible" there. I think that is realistic. Marxism for me is a theory and practice of how one might set about doing that. So I don't think there is any question that I am a Marxist or that I am a Marxist who believes in the possibility of progress. If you want to call that utopia, which could be a misleading term there, then that's fine, that's what I would sign on for.

ELC I am a bit surprised at your statement. You are a left-wing critic and a sociocritic, but if you are a Marxist, you are writing your own Marxism.

TE Well, let's remember that Marxism is a text, open to many different meanings and readings and has been from the very beginning, since the work of Marx and Engels. Within Marx and Engels themselves there are many different possible constructions of Marxism. If one has a very specific view of Marxism, that Marxism is this and only this, then clearly something else will be only questionably Marxist. It would be a deviation from it. Now, I do not accept that. I think that there are many different interpretations of Marxist theory. On the other hand, I am not open-minded to the point of being scatterbrained. I think there must be feasible limits on what is meant by the word Marxism, otherwise the concept, as with any concept, will cease to have meaning. So I am not prepared in some kind of sloppy and eclectic revisionism to say anything goes as far as Marxism is concerned. I think there are certain beliefs that are constitutive of Marxism. I don't, for example, see how anybody who rejected the idea of class struggle could call himself or herself a Marxist. But within that frame, of course, there are all types of nuances, many different versions of Marxism that are possible. I am surprised by your surprise, because I have never had any doubt, nor have the vast majority of my critics ever been in doubt, that I am in some significant sense a Marxist and that I continue to be a Marxist after the recent collapse of Stalinism. And certainly not a Marxism I am "writing myself." I have often found myself under fire from both sides, being criticized by a certain kind of Marxism for being too open to deconstruction, etc., and being criticized by deconstructionists for being too wedded to a Marxist orthodoxy and not going the whole way with them. As I said, if you get fired at from both sides, it probably indicates that you are pretty well in the right place, uncomfortable though it may be.

ELC I have talked to Michael Löwy, and his Marxism is quite different from yours. He accepts the idea of totality.

TE Me, too.

ELC Dialectics.

TE Me, too.

ELC Well, you very often oppose any totalizing effort.

TE You keep assuming that these terms have a fixed and given meaning, and therefore that either one is for them or against them. So Löwy uses the term in a sense that you and he agree on, therefore somebody who questions this notion doesn't agree with totality. The same with dialectics. Not at all. I don't accept that way of proceeding. There are many different notions of totality. There is not only Lukács's notion, there is a Hegelian one, there is a certain Sartrean notion of totality, there is a certain Althusserian notion of totality. Althusser is not opposed to totality; he is opposed to what he sees as expressive Hegelian notions of totality. The word "totality," once again, is a political battleground. One can't assume that it has an immutable meaning, and then say anybody else's meaning is not acceptable. I have constantly in my recent work criticized postmodernism for its fetishism of difference (I have also said positive things about postmodernism), *and* I have said that it is to me profoundly ironic that antitotalizing forms of thought should have developed over recent decades precisely at a historical point where in a sense the fact that we live in a total global system has never been more obvious. The interconnections between different levels of economy, of culture, of education have never been more flagrant. And I am interested in the question of why it is that precisely in that period antitotalizing thought forms have arisen, postmodernist, poststructuralist, Foucauldian, Derridian, or whichever, which are set against the notion of totality. However, it depends once again on what we mean by totality. If those antitotalizing thought forms are trying to take apart or criticize what we might call (to use an unduly demonized term) essentialistic forms of totality, where everything is seen as connected with everything else, where everything springs from a single, central principle which is self-identical, then fine, I will go along with that critique. If, however, we therefore conclude that that has taken care of the concept of totality, I would say, "rethink totality," rethink it precisely on the basis of these very cogent criticisms that have been made. I am therefore neither opposing totality, nor am I defending certain conceptions of totality that do indeed seem to me to be over-totalizing. I would not defend the concept of totality as formed and empowered by a single self-identical principle. I do think that's a metaphysical way of thinking, and I do think that sometimes the Marxist tradition has imported that metaphysical principle from Hegel into Marx. But my opposition to that is not in my view an opposition to reasonable notions of totality.

ELC You voice more criticism of Hegel than of Marx.

TE I am a great admirer of Hegel, and I wrote a chapter on Hegel in *The Ideology of the Aesthetic* which was by no means a purely negative assessment. But I would be suspicious of certain Hegelian notions of totality, certain readings of Hegel, certain understandings of the notion of totality that have come out of Hegel, that are often too quickly homogenizing and totalizing in an objectionable way. But, let me stress again, I want to criticize those notions of totality not in the name of sheer fragmentation, not in the name of sheer difference (which is impossible), but in the name of some feasible understanding of the system we live under as structural and as systemic, without which our critique is disabled from the outset.

ELC One of my favorite texts of yours is in a little book you share with Fredric Jameson and Edward Said on *Nationalism, Colonialism, and Literature* (Minneapolis: University of Minnesota Press, 1990).

TE Oh, good. Not widely known.

ELC I like this text very much because, in a very concise fashion, I believe, it reflects your temperament, intellectual preoccupations, and interests. I also found it very Camusian.

TE Hasn't occurred to me.

ELC You do speak of Brecht and identify with Brecht, with his comedy, his "deconstruction," his "carnavalesque" movements. You also speak of a philosophical and critical impulse, which you claim to have found in Brecht, but which to me seems quite typical of Camus. I thought that your Marxism, if it is a Marxism, was quite existentialist. To give you an example, you echo Kierkegaard in concluding that one should live the "dialectic passionately, ironically, in all its elusive impossibility" (38). Do you mean, in an absurd world?

TE No, I mean existentialist, insofar as an attention to the lived is very important to me, but I don't think that's exclusively existentialist. Existentialist in the more full-blown sense of the philosophical doctrine, no. I don't believe in the idea of the absurd, though I find it entertaining, I don't believe in individual acts of gratuitous choice; I am not a decisionist, ethically speaking. In all kinds of ways I am not an existentialist, but insofar as that phrase gestures to the presence of certain problems that can't be theoretically solved or even fully theoretically formulated, but can only be sensed and wrestled with, then yes, that's important to me. I would have thought that that was important to Marxists in general without necessarily calling themselves existentialists. Marxism is obviously much more than a doctrine, and people have not believed in Marxism in so many numbers for such a long time simply because they are enamored of a certain kind of doctrine. They have believed in it because they wished to be free, happy, and well-fed. To that extent, "the lived" is very central to Marxism.

ELC You made me think of Camus, of Meursault and Rieux, more so than of Sartre, but one of the major principles of Sartrean existentialism is the importance of the self, the individual, self-realization, a term I mentioned before since you use it so many times even in conjunction with Lukács. You have been interested in the idea of a "sensuously liberated society" (Rolleston, p. 99), the importance of "body integrity" (p. 91), the relationship between aesthetics and the body (p. 88). In reflecting upon your work and theories, two things come to my mind: there is this very rigorous philosophical development and, on the other hand, a rather sensuous, witty, playful breaking up within it.

TE Yes, I think this is much more accurate than the existentialist link which is misleading here, unless one uses existentialist in such a broad way to mean a concern with the lived or whatever. There is no way in which I am a Camusian, there is no way in which I am an absurdist, there is no way in which I believe in the lonely choice of the metaphysically isolated individual in an absurd world. Of course not. I wouldn't be a Marxist if I did. But you are right in the second point you made, which is much more accurate. I admire rigor in thought. I don't think, as is now sometimes disastrously thought by some people, that rigor is automatically authoritarian, oppressive or, God help us, male. I think that we need the utmost precision of thought to emancipate ourselves from the dismal situation that we are in, and any concession on that is simply a gift to our political enemies. My own concern, of which I am aware autobiographically, is probably inherited from my Catholic scholastic background. Catholicism has its uses. At the same time, I think you are right that my work, at least from the period after *Criticism and Ideology* onward, has been very much concerned with that which undermines rigor, or takes rigor apart, the ironic, the comic. Much of this has come out in my creative work more than in my criticism, and in the most broad and useless sense of the word could be called "deconstructive." I am not a card-carrying deconstructionist, but that does not mean that I can't learn from that current. That kind of tension, the need for a necessarily impersonal analysis which has not surrendered to some fetish of subjective experience, at the same time has as full as possible an appreciation of the lived, of that which does not fit into rigorous, philosophical terms, that tension seems to me one that can itself only be lived. It can be worked out to some degree in writing, and I think my writing is trying in some degree to do that. I am very suspicious of writing that seeks only to play and I am equally suspicious of writing that doesn't understand the meaning of the word play. My writing, I hope, is trying to negotiate a possible path between those two extremes.

ELC What made me say that is that sometimes in the midst of some rigorous philosophical development you use a quite incredible, unexpected example, like "ironing your socks" to demonstrate realism or referring to Fredric Jameson's enormous learning as a "California supermarket kind of a mind." It sort of blows your mind reading this.

TE Yes, yes, I suppose there is a bit of homespun English philosophy in that! My sensibility is attracted to those modes. It is partly, I think, because I believe in the importance of writing in a quite narrow sense. I believe that I pay attention to my style when I write. I am rather dismayed—this is a middle-aged grouse if there ever was one!—by the drearily utilitarian style of so much radical thought today. For all they may speak of play and *jouissance*, in fact this kind of turgid academicist left style, which I must confess I find very common in the United States, with eighty-three footnotes to every paragraph, I find very depressing. I don't find any difference, personally, between the experience of writing my creative work, plays and so on, and writing criticism; I think this is the same type of experience, and that has something to do with what you asked me about. I am a writer, a stylist; *what* mode I write in is to some extent secondary.

ELC I think your novel is somewhat theoretical. Like Umberto Eco's *The Name of the Rose*.

TE Yes. Though mercifully shorter.

ELC Another term that actually brings you again closer to Lukács is the importance you attribute to a certain "immanence." If you recall Lukács's *Theory of the Novel*, you will remember that Lukács finds the origin of the novel in the epic and says that, compared to the problematic hero of the novel, the epic hero enjoys immanence. My question is whether this idea of immanence is also a guiding principle for you?

TE Just tell me a bit more about it and how you see it in my work.

ELC Since I do not see you that much as a "totalizing" critic or even clearly a Marxist, I was wondering what your guiding principles were in establishing your morals and values. In some of your works, in particular the text on *Nationalism, Colonialism, and Literature*, it seemed to me that the body played quite an important role. You repeatedly stress the importance and the need of the body, and I was wondering whether you considered this immanence of the body as a guiding principle in your theories.

TE I am getting a bit impatient with the number of books that have to have the word body in their title in order to sell. At the same time, having said that, I do think that the body is a crucial category, and indeed in the chapter on Marx in *The Ideology of the Aesthetic*, I claim that the ambitiousness of Marx is that he is trying to work himself up, if that is possible, from the body itself, from what he calls species being. From what we are as material creatures, he tries to work his way up to a certain politics, to a certain ethics, and so on. Whether that project is entirely feasible, whether it is not philosophically too naturalistic, is a real question for me. But that is what I think Marxism is trying to do. The body is absolutely essential to Marxism. It is, of course, a body that is the laboring rather than the sexual body, and to that extent is at once crucial and limited. It suppresses the dimension of sexuality, but as far as the current fashionable concern with the body goes, there is no doubt in my mind that that is present from the earliest moment of Marx's work in his *Economic and Philosophical Manuscripts.* Now whether or not my own work is concerned with the body? My work is unequivocally concerned with socialist ethics. The conclusion to the *The Ideology of the Aesthetic* is my first attempt to write about this, about the question of whether one can derive an ethics from a certain view of how human beings as material animals are or could become. I think that's a vital project; I don't know whether it is answerable, but I think it is vital, for one thing, to oppose current postmodernist trends which either skirt the question of ethics or reduce it to the pragmatic subjective or the intersubjective. I don't think there is much future in that, and that is one reason why Marxism appeals to me.

ELC In Lukács, certainly, I have not found any references to a bodily presence other than to a social body.

TE But that is a body nevertheless. Marx's whole enterprise begins, as a very young man, in his 1844 manuscript, which we might say was almost entirely about that body. Marx is trying to look at the structures of the body and certainly sees the release of the sensuous, being able fully to experience one's senses and so on, as a key aspect of emancipation. That has been ignored or suppressed in the work of Marx, partly by later Marxists themselves. I wouldn't have thought that Lukács, for example, is a writer with whom one would automatically associate the concept of sensuousness or the body, not to speak of humor, which is notably lacking from his work. But I don't think it's unimportant to say that sensuousness, the enjoyment of the senses, the release of bodily powers and capacities, is the constant anthropology that underpins Marx's work, and in the *Economic and Philosophical Manuscripts* it is explicit.

ELC There is much talk today about the eighteenth-century Enlightenment. I am referring to recent Habermassian theories. Do you share this type of Marxism?

TE If anything is the test of dialectic thought for us today it surely is the Enlightenment. I neither back the case that present-day radicalism is simply an extension of the Enlightenment, nor do I support the case that the Enlightenment was the moment of the Fall, was some drastic catastrophe from which we never quite recovered. Both cases seem to me drastically undialectical. A dialectical assessment of the Enlightenment is I think, in principle, Marxism itself. Marxism understands itself, on the one hand, as the child of Enlightenment. It would not have been made possible without that marvelous bourgeois liberal enlightened overthrow of autocracy and absolutism. At the same time, Marxism tries to revolutionize Enlightenment, revolutionize the social order that it created. That kind of dialectical approach I find disastrously absent from most radical thought today. The hasty backing of horses, the manning of one barricade against the other, either on the one hand the Habermassian project of seeing socialism as simply the completion of Enlightenment, or the postmodern project of seeking to dismiss modernity as so much error, both of them seem to me so one-sided that any genuine radical thought has to negotiate itself in the space between them.

ELC In discussing Lukács you sometimes use terms that seem to modernize and update Lukács's thought. What you say about the proletariat could easily be said of women. In one of your prefaces you speak of Toril Moi and you say that with her you have nearly identical views, if I understood you correctly. I was very struck by that.

TE I say in the preface to the *Ideology* book that for the past ten years

she and I, Toril Moi and I, have argued the question of ideology together more than any other intellectual topic to the point where it is
not clear where her thought ends and mine begins. I don't say that we
have identical views, nor do I remember replacing the concept of proletariat with the concept of women. They seem to me to be very different political realities.

ELC I can see a resemblance between the two in their traditional positions in society, where they find themselves both on the exploited side
and need to overcome their exploiter. I think such a Hegelian master-
slave dialectic works very well for both but in the case of women the
situation seems to be more modern and more complex. The concept of
the proletariat today is really passé.

TE Not for me. Globally speaking, the proletariat has increased. I
would say two things on this, and again I hope in a dialectical way.
One is that I think that I have learned tremendously from feminism the
limits of a mere class analysis and the limits of traditional Marxism in
that sense, the blindness of traditional Marxism to the oppression of
half the human race and the cavalier way Marxism has sometimes
sought to approach that. The second thing I want to say is I think that
feminism, particularly in the United States, and to some extent in
Europe, has also displaced class analysis, and I think that is a grave
loss. I think that the struggles of sexual politics and the struggles of
class politics, while by no means in my mind synonymous or identifiable with each other, or even in many ways very parallel, have both to be
taken with seriousness. And what has happened, I think, on the negative side over the past two and a half decades, particularly in a society
like the United States which hasn't had recently much experience of
thinking in terms or class struggle, has been a disastrous abandonment
of the analysis of capitalism. If I remain a Marxist, it is that I want to
look at the necessary solidarity in the end of all these struggles rather
than narrow-mindedly attend to one rather than to the other.

ELC To me, as a woman, your theoretical collaboration with Toril Moi
seemed fascinating and encouraging. Just as I like the idea of having a
president of the United States whose wife is also very accomplished
and has a mind of her own. I think couples like this show us the future,
at least as I would like to see it. The two of you arguing the same
theories, such as ideology, is extremely interesting.

TE Let me put it this way. The feminist environment that I am aware
of here and in Europe has been by and large a socialist-feminist environment, where feminists would assume that they were on the left,
that there was much in common between their views about class politics and other issues. I don't think that can be assumed in the United

States. In other words, I don't find that I can assume automatically, although I am very glad to find it confirmed, that somebody in the U.S.A. who has progressive and enlightened attitudes on sexual politics necessarily has such attitudes toward socialism. I don't assume that there can be an alliance either intellectually or practically. I hope there can be, but I can't take that for granted. I think that my thoughts about feminism have been shaped in an environment where, as I said, what I have been in dialogue with was primarily a socialist feminism, and I found that very helpful as a kind of bridge between my own position and those of feminism.

ELC You mentioned Walter Benjamin and the importance of historicism and history. I may be misreading you, but when you speak admiringly of Benjamin's "sacred" reading (*Walter Benjamin or, Toward a Revolutionary Criticism* [London: Verso, 1981], p. 152) isn't that again somewhat idealistic?

TE I don't mean it's sacred to me, it's sacred to him.

ELC You admire him.

TE Yes, I can admire him without thinking that his reading is sacred. What I mean by this is not that in my view Benjamin's reading is sacred. I do think, incidentally, that certain things are sacred. I can't imagine anybody who didn't. Certain things are so valuable that "sacred" is the word one could use. I don't see why one needs to be unduly frightened by its theological implication if it doesn't have any for one. Benjamin's readings are sacred in a theological sense, of course. I am interested in that very strange cabalistic way of reading, whether it is reading text or history. I don't share that theological belief, but I find it profoundly suggestive and creative and one which, as in Benjamin himself, can be transported into secular uses.

ELC How could you read the text of the history of World War II in a "sacred" way? Do you mean in all its crudity and violence?

TE No. For Benjamin it would mean reading it with a due reverence for the victims of that violence.

ELC But how would you "read" it?

TE In a manner that Benjamin attempts, by scanning or fanning history in order to find the redemptive, emancipatory moments, crevices, sparks within a text that is largely oppressive and negative. That is what Benjamin does. There is a whole messianic ideology behind that in Benjamin which is why he can discuss this as "sacred." He wants to look for the strait gate, as he says, through which the messiah might always enter. Now, one doesn't have to subscribe to that Judaic theology in order to see the power or suggestiveness of a certain reading of history that is rather like a materialist reading (which Benjamin's was also), that looks for certain emancipatory impulses, certain moments of the past to be rescued and protected as he wished, certain attempts, as in the Cabala, to make correspondences between the present and disparate moments in history. All that is to him "sacred," part of the sacred methodology, and I find much of value in that. As I said, that does not mean that I am a Jewish metaphysician or that I believe in messianism, but it's opposed to the secular by which Benjamin means essentially bourgeois historiography.

ELC Doesn't it have an idealist bent to it?

TE Well, I think it does. But where would Marxism have been without philosophical idealism? Every major Marxist thinker has learned enduringly from the results of that idealism.

ELC You mentioned the Kadarkay biography of Lukács. He presents a Lukács who was profoundly influenced by Judaism and who is messianic. There is also a searcher at the Lukács Archives in Budapest, Miklós Mesterházi, who wrote a book about Lukács's messianism. Yet unlike Benjamin, Lukács never talked about his Judaism; it did not seem to matter to him, he seemed to even turn away from it. Only recently have we received more and more evidence about how much all this mattered to him and how much his religious background influenced his theories.

TE My point is not so much about that, although it is very interesting, but rather about the role of idealism with regard to Marxism. Marxism began from certain idealistic sources, Hegel and so on. It has always raided the illuminating insights of idealist thinkers and has tried to use what it can. There is to my mind no pure materialism. There has been a running battle between, if you like, idealism and materialism. Most major Marxist thinkers are some amalgam of insights that come from the great bourgeois idealist tradition, some coming more directly from materialism. Idealism is not for me an altogether negative word, that's what I am trying to say.

ELC You frequently criticize idealism and idealists.

TE Oh, yes. And they often asked to be criticized. But there is not one single thing for me called "idealism," which is a kind of heresy and has in a blanket way to be opposed. The word idealism means many different things, and idealism in philosophy played a very important role in the period of mechanical materialism in keeping alive certain values and meanings, certain human possibilities, that were not explicable by mechanical materialism. No rich and complex philosophical tradition is for me valueless. That's one way in which I will see myself as a dialectician. It would be disastrously nondialectical to write that off as absolutely worthless. What a dialectician has to do, and what I think

Benjamin, to come back to your point, is doing with the notion of the "sacred," is scanning that tradition for its potentially usable points, for its redemptive role, and so on. But of course to do that you would indeed have to negate, deny, and refuse much of its negative side, much of its false utopia, much of its false spirituality, much of its displacement of the material world into bad kinds of transcendence. Surely. But both go hand in hand.

ELC I am coming to my more global questions about Marxism. In *Against the Grain* you spoke of "young post-Marxist intellectuals" who "race to deconstruct its drearily metaphysical basis" (p. 62). Where do you see Lukács? Do you see him as a metaphysical or a materialist Marxist?

TE That is a difficult one. My impressionistic answer to that would be that Lukács retains the form of the metaphysical while changing the contents. That's what I meant when I said somewhere that he replaces the world spirit with the proletariat. In one sense that is a materialization, that's a bringing down of those rather grandiose concepts to the earth. In another sense, you don't transform a problematic just by changing its content. Walter Benjamin knew that in order to transform, you had to change the form and not just the content. My own impression would be that the structure and the architectonics of Lukács's thought remained thoroughly Hegelian, but the content changed. Whether, however, such a disparity between form and content can itself be said to be Hegelian is a different question. So Lukács does carry a lot of Hegelian baggage in that sense, but then if that's what allows him to think totality, to think historicity, if Second International mechanical, materialist Marxism can't provide him with that, then in my view better to go to the Hegelian tradition than nowhere at all. And that again I would see as a dialectical assessment.

ELC You know that Lukács himself described his *Theory of the Novel* as characterized by left ethics and right epistemology. So you, too, see him somewhat between the two. Lukács has always been criticized by both sides, the right and the left wing. I remember during a visit to Budapest in 1976, I spoke to an official Lukács scholar, István Hermann, who was extremely critical of Lukács. Shortly after that, in the United States and in Australia, Lukács's own disciples were equally tearing his work apart, in particular his *Ontology.* So he is, as usual, between two extremes.

TE The fact that his work polarizes people so sharply is in itself symptomatic of something about it. It is symptomatic of a set of contradictions or ambivalence in that work, of what happens when we rewrite Hegel, when we rewrite Marx through Hegel. Again, to put the point as it were dialectically, you might say both cases you allude to are right. Those who criticize Lukács home in upon the negative consequences of what he does, and those who defend him on the positive ones, but both of those things are there, in my view. You can't take one without the other.

ELC With regard to Marxism, you comment somewhere upon Foucault's statement that Marxism belongs to the nineteenth century by saying more or less: "so what?" Where *does* Marxism belong? To the nineteenth century? You identify yourself as a Marxist today. What do you mean by "so what?"

TE Marxism understands itself as a response to capitalism, understands itself as something that could only have grown up within the categories and the realities of that epoch. Marxism doesn't understand itself as having dropped from the sky. So when Foucault says, poof, this is just nineteenth-century, old-fashioned thinking, he is not saying anything to Marxism that Marxism itself is not aware of. But as long as that nineteenth-century system of capitalism is still with us, in a transformed way in the twentieth century, then Marxism must be with us, too. So to say that Marxism is a nineteenth-century phenomenon is to make a dialectical point about the conditions of its emergence and its necessary historical relatedness to the system it opposes; it is not to say, as Foucault implies, "therefore it is redundant." Darwin is a thoroughly nineteenth-century thinker; but that's not to say that he is not relevant today or was not in principle relevant to the eighteenth century. Freud is highly relevant to the Middle Ages, even though they had never heard of him.

ELC What happened, in your view, in Soviet Russia and Eastern Europe with the end of communism? Was it the end of Stalinism, or has it also affected Marxism?

TE The concept of Stalinism is in itself a complex one that perhaps can't be unreservedly used for whatever those societies were, but certainly I find surprising the assumption on the part of some liberals and conservatives that Marxists should be disillusioned by what has happened. You can be disillusioned only if you are illusioned. Hardly anybody I know on the far left in Britain has ever entertained serious illusions about the nature of those societies. The last time when widespread illusions in this country and in Europe were entertained about those societies was in the 1930s. The 1930s were a long time ago. Most, almost all, of the creative forms of Western Marxism have been deeply critical in one way or another of the postcapitalist bloc in the East, whether one is talking of Trotskyism, whether one is talking of the

Frankfurt School, and so on. The collapse of those systems poses severe problems for Marxism, but not, I think, problems of disillusionment.

ELC What is the lesson?

TE The lesson is, I think, a very old and a very classical lesson of Marxism: You can't build socialism in isolation in backward societies. As all of the major Marxist thinkers from Marx to Lenin understood: to build socialism, you need some material basis. If you are trying to do it in desperately backward societies, and if those societies have to go it alone in the face of a hostile world, then they are very likely to be forced down the Stalinist road. "Stalinist" has to be understood as a particular response to, or a consequence of, the attempt to build socialism in those material conditions. In other words, the strength of Marxist theory is that it has contained a theory of the nature of Stalinism, of its structure, of its emergence, and of its potential far more powerful, cogent, and comprehensive than anything that Western liberals, postmodernists, or conservatives have been able to produce. If you want a historically grounded, materially based critique of Stalinism that is relentlessly politically hostile to it, you have to go to Marxism. You can't go to the somewhat feeble, even though well-intentioned, humanitarianism or moralism of Western liberals. It just doesn't go far enough. The Trotskyist tradition has argued well over half a century that those societies were not to be reformed, they were to be revolutionized, and the precondition for transforming them into genuinely socialist societies is dismantling the state apparatuses they have. The dismantling of the state apparatuses has now taken place. Suddenly revolution, in the classic Marxist sense, broke out in the places where everybody had least expected it. But Trotsky had always warned that a result of the collapse of Stalinism might be a reversion to capitalism; this is something else that Marxism has understood for a long time.

ELC You actually credit Marxism for the recent revolution in Russia?

TE No, that's not at all what I said. I said that Marxism has contained within itself the critique of Stalinism, a critique, and I say it again, much more powerful, more historically based than anything that Western liberals have managed to produce. That is not to say that Marxism created those revolutions; of course not. But just at a point in the West when the concept of revolution itself had been apparently utterly discredited—it was metaphysical, it was passé—revolution in quite a classic Marxist sense, namely, the overthrow of the state by a popular movement, took place exactly in situations where it was least expected.

ELC In the name of money!

TE No. Let's tell both stories. I just told the first story. The second story is the story that you just broached: the bringing down of the Stalinist state is not *sufficient* to create socialism. It is a precondition of socialism, but not the achievement of it. But what Marxists have said, ever since the work of Trotsky, is that in that situation there will be a dire possibility that those societies will adopt capitalism. Marxist theory has long anticipated what has now happened in those societies. Trotskyists argued in the Second World War that there should be popular revolutions against the Stalinist bureaucracies. They came, a bit belatedly, but they came in our own time. Trotsky was also arguing that if this happened, that there was a real danger that capitalist systems would move in. There is nothing that has happened—I don't wish to appear conceptually arrogant—but it is simply the fact that there is nothing that has happened since Tiananmen Square that many Marxists have not been clamoring for or envisaging as a dangerous possibility for generations.

ELC Why is it that we do not have a communist state or, let's say, a Marxist state that is flourishing?

TE Because building socialism requires very definite preconditions. It requires that you, for instance, are not attacked and invaded all the time by other hostile societies, it means that you are not desperately economically backward, it means that you have the material resources to build up production, you have the culture and the expertise, you have the time for genuine participatory democracy, you have the international cooperation and help. You give us all those things, and the possibility for real socialism will of course be better.

ELC How about Sweden?

TE Well, social democratic societies are not the same as socialist societies. I am talking about societies that are genuinely socialized.

ELC Mitterrand's France?

TE Societies that have genuinely popular self-government and democracy, workers' control, the abolition of private property, the abolition of class systems, that is what has classically been understood to be a socialist society. Now, can this be feasibly created? Of course, if all of those conditions that I have just mentioned were there. The reason why we don't have those societies is because those conditions are not there.

ELC Coming back to Lukács. What is Lukács's role today after all that has happened? Is he still here? Are you working on or with him? How do you see his future?

TE I would say that the immediate future for Lukács doesn't look too bright, in the sense that it is not likely that in the wake of the collapse of the Stalinist systems for which he was sometimes a craven apologist—not always, sometimes also a brave critic—it is not likely that a major classical Marxist figure associated with those systems will move to the center of intellectual attention. The other story is that we will perhaps realize that there are enormous theoretical resources in his work that we have too hastily displaced. This goes back to what I said earlier about Althusser and so on. Now that the dust and heat of some of those arguments have settled, I think the way is clear for people at least to go back and look at Lukács, though not uncritically. I would hope that now there would be more possibilities for people to go back and appreciate his work.

ELC For you, *History and Class Consciousness* is still Lukács's greatest work? You don't appreciate his work on literary criticism as much as this one?

TE Not as much, although I rate his literary criticism very highly. I think that one of the limitations of his literary criticism is a certain repetitiveness. Lukács has a marvelously interesting and I think original case, which in a sense you can do no more than state again and again about different authors, different movements. But I would think that *History and Class Consciousness* will go down in the annals of radical social thought as an absolutely major and classic text.

ELC Even though you criticized Jameson for being in awe of it.

TE My greatest hope—although I don't have much hope for it right now—is that people would understand that one can criticize and affirm simultaneously, and if one doesn't do that, one is simply not being dialectical. I reject the Manichaean demand that is wholly for something or wholly against it. To praise and to criticize in the same breath seems to me the most natural attitude; we do it every day, we do it about people, we do it about institutions, we do it about critical thought. But that it should be thought extraordinary to say: I think this is a major writer, a major artist, but look how awful he or she is, too—the moment that is seen as extraordinary or slippery or evasive, I will sign off. The integrity of intellectual thought to me, and I don't honestly find this much supported in present radical culture, is that one gives the devil all his due. At the same time, one says he *is* the devil, and if you can't do that, if all you can do is boringly praise or boringly condemn, then there is no possibility for dialectical thought. Lukács therefore would be for me an exemplary case because in central ones I disagree with him, and I see absolutely no conflict between saying that and saying that there is no doubt he is of towering intellectual stature, which is to say he is worth arguing with interminably in the way that Jean Baudrillard simply isn't. Look how far we have declined. I wouldn't regard a figure of that kind as somebody worth having interminable, complex arguments with, whereas one can bounce off Lukács and get passionately angry or admiring.

ELC So he is a devil, but a great devil?

TE Or if you want, you could put it the other way around and say that he is a great figure with diabolical leanings.

INTERVIEW WITH SUSAN R. SULEIMAN

31 July 1993, Princeton

ELC I should like to tell you how much I appreciate your agreeing to this interview. You are a very special "subject," not just because you are the only woman to participate in my project, but for other reasons as well. You had a relatively early exposure to Lukács, I believe, through Lucien Goldmann. In 1975 you were the only reader of my Ph.D. dissertation on Lukács who could actually understand my quotations of him in Hungarian. You have also just returned from a year of research at the Institute for Advanced Study in Budapest, where you might have observed current attitudes toward Lukács by his own countrymen.

In *Authoritarian Fictions** you deal quite extensively with Lukács. Do you remember when you first met Lukács's work?

SRS I think the first place I encountered Lukács was in reading Thomas Mann's *The Magic Mountain*, where the figure of Naphta, a very strange, brilliant, paradoxical, East European intellectual who commits suicide in the end, is always said to have been modeled after Lukács. I read *The Magic Mountain* when I was in college and I loved Mann. It's funny because while I was in Budapest several Hungarian intellectuals told me, "You know that Naphta figure in Thomas Mann is really Lukács."

ELC You also know that Lukács did not like this.

SRS Yes, because in the novel Naphta is very brilliant but also a kind of dangerous, strange, and strangely destructive man.

ELC Do you remember when you first read Lukács himself?

SRS I think when I was in graduate school. I read his *Studies on European Realism* because I was interested in Balzac, Stendhal, and so on. It could have been with Fredric Jameson who was my teacher in graduate school. He was a young professor at the time. But this might just be my afterthought—at that time, in the mid to late sixties, Jameson was not a Marxist.

ELC At the beginning, I believe, Jameson was quite interested in *The Historical Novel*.

SRS That's right. There was also a historical novel I was interested in, Vigny's *Cinq Mars*, and some of the nineteenth-century historical fiction, so that I was at least aware of Lukács's book.

---

*Susan Rubin Suleiman, *Authoritarian Fictions: The Ideological Novel as a Literary Genre* (New York: Columbia University Press, 1983). Page numbers within the text refer to the new edition (Princeton: Princeton University Press, 1993).

ELC From then on, did Lukács have any effect on your theoretical development? on your preferences?

SRS One really lasting impression that Lukács made on me, both positive and negative, was in his writing about Zola: the notion that certain kinds of formal features of writing had deep ideological significance. For instance, he hates Zola's descriptions because they dissolve reality and don't really get you to see the complications of society the way Balzac's descriptions make you see everything. He loves Balzac as someone who gives you a total picture of the world, but he hates Zola because Zola sort of dissolves the world and doesn't give you a total picture. So this really struck me. How can you use certain kinds of formal features of writing as an index of ideological correctness? For instance, to say that the sonnet is bad, bourgeois—and this is the kind of thing some theorists do—or at one point people in France were discussing the realist novel as a hopelessly compromised bourgeois form. So it's the relationship between form and ideology that I probably got for the first time from Lukács, as well as his violent critiques of naturalism and, of course, of modernism.

ELC We were together at Columbia for a few years, and I remember seeing you at Lucien Goldmann's seminar, so I wondered whether you encountered Lukács there, since Goldmann's seminar on Sartre was really a seminar on Lukács.

SRS As you know, I was teaching then and did not attend his seminar very regularly, although I read Goldmann and heard him speak and knew his work. I had read his *Le Dieu caché* in graduate school and thought it was very, very good and I also read his *Sociology of the Novel.** No, it was not through Goldmann. I think I had read Lukács before, in graduate school. I encountered both Lukács and Goldmann pretty much at the same time, in graduate school, around 1964.

ELC If you were to characterize your method, would there be one figure or one philosopher more than another who influenced you?

SRS Do you mean Goldmann versus Lukács or in general?

ELC If you wish to say something about that, yes, but I meant it more generally. I know you mentioned Sartre; you also mentioned Barthes and Todorov.

SRS Yes, and Genette. Genette for a while became my hero for his theories on narratology, his "Discours du récit."** Also Greimas, and in general the French structuralists. I cannot say that Lukács was one

*Lucien Goldmann, *Le Dieu caché: Etude sur la vision tragique dans les "Pensées" de Pascal et dans le théâtre de Racine* (Paris: Gallimard, 1959); Goldmann, *Pour une sociologie du roman* (Paris: Gallimard, 1964).

**Gérard Genette, "Discours du récit," *Figures III* (Paris: Seuil, 1972).

of my heroes, although I really admired him. I think he was an important figure for me because I was struggling with those questions about the relation between form and ideology. Here was a man who sometimes made, in my opinion, very wrongheaded judgments.

ELC So your first reaction was negative?

SRS My reaction was, "This is really brilliant, but he is totally wrong." What a curious and strange notion that Beckett and Kafka are in some way terrible writers because their vision of the world is not "total" enough. Lukács considers their vision too partial, too egocentric, almost "sick."

ELC For Lukács it was "irrational."

SRS What Lukács is saying is that they are giving us characters who are actually sick people, but they want us to believe that this is the world, this is what modern life is like, that those characters are metaphors for modern life. And he holds that against them. So, even though I have never thought of Lukács as one of my intellectual heroes, he was ultimately someone who loomed in my world along with people like Sartre, Goldmann, and my then teacher Paul Bénichou, whose book on seventeenth-century literature and ideology (*Morales du grand siècle* [Paris: Gallimard, 1948]) always interested me.

ELC As I said, I did not find much of Lukács directly in your writings, except in one chapter of *Authoritarian Fictions.* However, I find Lukács in many of the things you say, even in your feminism, so I should like to return to this later. You mention somewhere that all you had was a "smattering" of Marxism. I guess this means that you were never interested in Marxism or the later Lukács and his Marxist writings except for the studies you mentioned on Beckett and Kafka. Have you read *The Theory of the Novel*?

SRS *The Theory of the Novel* is one of the works of Lukács, besides the ones I mentioned, that I know really well. I don't know his deeply philosophical works like *History and Class Consciousness*, for example—I am not enough of a philosopher or enough of a Marxist—but his critical works I know quite well, and *The Theory of the Novel* I know very well, and that is the one work I discuss in some detail in *Authoritarian Fictions.*

ELC You state quite emphatically in your introduction to *Authoritarian Fictions* that "this study is not Marxist in approach or allegiance" but it might be said to be "formalistic" or "ideological" (not in the Marxist but rather the Barthian sense where no discourse is said to be "wholly free of ideology") (p. 2). Does this mean that you are very opposed to Marxism? Are you an anti-Marxist? Have you ever had sympathies for Marxism?

SRS Of course, I had sympathies. In fact, it is hard for someone who has studied the 1930s in Europe not to have taken sides against the fascists and for the Marxist writers. So I have never been an anti-Marxist. When I wrote that in *Authoritarian Fictions*, I simply wanted to protect myself from accusations of people who might say "You haven't read *Das Kapital*," or whatever. I wanted to say my approach is not particularly Marxist, and specifically it is not Marxist because it doesn't place class above everything else as an analytic category. I did not want my writing to be ideological, but rather, inspired by the structuralists, I wanted it to be "scientific." As it turned out, of course, it became very clear that I had strong values and judgments about the books that I was talking about.

ELC When you wrote your Ph.D. dissertation on Paul Nizan, who became a Marxist, did you deal with Marxism then at all? Who was your advisor?

SRS W. M. Frohock. What I had was a kind of romantic version of Marxism, especially of Marxism as an antifascism. I was extremely attracted to the interwar period in Europe, which is my own prehistory. I was born a month before the outbreak of World War II. So the interwar period, the things leading up to the war, the rise of Nazism in Germany were my prehistory. My life—and maybe my scholarly interests, too—would be very different if I had not been a Jew born in 1939.

To get back to the question about Marxism, I had a romantic attraction to people who were staunchly anti-Nazi in the interwar period. Obviously, they were of the previous generation to mine or even quite older, Sartre's generation, people born between 1900 and 1915. Most of them were Marxists. There were also some anti-Nazis who were not Marxists. But if you think of the 1920s, after the founding of the Communist Party in France, there were many people like Léon Blum who were Marxists even though they weren't communists. There was the whole question of socialism versus communism. I was drawn to the antifascists and to some communists like Nizan—but as you know, he left the party after the war broke out.

ELC The interest in socialism and communism was in the air among intellectuals at that time and even after the war. My hero at school in the 1950s was Camus. I never heard of Lukács until I met Lucien Goldmann and embarked on my Ph.D. dissertation at Columbia University. At that time, my father told me that he knew of Lukács since he studied in Budapest in 1919 when Lukács became the notorious cultural "Kommissar" who terrorized the bourgeois students at the university in favor of the proletariat.

SRS In my case, as a graduate student, I did not know enough about

Marxism yet to be critical of it, even though I knew, of course, of the show trials and the horrors, but nobody knew that much about the Gulag yet. But as I said, I had the romantic vision of those writers of the interwar period who were my heroes and who were firmly anti-fascist. Camus would fit that description, except that later he had the famous fight with Sartre (around 1950) after he had criticized the communists in *The Rebel.*

ELC For me, Camus was the first sociocritical writer I encountered. I read *The Plague* at school and lived in Paris when he died, in 1960. I feel quite influenced by him. He no doubt played a role in my "road to Lukács."

Let's come back to you and Lukács. I have a question that relates to *The Reader in the Text.** In your introduction you are saying that "An audience . . . remains irreducibly itself, appropriating the text for its own tastes and purposes . . . both possessing it and being possessed by it" (p. vii). It seemed to me that one could say this also of Lukács's relationship to the text. He takes the text and kind of "possesses" it, reads things into it. Having studied many reader-response theorists, what do you think of Lukács's "reading"?

SRS I think he is a very brilliant reader. He is also a very prejudiced reader. He comes to the text with a grid already in his mind. He knows what he likes and he knows what he is looking for. He is the kind of person who gets really furious when he reads Beckett or Kafka or Zola, saying, "No, they do not give me enough reality which is what literature should do. They are not giving me a total picture of reality and a total perspective. So I will demonstrate exactly why it is that they failed." He is a brilliant reader because he is able to prove his point and look for the cause of his fury and show exactly why it is that he rejects those writers. I think he is wrong, because I don't believe that there is a one-to-one relationship between certain kinds of formal features or procedures and ideology.

ELC You think that he goes too quickly from form to ideology and hasty value judgments?

SRS From form to ideological meaning. That is my argument in *Authoritarian Fictions*, at the very end: It is not the case that all realist novels are by definition, and because of their very form, reactionary or right-wing or not progressive or "bad."

ELC Do you have similar reservations about Goldmann's work, for instance *Le Dieu caché*? You do criticize him in *The Reader in the Text* for the "total homogeneity" he assumes between the writer and his

---

* *The Reader in the Text: Essays on Audience and Interpretation*, ed. Susan R. Suleiman and Inge Crosman (Princeton: Princeton University Press, 1980).

public (p. 33), his reductionism (p. 34), and his reflection theory. I think you say this in reference to Jacques Leenhardt's text, which constitutes one of the chapters of *The Reader in the Text*. How do you see the relationship between the text and the social?

SRS That's really an interesting question. *Le Dieu caché* got me very excited. I remember going to Bénichou and saying, "What do you think?" Bénichou at one time (before I knew him) was flirting with the Marxist approach too; his book, *Morales du Grand Siècle*, clearly suggests that kind of approach.

ELC It was the first Marxist critique I remember.

SRS Yes, except that in the 1960s Bénichou was no longer a Marxist. He pointed that out to me when I was a graduate student at Harvard and went to see him about Goldmann, saying, "Look at this wonderful, interesting book by Goldmann." He said, "Ah, oui, oui, oui, mais c'est un Marxiste!" But I thought that *Le Dieu caché* was absolutely brilliant because of its reading of Pascal. His reading of Pascal was very interesting to me, but the part that I guess is the problematic part would be to say "this is the vision of a certain kind of *noblesse*, the *noblesse de robe*" and make a very clear link between a certain theology and a certain social position. Goldmann sometimes sees too simple a relation between an individual writer and the social group whose "vision" the writer supposedly represents.

ELC Actually, this leads me to another quotation. You mention Stanley Fish's argument, in the late 1970s, that "How one reads is entirely a matter of shared conventions or interpretive strategies" (p. 20). Do you agree with this statement? Are Lukács's theories expressions of shared "interpretive strategies" belonging to the first decade of the century more or less? How much room is there for individualism and originality? How much is Lukács, or any of us, just a product of the historical moment?

SRS I don't know enough about all the people around Lukács to be able to say to what extent he shares the reading strategies of his contemporaries. But I do agree with that statement by Stanley Fish because we all have categories that we learn somewhere at school or elsewhere, implicitly or explicitly, and that determine what it is we are looking for when we read. Is it complexity or irony, or wholeness, totality? It would appear that for Lukács it was very important to see, for instance, typicality. I assume that his categories came from Hegel and Marx, the extent to which you could read individual works of literature but always with the view of seeing how those works express their moment. That notion that the writer expresses a moment and also expresses a particular understanding that comes from his belonging to a particular class, those categories are already Marxist categories.

ELC It is maybe interesting in this context to bring up a book I just reviewed which tried to bring together Lukács, Freud, and the novel. I thought that in this particular case it did not work too well because the person had not read Lukács carefully enough and made many unfounded assumptions; but according to Marxist theory there should be many similarities between Lukács and Freud since they lived and wrote some of their works at approximately the same time in a relatively close proximity to each other; yet, in fact, their approaches and conclusions are quite different. This brings us back to the question as to how much we are a product of the historical moment. You and I would have to think very much alike according to this theory. We have gone through similar experiences, both having been born in Hungary, both specializing in French, and I have noticed while reading you that we have had similar theoretical influences on our intellectual work, not only Sartre, but also Todorov in addition to Goldmann-Lukács and the general French structuralist-poststructuralist group. I did not go as much into feminism as you did, with the exception of Cixous. So when I am reading your work that is maybe why I find so many thoughts that I can share, many of which to me seem actually Lukácsean in inspiration, even though you are more explicitly interested in formalist approaches. There was also the Maison Française of Columbia University, which I attended religiously in order to listen to all the theoreticians passing through New York. I often saw you there. You were already teaching as an assistant professor while I was still an instructor and graduate student. There was definitely an "affinity" or solidarity I felt which made me want to talk to you about the part Lukács may have had in your intellectual development.

Going back to our question and one of the major tenets of Marxist criticism: how much are we influenced by the historical moment and shared social experiences? How is it that Lukács and Freud wrote at the same historical moment and that their work is so different?

SRS Well, I think if we go back again to Stanley Fish's statement which you quoted, the implication is not that we are the playthings of history or merely little puppets that are moved by context but rather (at least the way I read it) that within this large historical moment and context there are what Fish calls "interpretive communities"; in other words, there are very specific shared understandings among people within specific groups. The fact that Freud and Lukács wrote at the same historical moment in more or less the same place does not mean that we should expect them to belong to exactly the same "interpretive community." Although one probably could say, yes, at some level they were bathing in the same ideas. . . .

ELC In the same totality?

SRS If you will. But they also belonged to different interpretive communities, they used different categories.

ELC People often say that one develops theories that usually reflect personal experiences, and that we are drawn to theories that speak for us. I am sometimes asked why I became interested in Lukács. When I was first asked the question, I thought about it and, yes, I found ideas in Lukács that explained to me many of my own experiences in society.

Have you turned to the specific theoreticians that influenced you because you felt that they addressed and explained some of your own experiences? Sartre? Genette? Barthes?

SRS What do we call my "theory"? I don't seem to have a single theory, although I am identified by many people as a feminist or as a one-time narratologist, or as a person who is interested in reader theories. I am sort of a jack-of-all-trades as far as theory is concerned.

ELC You have done many things, but I feel there is some thread going through it.

SRS Well, you tell me that. Other people find more unity in my thinking than I do myself.

ELC I find that you have definitely a sociocritical interest. Look at the titles of your books, or your feminism, or your writings on modernism.

SRS Yes, there may be an attempt to link individual works with larger historical moments.

ELC You stress your interest in formalism. Your work is not that formalist to me as a reader.

SRS I am glad you say that, because some of the reviewers of *Authoritarian Fictions* said that it was very formalist. It is true that history is always there in the background. Even though I do not give a historical account, history is always assumed as a given. I talk about the Dreyfus Affair, the 1930s. . . .

ELC You discuss form but in a sociocritical context toward which you have an implicitly critical attitude. This is certainly true also in your feminism, for instance, when you talk about patriarchy, which I should like to discuss a bit later.

SRS Yes, maybe in this I would certainly want to give credit to Lukács and a few others. This is an awareness or a kind of personal engagement with the text because you take it seriously, that is to say, you read it because it means something to you other than mere entertainment. It seems to say something about the world and things that matter to you.

ELC I would call your writings *engagé*, despite your protestations. Also, have you been influenced by Adorno and his notion of "the authoritarian"?

SRS I probably got the title for *Authoritarian Fictions* through Adorno and Horkheimer, from *The Authoritarian Personality*, which I read when I was finishing my book.

ELC You certainly have a resentment against "authoritarianism."

SRS Not a resentment but a strong resistance to it. Resentment implies a sort of helpless rage, whereas resistance suggests, for me, an informed opposition. I have a resistance to authoritarian techniques and methods.

ELC This may seem paradoxical. Lukács is quite authoritarian as well, yet at the same time he teaches you to resist what he calls "establishment" authoritarianism.

SRS The authoritarian side is the heavy Marxist side in him, when he says, "This is the truth," and so on. That's why I say he is often wrongheaded and provokes your fury, but that's okay.

ELC You say that you usually favor the "hybrid" rather than the homogeneous, which is in line with your critique of the *roman à thèse*. Lukács was also critical of the *roman à thèse.* He felt that it was not realist and was not artistic. He did have a sense for good literature. Here again, I felt, you were quite close to Lukács. But at the same time, Lukács liked norms and "organic developments"; for instance, he would have been in favor of the organic, historicist criticism of "Racine" and "racine," which you probably reject if you favor the "hybrid."

SRS The notion of organic development in a single work or historically?

ELC With reference to the whole historical development of genres, for instance, as opposed to the Deleuzian rhizomatic theories of the 1970s, when everything and everybody was "anti-(R)racine." Barthes was somewhat in that line, and you were influenced by him, weren't you?

SRS I met him, but I was not his student. He actually read my first article which appeared in *Critique* and became the first chapter of *Authoritarian Fictions.* We had only one meeting, but I admired him. His work was very important to me.

The organic metaphor is not one, particularly, that I have used, and I also haven't gone totally to war against it. The organic metaphor has so many versions, for instance, *déracinement* and *enracinement*, and in that sense I am very heavily critical of it because it is used by people like Barrès and other proto- (and "regular") French fascists as a way of attacking what they consider the "rootlessness" of the cosmopolitan, namely, Jews or other nomadic creatures. The metaphor of the tree can be a wonderful metaphor for "growing," "spreading," "vibrant," "alive," and so on, but if they carry it too far, it can also become abusive. My thinking would be, never to interpret any metaphor as having only a single possibility. It always depends on who is using it, to what purpose, when, and with what consequences. When Barrès talks about *déracinement*, I just want to close the book or I want to scream. But Yeats has a wonderful poem with the verse "O great-rooted blossomer," referring to a tree, which is beautiful. I wouldn't want to build a whole theory on organic development because I believe in things like. . . .

ELC Like "hybrids"?

SRS Like "hybrids." They are also organic in a way. You can produce hybrids by growing them, "breeding" them if you want an organic metaphor.

ELC So you have no nostalgia for *enracinement*, in the sense that you have your origins in Hungary? Have you not had this urge, which I have had all my life, to go back, find your roots and somewhat "recuperate" your origins?

SRS Oh, I have done nothing but that in the last six months, while I was in Budapest. But it does not mean that I want to go back and settle down. You can't go back and start all over again. It would be artificial for me suddenly to put down roots in Budapest, even though I may want to go there and live there for a few months or a year. No, I am not nostalgic for it.

ELC You mentioned ideology a few times, particularly in relation to the *roman à thèse*, in *Authoritarian Fictions*. Is every text for you "ideological"?

SRS I deal with this in the introduction to the book. It depends on how you define "ideology." If you define it in a very broad sense, if you say that a person's ideology is the way they view the world, or that ideology is the whole set of unstated assumptions that don't even need to be stated because they are what goes without saying, then of course every text is ideological.

ELC Do you mean in a context?

SRS Yes, within a context. For instance, part of the American ideology is that individuals are sacred and so is property. You don't really need to state this. It is an ideological assumption. So, if you define ideology in that broad sense, as the set of unstated assumptions that make up your values, then every text is ideological, because every text bathes in certain values and criteria for judgment. In *Authoritarian Fictions* I say at the beginning that the *roman à thèse* is not ideological in that broad sense but in a more specific sense, because there are also ideologies defined as isms, as doctrines. In my book I am interested in ideologies as isms, as very clearly and consciously shaped sets of beliefs.

ELC They would not be political but rather more broadly cultural?

SRS They are either political or theological: communism, fascism, Catholicism, liberalism. . . .

ELC It is not always an intentional content of the text; it can be intrinsic, hidden in the form?

SRS I think it's always intentional.

ELC It seemed to me that, at least at one point, you seemed to equate *roman à thèse* and ideological text.

SRS I equate the *roman à thèse* with a conscious ideology.

ELC You also mentioned "realism" in relation to the *roman à thèse*. What is your attitude toward realism? You say somewhere that the *roman à thèse* is written in a realistic mode, based on verisimilitude and representation (*Authoritarian Fictions*, p. 12). Is the realist novel according to you a didactic text? Isn't the *roman à thèse* quite different from realist fiction?

SRS Yes, that's the whole point. I define the *roman à thèse* as a novel written in the realist mode to distinguish it from, let us say, didactic novels that are science fiction mode or pure allegory mode, for instance, taking place among rabbits or horses that talk. *Animal Farm*, you can argue, is a *roman à thèse* because it has a very clear didactic intent. It's a fable. So the *roman à thèse* is just a realistic version of a fable. But *Animal Farm* does not come under my definition of *roman à thèse* (the way I define it in *Authoritarian Fictions*) because it is not written in the realist mode. A novel in which animals talk is not a realist novel. What I am saying is that the *roman à thèse* is interesting because it combines two different modes: the realist and the allegorical. The mode of realism is based on verisimilitude and representation, that is, we expect in the realist novel to find a world that corresponds pretty much to the world we know, where people don't spread their wings and fly off to the moon and where tables and chairs have certain functions, and events occur in some form of causal sequence. The other mode is the fable or allegory, which has a clear demonstrative, didactic purpose. When Christ tells you a parable, there is a demonstration involved.

ELC So is that a *roman à thèse*?

SRS Yes, except that it is not a *roman*, it is not a *roman à thèse*, because parables are not novels. The interesting thing for me is that the *roman à thèse* is a hybrid genre, between the realist novel and the fable, the parable, the allegory. My attitude toward realism, to come to your question, is that I see nothing wrong with it; I like realist novels. I don't even mind some *romans à thèse*. It's just that there is a clash in some way between the impulse of realism, which is to represent the world in as complex a way as possible, and the impulse of didacticism which is to simplify, to reduce, and to demonstrate. The *roman à thèse* is caught between those two impulses: it claims to be a realist novel and "wants" to be a realist novel, but it also wants to prove a point.

ELC And the point could be completely wrong? A *roman à thèse* could be completely wrong, whereas a great realist novel would represent reality, a totality, it would have a realist value. According to Lukács, for instance, Balzac, the Catholic and royalist, nevertheless wrote realist novels of great value because he narrated things as they were. He was not doctrinaire.

SRS You see, there is where I part company with Lukács, because my criterion for realism is not, "Is it true?" For me, realism is not determined by "Is it true?" but by verisimilitude, which is not a question of truth but of what is considered *plausible* at a given time. I adopt more the Barthesian definition of realism, as the mode of writing based on verisimilitude, redundancy, and realist effects. Why does Lukács hate Zola and like Balzac? He thinks Zola does not see the real world. . . .

ELC He said that he was not a realist, that he exaggerated. He was an experimentalist, a naturalist.

SRS For me, as I have said, the difference is between someone who attempts to show complexity and ambiguity, versus someone who attempts to demonstrate, which involves reductionism and simplification in order to make a point.

ELC Let me bring in Riffaterre here who says in *Fictional Truth* (Baltimore: Johns Hopkins University Press, 1990) that the didactic and doctrinaire, and so also the realist, are in the eye of the beholder, the reader. You quote Riffaterre saying that the genre is "a phantom form that exists only in the mind of the reader" (p. 8). So what is the role of the author? Is he the realist? What does he put into the text? Is there anything in the text? Is it all in the eyes of the beholder, the reader? Riffaterre seems to go to an extreme.

SRS Yes, except that Riffaterre is talking here about genres, not individual texts. Certainly, there are genres that have developed historically—you could say, for instance, that the sonnet exists independently of the mind of the reader. The sonnet is a fixed form, but the *roman à* *thèse* does not exist in the same way. They are different kinds of genres. I was trying to deal with a genre that I was defining, constructing, and creating at the same time as I was describing it. My quote of Riffaterre refers to that, but generally speaking, I would say that indeed it is true that you could read almost any work bringing to it your own classifications and categories. What I read as a *roman à thèse* you could read as a novel that uses certain kinds of metaphors or whatever. But I also do believe, as I say in the conclusion of *Authoritarian Fictions*, that there are limits set by the text; some novels are more *à thèse* than others. Not all realist novels are the same; you have to make distinctions.

ELC I know that your intention in *Authoritarian Fictions* is to define the *roman à thèse*, not the realist novel. Coming from Lukács, however, your terms could be easily criticized, particularly if you equate one with the other. You probably do not want to go that far.

SRS No, I don't. In fact, at the end of my book I strongly criticize Charles Grivel's book *Production de l'intérêt romanesque* (The Hague: Mouton, 1973). Grivel makes no distinctions between the novel, the realist novel, and the *roman à thèse*. For him, they are all the same bourgeois ideological practice. I make a very strong claim that it is important to make distinctions. I am saying, yes, there is a great leeway for readers to impose their own structures on works, but I do believe that authors are also responsible for the text.

ELC With respect to genres, you seem to disagree with Fredric Jameson about the way to ask the question of genre. You write: "The question one must try to answer in describing a genre is not, as Jameson suggests: 'What is *the* structural model that corresponds to a given mode in order to constitute the genre'? but rather: 'How does a given mode "appropriate" a given structural model in order to produce a work that we call tragedy, epic, melodrama, fantastic tale?' or whatever genre happens to interest us" (*Authoritarian Fictions*, p. 64). Does that mean that according to you genres did not originate at a particular historical moment, that they are givens? I don't quite understand how you see the origin of genres and what you mean by givens? Lukács has very clear and definite theories about the historical development of genres. If you look back into history, it is true that certain genres work better at certain historical periods. For instance, tragedy, even though Voltaire tried to revive it, does not really work in the eighteenth century any more. So could you explain a bit more what you mean by a mode that is "appropriating" a genre.

SRS When I use the word given in the passage you quote, I mean it simply as a synonym for particular—a particular mode, a particular structural model. These terms are Jameson's: by mode, he means "the essence of the genre," however one defines it; and by structural model, he means a syntactic model such as Vladimir Propp's model for fairy tales, which defines the "typical" narrative sequence of a fairy tale. Jameson is not concerned, in this essay of his, with the origin of genres; similarly, in my book I am not really interested in discussing the development of genres. I don't discuss, for instance, the move from epic to novel, which is very important, and both Bakhtin and Lukács deal with it in some detail. My book is structuralist in the sense that it seeks to describe a genre the way Todorov, for example, describes the fantastic. He is not primarily interested in the development, the historical evolution that produced the fantastic. My approach in *Authoritarian Fictions* was not to try and trace the historical growth of the *roman à thèse*. It was also not my concern to ask, "How did the *roman à thèse* come into being?" I claim that from the beginning, the novel as a genre has had a didactic impulse, which can be more or less emphasized. I read very widely among other didactic genres: the parable and the fable, for instance, are not confined to a single period, right? My approach is more structural than historical.

ELC I think you have also been interested in Maurice Roche. How do you see his novels? Are they novels? If you speak of "appropriation," could one say that he took the novel form and appropriated it to his needs?

SRS I think he uses the word novel as a provocation, the way Sollers sometimes used it.

ELC I interviewed Roche about ten years ago about his theory of the novel. He told me then that his novels were realistic, in a modern interpretation of realism. He took the genre of the novel and put all kinds of things into it, music scores, pictures, calligraphy, and transformed the whole genre, saying that that was the modern realist genre of the novel.

SRS Every generation of novelists always thinks they are more realistic than the preceding one.

ELC Do you think that the realist novel is passé? That it belonged to the nineteenth century and cannot be updated?

SRS No, I don't think that. David Lodge, in his book *The Modes of Modern Writing* (1977), claims that instead of a linear progression from realism to, say, modernism, there is rather an alternating series moving between realism and experimentation, or realism and antirealism. We certainly see empirically that there are many contemporary novels, good novels, that are written in the realist mode. Look at Saul Bellow or Nadine Gordimer. There are great novelists who are writing in the realist mode today.

ELC Are you saying that they have not transformed the mode of realism? My question is really whether realism in its *form* can be updated, whether there is, for instance, a late twentieth-century realism. Can the novels of Robbe-Grillet be considered realist for the 1950s? or Maurice Roche's in the 1970s? Realists, in the Lukácsean interpretation, tried to represent the totality of an experience. Now, does a Maurice Roche represent his view of a realist totality? Can this be called in any way "realistic"?

SRS I think he represents his view, but according to Lukács, the realists did not just represent their view, they represented things as they were. They understood how society worked. Balzac was great because he realized the new developments in the nineteenth century and could analyze them for us; for instance, in *Illusions perdues*.

ELC We also have Thomas Mann in the twentieth century.

SRS Thomas Mann did the same in *Buddenbrooks* (1901). He showed the decline of a family not simply as a process involving individuals but as a historical phenomenon. It all depends on how you define realist. Is it just the "truth" or—I am again influenced by Barthes and the structuralists who say that it is not a matter of "truth" versus "untruth," corresponding to the real or the unreal—is it a certain mode of representation? In order to have a realist novel you must have a narrative that tells a story with an identifiable beginning and ending: A to Z. Besides the narrative, you also need characters whom you care about and who are more or less recognizable individuals living in society, and then you also have to have a world, a decor, a setting, all of it adding up to something coherent. That is Barthes's definition. I think it is difficult in Roche's novels to say that we have a story, characters, and a world. We certainly have elements and fragments, fragments of a story, fragments of characters, and fragments of a world, and maybe it is more "true." Certainly, there is a lot that corresponds to the facts of modern life. He gets a lot of material literally from advertisements, for example. I think it is more exact to speak of Roche as someone who writes texts, often extraordinarily inventive and challenging texts; I would not say that he is a realist novelist.

ELC I think that for you the realist novel is simply a nineteenth-century genre.

SRS But also a twentieth-century genre. Take a contemporary American like Mary Gordon, for instance. She writes realist novels, very good ones. So does Anne Tyler, so do many many other novelists.

ELC A realist novel according to you always tells a story, has a logical development and realist characters?

SRS Yes, that's what the realist genre means to me. Within that genre, as within all genres, you can have great works and also mediocre and trashy works. Personally, I like many postmodernist novels which contain realist elements but are much "crazier." Angela Carter, for example, is one of my heroines. Her novels are not realist—they are too full of fantastic creatures and events for that.

ELC From the notion of realism, let's move on to your ideas about "redundancy." You say somewhere that without redundancy there would be no thesis, no *thèse* in the *roman à thèse*. Would you like to comment on that?

SRS Redundancy is a very interesting notion, taken from linguistics. Linguists have shown that every sentence must have redundancies because without them we would never understand anything. In speaking or writing, you have to repeat certain bits of information. In the chapter in *Authoritarian Fictions* which is my wildest attempt at being scientific (if I can put it that way), where I provide tables and formulas, I try to categorize the different ways in which realist fiction builds up its redundancies. It is an idea first proposed by Barthes and then by Philippe Hamon that in realist fiction the same pieces of information are communicated very often. What I did in that chapter, which no one had done before, was to construct a "scientific," formal, exhaustive typology of the redundancies possible in realist fiction; and then to say which ones among those redundancies are particularly preferred by the *roman à thèse*. As one might expect, they are the ones that involve interpretation and judgment of values.

ELC I find interesting that you are always focusing on form and are providing formal rather than sociocritical responses, even though, I think, that the message implied in your work is sociocritical. It is against authority and power over others. I had to repeat this one more time but shall part from it.

Let's move on to your feminism. Have Marxism and Lukács been of any help?

SRS I mentioned earlier that Marxism is a way of dealing with texts that is clearly committed to some kind of critique. I suppose feminism can be compared to it because of its own kind of political commitment and critique of the status quo. There are also critics who think of themselves as Marxism feminists, but I am not one of them.

ELC Have you worked with ideas such as, for instance, "reification"? The transformation of a woman into a thing. . . .

SRS Yes, but I do not use the term "reification."

ELC I thought that you may have come upon it in your work on Sartre. The notion of "patriarchy," I think, could correspond quite easily to the idea of "establishment" in Lukács, except that Lukács is using it for a critique of society as a whole; he makes no gender distinctions. Nevertheless, I think the idea of patriarchy in feminist critique could be approached quite well with this Marxist model.

SRS Certainly.

ELC We have not mentioned Hegel yet. Has he been of any help to you? His idea of overcoming the master in his master/slave dialectic, which became so important to the Marxist concept of the role of the proletariat, I think could be seen as corresponding to the patriarchy/women dialectic.

SRS The most interesting idea for me in Hegel, as far as I know him at all, is the struggle for mutual recognition in the master/slave dialectic. But my own approach, I think, tends more toward the psychoanalytic. You are thinking of me in terms of the sociocritical, and maybe I am, but my real investment in much of my feminist critical work is in psychoanalysis. For me, subject/object has to do with "I" and the other, and that does not necessarily mean that I have to apply categories such as reification but rather some other, more psychological notion—intersubjectivity, for example.

ELC What makes me see you, in a broader sense, as a sociocritic rather than a feminist is your more moderate approach to feminism compared to some extreme forms that have sprung up all over the country in the last few decades. You do not seem to have the need of leaving everything behind and flying away, as Cixous does, or Irigaray. I feel that these feminists sometimes just want to leave behind reality, whereas you maintain a more moderate, balanced attitude and attempt to integrate your views within a realist social context. I think that is the reason why I have no problem with your feminism. In my mind, the explanation for this was that you had established your feminism within the broader context of sociocritique.

SRS You mentioned Cixous and Irigaray. What do you mean by feminists who are taking off, leaving society behind?

ELC Many, a surprising number of those I knew personally around Columbia, have moved away from the heterosexual world. I analyzed this tendency in Cixous with the help of Todorov's theory of the fantastic in the seventies, with reference to one of her early novels, *La*, actually before Cixous openly took this course, to my knowledge. Her novel was filled with the desire of flying away and leaving behind the society of fathers, husbands, and so on, who did not know what "woman" meant.

SRS Well, it's true that I happen to like men. I guess that's a personal prejudice. I like individual men. I also recognize, however, that men throughout history, insofar as they have been oppressors and dominators, have done an awful lot of harm.

ELC In looking ahead, you say that maybe there will be a "blurring" of differences (*The Female Body in Western Culture* [Cambridge: Harvard University Press, 1986], p. 4) between men and women, which again is a sociocritical notion. It is opposed to extremes, to dominators and dominated.

SRS A mixing, yes, a crossing of different boundaries. To do away with very strict hierarchies would be something that I firmly believe in. To do away with oppressive categorizations of every kind.

ELC Naturally, the "blurring" could go too far.

SRS That's why I think that "blurring" is probably not the word I would use any more because it may imply that we all would get into this soup and that we would all become the same. That's not what I mean and that's not what I had in mind. It is more, I think, the possibility of recognizing different combinations, going beyond very clear-cut, very rigid categories, whether in the realm of ideas or in the realm of behavior or of identity.

ELC But is this desire limited to women? Isn't that a general status that you would like to have for everybody?

SRS Oh, yes. It can't even work unless it is for everybody. Women alone can't do this. If we are talking about going beyond strict and rigid notions of identity, clearly they cannot go it alone.

ELC This again, for me, leads to general sociocritical theory. It's feminist, okay, you want the freedom and possibility of expression, development, and creativity for women. But it should also be there for men, and not everybody, not every man, has that. So in that sense, it is not a specifically feminist concern.

SRS Right. Except that it is feminist insofar as many of the notions such as doing away with rigid categorizations came out of feminist thinking, feminist critiques, for instance, of Freud. You mentioned Irigaray, who says, "Let's look at Freud's theories of the feminine and let's see some of the blind spots and the way he tends to categorize, the way he bases everything on a single model." My own brand of feminism, the very thinking that went into this notion of doing away with strict hierarchies and categorizations, at least the way I have always thought of it, has been influenced by feminist theories of the 1970s and 1980s. But now you are interestingly pointing out that maybe it also has something to do with this "other stuff" behind me, all the Sartrean, Nizanian, Goldmannian influence.

ELC How confident do you feel in your feminism? Do you know exactly that what you want now is what there should be for women? Are you sure of what the role of women should be in society? Some women are not that confident about their own critique and vision of the role of women in society.

SRS When it comes to certain social policies that will make women's lives less stressful, I am totally clear about my feminism.

ELC Do you believe that the possibility of a totally equal existence between men and women can ever be realized? That women professionals will be as free as men to pursue their careers?

SRS I think that we have to work toward that. There is the realm of theory and doing away with all hierarchies, strict categories, and then there is the realm of everyday, concrete living and politics. I don't know whether we will ever achieve a world where everybody does a multiplicity of things and moves freely between work, home, and play, where women and men exchange roles easily. That would be the ideal, wouldn't it? I think we can do a lot better than we are doing. Young workingwomen wouldn't struggle as much if there were flexible work hours for both men and women. They would be doing better if there were a really reliable system of infant care in this country with good, trained, warm, loving people taking care of young children while the parents worked; if there were an attitude that men aren't sissies if they share the first few years of the job of caring for their children. There are so many social policies that could be adopted to make life easier for women. I am very clear about that.

ELC You don't think that there will be a backlash after a few years that could push the whole development back to zero?

SRS I hope not. I certainly will do my best, along with many others, to prevent this from happening.

ELC I am just reading Peter Bürger who makes a clear distinction between modernism and the avant-garde. You have used the term avant-garde in relation to the women's movement (in your book *Subversive Intent*),* and I was wondering whether you make a similar distinction in your feminist theory. For Bürger, modernism is much less critical than the avant-garde. Modernism is something that we allowed to happen in bourgeois society, whereas the avant-garde, for him, is more revolutionary.

SRS Modernism does not necessarily have the avant-garde's political ambition. I don't refer to the women's movement in general as an avant-garde but rather to women artists and writers who are feminists and at the same time are engaged in experimental work. There was a

---

*Susan Rubin Suleiman, *Subversive Intent: Gender, Politics, and the Avant-Garde* (Cambridge: Harvard University Press, 1990).

feminist avant-garde in France that flourished in the late sixties and the seventies; and there are many contemporary English and American artists who qualify as well. Unlike Bürger who seems to think that the avant-garde played itself out sometime in the 1930s, I use the term avant-garde also to refer to contemporary phenomena.

ELC Many important contemporary critics, for instance in France, were marginal people, in the sense that they were all born and grew up outside France, and yet they became France's leading critics. I am thinking of Kristeva, Todorov, Goldmann, Derrida, and so on. Do you think that we could think of women also as marginal in the sense that in the past they were marginal to the establishment but that this same marginality in the end has helped them recognize their predicament? Has the very marginality provided women with a superior critical strength?

SRS I think it always helps to look at things from a position that is not entirely within the mainstream, or within the center, because people who are right there in the middle probably have a greater number of things to which they are blind than people who are off in some other less central place.

ELC Those in the center are blind because it is not a problem to them?

SRS Yes. The world seems natural to them, so they don't notice the things that aren't natural; whereas if you take a slightly eccentric position, you can probably see certain things as not "natural" at all, but rather as created by a given society for specific purposes—and therefore subject to change.

ELC One of your metaphors is the "laughing mother." You see this as a highly positive image. I agree, but, again, shouldn't everybody be free to laugh?

SRS The laughing mother is a kind of allegorical figure. There are other allegories of the mother in our culture (the best-known one is the *Mater dolorosa*, I suppose). Mine is the laughing mother. Sure, everybody should laugh as far as that is possible in our contemporary world. What interests me in the image of the laughing mother is that it goes against the grain of psychoanalytic theorizing where the mother is a still center, as she was for Barthes; a still, silent figure, always there for her child and therefore making it possible for the child to play. With the laughing mother, I wanted to emphasize the mother's subjectivity and what would happen if we integrated it into our theory. To put it in the simplest terms, it is a matter of recognizing that in the story of human development it is not only the child who is a person. The mother also is a person who has a function and a life other than simply providing nurture to the child. It means recognizing the independent subjectivity of the mother. Jessica Benjamin, who is a feminist psycho-analyst, has talked a lot about the need for interrelationship and mutual recognition between mother and child, in contrast to more traditional views of child development. In the traditional developmental story, the child is always trying to get free of the mother, developing its own personality independently of the mother. The mother is like a blank whose sole purpose is to allow the child to develop. The point is that we have to recognize reciprocal interactions between the mother and the child, where both are genuine individuals, people who are persons and who have needs.

ELC In one of your recent articles you speak of Freud who says that the mother's purpose is just to be there.

SRS That was probably D. W. Winnicott, actually. He speaks about the child being alone in the presence of the mother. But there are other possibilities. That is what the laughing mother is meant to suggest.

ELC You have just come back from Hungary. Did anything change your views while you were there or challenge your previous positions in any way?

SRS It isn't so much that being in Hungary challenged my views. If anything, I moved closer—if I could move any closer, since I have been moving more and more in that direction in the last few years—toward the realization of the immense importance of certain kinds of shared historical experiences in peoples' lives. And there I must also say that the category of gender becomes complicated by other categories, categories of ethnicity, categories of religion, categories of shared historical experience—which means that, in your terms, my feminism has become even more sociocritical, I suppose.

ELC Do you have family in Hungary?

SRS Almost none—my mother's two cousins, two sisters who are in their seventies. Living in Hungary for six months, aside from the immense personal significance it had for me and the deep personal satisfaction it brought me, has made me aware of the importance of other categories, so many other categories, besides gender. You cannot be in Hungary for long before becoming aware, for example, of the Second World War. Even by looking at the buildings—I am talking about Budapest—there are many buildings that still bear bullet holes. I lived in a house in which I had a very beautiful apartment, it was just a three-story house, but the front, the facade, still had bullet holes from the war. As a Jew, I discovered many other traces of the war as well. At a dinner party once, a woman who is about in her thirties suddenly announced, "Yes, my mother was at Auschwitz." Obviously, her mother came back from Auschwitz and married and had children, and she was one of them. To me it felt very strange, very shocking. You are also constantly aware in Budapest of 1956; and now, more recently, of what they call "the change," the fall of communism. All the streets have gotten back their old precommunist names. Being in Eastern Europe, you cannot not be aware of the importance of historical catastrophe in people's lives. I think we have much less of that in the United States.

ELC Did your anticommunism intensify?

SRS While I was there now? I am not an anticommunist.

ELC But did you say: okay, that proves it, communism was a failure?

SRS No. Because, if anything, many Hungarians now are saying, "We had it pretty good under the old regime. Prices were lower. Sure, we couldn't find certain luxury items, but at least we all had a roof over our heads, medical care, and we even had a car, we could afford a little country house, a little parcel of land somewhere, and we had our paid vacations on Lake Balaton. Now, suddenly things have gotten terribly expensive, and people who live on fixed incomes can't afford them. There is a huge degree of unemployment which never was there before." I believe that many of my friends who are saying these things are also saying that these are unfortunate but temporary developments. On the whole, it is a good thing that Hungary is no longer communist, because there has been a great deal of liberalization of everyday life. In the old days, even in the best of times you could only leave the country every three years to go to the West. I think most people feel that they have gained something, but there is an immense sense of fear and worry about the immediate future.

ELC Did you hear about Lukács in Hungary? Do people talk about him?

SRS Not much. One of my colleagues at the Collegium, the rector, has fond memories of Lukács. Lukács was a teacher of his, and the students loved him because he went to the movies. Hungarians love movies.

ELC Lukács wrote an article on film.

SRS They liked him, because even as an old man, in his seventies, he would show up at a movie showing. In Budapest, one sees an awfully large number of young people at the movies and generally many fewer middle-aged people. So when Lukács would show up at the movies, his students were very happy.

ELC That's interesting. Because he also went to concerts and gave talks about Béla Bartók, even though he was not a musician. Rumors are that he could not carry a tune.

In your own work, do you think that Lukács will have any place in the future?

SRS From now on? Are we going to read things that we haven't read?

ELC Yes, just as people have read Marx, Engels, or Mao? Do you see a need for Lukács right now?

SRS I don't. I have to say, I don't.

ELC You would not reread some of his works on modernism or realism?

SRS In my courses, I do. But would I now go and really seriously read things I haven't read by him? I always advise people to read *The Historical Novel*, *The Theory of the Novel*, and some of his essays, so he is always there in a way, and maybe more so for me than for most of my colleagues in literature. But in my own work, am I starting to quote Lukács again? No.

ELC Was Lukács, for you, one of the great twentieth-century philosophers? How do you see his importance overall to the critical discourse?

SRS I think he was important. He was one of the great philosophers and critics of our century. It would be interesting to ask people: who was more important, Benjamin or Lukács? Nowadays, there is no question about this. Benjamin is much more visible and appreciated than Lukács.

ELC Adorno is much talked about today.

SRS Yes, Adorno. I think also, partly, because Lukács for many people is identified very closely with a kind of hard-line communism, even though he criticized socialist realism. He was a good "comrade." He spent many years in Moscow. He started out being involved in the Kun government right after World War I, so for many people he seems a much more dogmatic character than Benjamin or Adorno. And I think we have a great deal of suspicion against dogmatism. He was dogmatic. But he was also brilliant, so that even when he was wrong he was interesting.

INTERVIEW WITH ROBERTO SCHWARZ

15 August 1994, São Paulo

ELC As I mentioned earlier, I was fascinated by *Misplaced Ideas** and was wondering about the role Lukács might have played in the creation of this brilliant critique of Third World and in particular Brazilian culture. Having been in Brazil for only a little more than twenty-four hours, I can already sense that Lukács is alive and well in Brazil, more than in the Northern Hemisphere, and I can see why he would be, even though, I am sure, you will tell me that his theories are "misplaced" in Brazil as well. So, to assure a relatively safe ground for the beginning of our discussion, I should like to quote you: "My work would be unthinkable without the—contradictory—tradition of Lukács, Benjamin, Brecht, and Adorno, and without the inspiration of Marx" (p. 13). Since you name Lukács first, I should like to ask you when and how you met his work and what you think his influence might have been on the development of your own ideas?

RS I heard of Lukács at home, as a boy. My parents had attended lectures he gave in Vienna in the early twenties when he came as an exile from Hungary. Then, as a student in the late fifties I got hold of some of his essays on literature, two publications by the Aufbauverlag in East Germany, *Schicksalswende* and *Essays über Realismus*. I was particularly impressed by "Erzählen oder beschreiben?"

ELC The later works first!

RS Yes. But Lukács was to become an important presence in Brazil around 1960 with the French translation—a pirate edition—of *History and Class Consciousness*. At that moment we had a sort of resurrection of Marxism, of nondogmatic Marxism, linked to a fast industrial expansion, which opened the way to a lively and many-sided struggle against underdevelopment, imperialism, and, at last, against capitalism itself. Here the great Lukács from the early twenties came in as an important stimulus, together with Sartre's *Critique of Dialectic Reason*. These books were read more or less at the same time, in a spirit as subversive of capitalism as of official communism, and were decisive for the elaboration of an independent stream of Marxism. This was going on mainly at the university of São Paulo and was quite productive. Several of the better pieces of recent Brazilian writing in history

---

*Roberto Schwarz, *Misplaced Ideas: Essays on Brazilian Culture*, ed. John Gledson (London: Verso, 1992).

and sociology date from those days and include a certain amount of Lukácsean inspiration.

ELC Have you studied in Brazil?

RS Yes, I studied social sciences at the University of São Paulo.

ELC So, there you had your first real encounter with Lukács's work?

RS Yes. At that time I participated in a seminar on Marx's *Capital*. It was organized by a few young professors who allowed some lucky students like myself to drop in. We read all three volumes of *Capital* quite conscientiously and were more or less prepared to grasp the importance of *History and Class Consciousness*. Lukács helped us understand more fully the originality of Marx as opposed to the academic social sciences and as opposed to the communist vulgate.

ELC Had any text by Lukács been translated into Portuguese by that time?

RS I don't think so, but people at the university read French. Then, in the early sixties, the anti-Stalinist faction of the [Brazilian] Communist Party began to translate and to publish Lukács's essays on literature so as to push the party into a line more respectful of artistic freedom. This was part of the struggle for de-Stalinization. Lukács became a well-known figure in literary studies at that time. His essays, such as "Narrate or Describe," became fashionable and were taught at the university.

ELC In your work the question of national identity seems to play a considerable role, what I think could be called "Brazilian self-consciousness." You criticize others, including the Communist Party, for having approached the problem in the wrong way, for instance, for having put too much emphasis on imperialism. I was wondering whether Lukács's *History and Class Consciousness*, which you read as a student, has influenced you in developing your own critical direction which, more than other Brazilian left-wing criticism, seems to be focusing on questions of "class."

RS The concern with national identity, a very powerful topic, was usually a specialty of the right in Brazil. National identity was bound up with tradition and with ancient Brazil against anything modern, cosmopolitan, and international. It was a conservative domain. The point for me was to make it change sides, to win over this conservative stronghold to the left, to turn it against privilege. Instead of the usual celebrations, I tried to look into it from a critical point of view. I did not write in order to enhance it, nor to deny it, but to show the class content it had, the class content that underpinned it. So, in a sense, my work is a critical appraisal of current national identity.

ELC In your essay "Culture and Politics in Brazil, 1964–1969" (*Misplaced Ideas*, pp. 126–59), you criticize the Communist Party for putting too much emphasis on the problems caused by imperialism and neglecting those arising from class differences.

RS Yes, that is right. In cultural matters there was a considerable convergence between the Communist Party and conservatism through nationalism and anti-imperialism. The point in common was the hostility both parties felt toward everything modern, which was understandable, since in a backward country all that is new must by necessity sound foreign. The conservatives feared social change, the communists feared American influence, and both felt more at ease with traditional Brazil and its indecent class structure.

ELC So you were in between the two?

RS I was critical. I have been critical of the Communist Party since my school days.

ELC As you know, Lukács was also critical of the Communist Party but joined it nevertheless as a lesser evil than the right-wing conservatives. Lukács frequently spoke of the necessity of "finding a home" in the way you seem to wish to discover a true Brazilian authenticity, a kind of Brazilian "immanence"—another typically Lukácsean concept. How do you envisage going about discovering, listening to what you often refer to as an "inner necessity"? How do you want to create an "unadulterated existence"? How do you approach it? What is your method?

RS This theme of authenticity is also conservative. To Brazilians, it means mainly whatever has not been affected by modern foreign developments. Yet if you look more deeply into the question, you will soon discover that it has no substance. In fact, it is foreign influence on the former generation which by now looks national, authentic, natural, etc. If you go back one step farther, you will not be better off. You must step back and back and back, until you reach the only authentic thing, which is the colonial world, the one that is least affected by modern European developments, although, of course, it is a completely European and modern development itself. So the quest for authenticity, in the sense of the unmixed, leads nowhere. Yet it may serve as a barrier against anything progressive, mostly against civil rights. My point is not only to criticize the argument of the conservatives, but to explain why it carries so much weight, why it is that in Brazil modern influence *looks* so unnatural. Here the quite paradoxical explanation is that modern developments do not seem artificial because they are forced onto the people, but because the poor have no access to them. The key to the regretted lack of organicity in the culture is not the presence of foreign developments but the iniquitous social structure which enforces their segregation from the poor, therefore producing a kind of social dualism. Thus the argument about the authenticity or the foreignness of modernity in Latin America turns out to be a distorted mirror of a world-historical class exclusion. I tried to turn the question the other way round.

ELC There is then no preoccupation with the authenticity of the Brazilian poor in either colonial or in modern times?

RS As I tried to explain, these worries are double-edged. They are influential ideological facts, and they function mainly so as to keep the poor away from progress. The democratic point of view, as far as I can see, does not concern itself with cultural purity, but rather with the more productive or less destructive ways in which the poor are "exposed" to international modernity. As you see, here too among the democrats there are paternal worries. They are dictated quite unavoidably by the dualism in the social structure itself. Of course, there are many nuances in between. But as a matter of fact, once commercial TV came in, the whole idea of a responsible cultural leadership became a hopeless fantasy.

ELC Do you know the percentage of the poor in today's Brazilian population?

RS That depends on definition. Official statistics say about 30 million people live below the line of absolute poverty.

ELC To what extent can these Brazilian poor functionally be compared to Lukács's concept of the proletariat, or is this a completely different situation?

RS Well, they should be compared to the proletariat, but in order to stress the difference. In fact, what you have in Brazil is something like this: in the thirties begins a sort of effort at national industrialization which bears some resemblance to what happened in socialist countries. Under the leadership of the state, a huge effort was made to industrialize, which attracted the people from the countryside to the city. These were people who had lived under colonial conditions and then came to town to become part of the labor force. But the industrialization did not happen on the full national scale at which it had been expected or promised, so these people were left dangling in the air. They had lost their former integration and then were not absorbed by industry and so became a specific and new social category, the work force of an industrialization that did not come off. There is a German theoretician of modernization, Robert Kurz, who calls them an ex-virtual-proletariat, a huge mass of monetary subjects with no money.

ELC What are they doing? How do they survive?

RS Since the present-day industrialization will not create the employment it used to promise, they live by all sorts of marginal work, informal buying and selling, informal services, often on the fringe of legality. It would be very farfetched to call them proletariat.

ELC So any Hegelian dialectics which Lukács adapted to modern times would not work?

RS If you stick to the classical terms, it will not work.

ELC The master and slave relationship could be envisaged in the sense that there is a master represented by the bourgeois rich, and the poor would be on the other end of the scale, on the side of the exploited.

RS The main point is, though, that the large part of these poor are not really exploited in the full capitalist sense, although of course they are victims of capitalist development. They certainly would want a job that would allow them to be decently exploited by capital. But capital does not want them. If they were exploited, they would be much better off.

ELC You said that many of them were drug addicts. Isn't that a form of exploitation? I think in the United States there is an exploitation exercised by the drug lords, there is a master-slave relationship between specific groups.

RS Again, the difficulty is that the poor in Brazil are not even potential labor from the point of view of a profitable investment. Capital has no possibility and no visible intention of exploiting them. They are simply left aside, which is much worse. All they do in order to earn a living or to defend themselves must look menacing to organized society. The two forces that would be interested in them are the church, which, out of Christian feelings, of course, has an eye for their misery, and then there is narcotic traffic. I am told that in terms of numbers the last one is not important. Yet it certainly is a powerful presence.

ELC Religion and drugs.

RS Yes. In principle, government should be interested as well, at least so as to get votes. Capital does not need them.

ELC In your attempts to find some help or change for Brazil you also say that one should beware of foreign ideologies. You caution against imitation. You identify as one major Brazilian problem, which you see as tragic, the need for imitation. You say: "We Brazilians and other Latin Americans constantly experience the artificial, inauthentic and imitative nature of our cultural life" (*Misplaced Ideas*, p. 1). You speak of a "mirror culture." You also say that "There is historically no such thing as a repetition" (p. 151). Are there any good models? How dangerous are left-wing ideologies? How dangerous is Lukács for Brazil?

RS The point is that I am not at all against imitation. Quite to the contrary. I am afraid I did not make this clear in my book. My cautions against imitation were ironic, a parody of the conservative concerns over national purity. What I try to explain is something else, i.e., *why it is* that modern culture *is felt* like an imitation in Brazil. The reasons are thoroughly related to class structure and to world history and have nothing to do with an "authentic" national path that should be kept clean.

Imitation was a treacherous word once it got its romantic and silly undertones of contempt for everything that is not original. This sort of feeling entered a confusing alliance with the ideological situation in our newly independent countries with their "colonial complex." What was the context of the argument, which to a certain extent and with some changes is still alive today? You had an upper stratum that was linked to the modern world and whose self-styled historical and national mission it was to change the social relations inherited from colonial times so as to transform the colonial crowd into modern, free citizens. Of course, this upper stratum, which benefited in many ways from the former iniquities, was soon to oppose those same modernizing changes, besides having very mixed feelings about them. The quarrel about national authenticity, which often could get really hysterical, reflected this sort of ambivalence of the educated. Yet it hid the effective questions of social progress, which have little to do with these alternatives between imitation and originality and obviously suppose a mix of the two, as does the absence of social progress as well. In itself, imitation is neither bad nor good, and it must be examined in terms of its results, which may look different to the different social classes.

ELC You do say that Machado de Assis knew how to imitate and how to use other cultures for Brazil. You name a few people who knew how to imitate. For instance, with respect to the novel, you say it came here and was sometimes just simply imitated, but then there were those, like Machado de Assis, who knew how to adapt it to Brazil.

RS Yes, there is an interesting distinction to be made in Brazil between a judicious and a dazzled relation to modernity. Machado de Assis is a nearly miraculous example of the first one. He has a keen eye—a bit like the nineteenth-century Russians—for the grotesque and yet functional combinations of modernity and its opposites, such as slavery and patron-client relationships, which were at the center of Brazilian life. Besides the comicality of these extravagant combinations, he understood their historical basis as well. His last twist, which made him a really superior writer, was that he did not envisage these maladjustments only as signs of national backwardness, but as essential aspects of modernity itself, of its shallow formalism, which easily lends itself as a cover for the persistence of evils that the modern spirit is supposed to eradicate.

If you look at the work of lesser writers, the destructive effects of an uncritical relation to modern European forms are easy to notice. It was only natural that Brazilians in the second half of the nineteenth century would try to write novels on the French model, say, of Balzac. What was the result? As we all know, at the center of the Balzacian novel you have an energetic figure who takes the ideals of bourgeois society at face value and wants to make them real, also as a form of self-realization. In the process, these figures must face the realities of money and discover that the hoped-for self-realization is not possible, which is the lesson to be grasped: bourgeois society does not keep its most cherished promises. This narrative model requires characters of superior strength, but who go through a process which is at work in the lives of the secondary figures as well. The central contradictions reverberate on the periphery of the plot, making for a consistent whole, with an immense critical scope. Now when a Brazilian writer, eager to bring modernity to his country, tried to *apply* this model to local realities, the outcome was bound to be different. Like his master, he would invent a central character that takes up a grand question of bourgeois society in a consistent and energetic manner. Yet, out of faithfulness to the local context, to local color, the secondary figures would be "Brazilian," which means that their drive and their problems would be of a different kind. These characters belong to the world of slavery and paternalism, where personal favor—with its peculiar meanders of submission, flattery, and negotiation—is the universal thoroughfare. Now, if there are no individual or universal rights, if there is nothing but personal dependence, who would be so foolish as to behave in the absolute manner of a Balzacian hero? The architecture of the novel will not work, because the central figure, who is imitated from Balzac, does not belong to the same world as the peripheral figures, who are imitated from local reality. Thus the form splits apart. Here again, the clear-sightedness of Machado de Assis will show that he understood the historical truth of this maladjustment and managed to make appropriate use of it, turning it into comedy. The incongruous ambition to be both as "modern" as the characters of a European novel and as "traditional" and "comely" as a well-to-do Brazilian became a sort of stabilized national feature and a problem in itself, full of interesting implications. This rather absurd combination, which was at the bottom of the artistic failure of his fellow novelists, became the source of Machado's strength. A good example of literary dialectics.

ELC What impressed me in your analysis of Machado de Assis is that you tried, in a way, to deconstruct the model of Europe, the "originality" of Europe, saying that it does not work in Brazil. If Europe is considered an "origin," it does not work here. This idea, it seems to me, is not really Lukácsean but rather Derridian, an erasing and deconstructing of origin. Has Derrida helped you in formulating this idea?

RS What helped me was that I noticed that the Lukácsean model would be out of place in Brazil.

ELC I am curious to hear why you think so.

RS The presence of Lukács in my work is basic—as a term of difference. I think it is quite productive to work out in what sense his construction is inadequate to Latin America. I do not mean this as a criticism. Lukács has put together a model for the European history of ideas and for the European history of the novel which depends upon the general historical evolution from feudalism to capitalism and then to socialism. It is a powerful construction. He shows how this development is active in the work of philosophers and novelists. If you then turn to Latin America, you will observe that this sequence is not there and that, therefore, it is not universal. The sequence here goes from colonialism to the attempt at a national state. It is a widespread mistake to make these terms coincide with feudalism and capitalism. You know that colonialism and colonial slavery do not come before the mercantile states and that they are a thoroughly modern phenomenon. So the relationship is of a completely different order.

ELC There are similar explorations of this colonial problem in the literatures of other countries, for instance, in the Algerian novels that began to be written in the 1960s. It seems to me that these Maghrebian novels can be looked at through Lukácsean theory, and I do not quite see why the same could not be accomplished historically and structurally with respect to the Brazilian novel, the novels of Machado de Assis, and also more recent Brazilian fiction. Even the deconstruction of the origin I mentioned above, and the prohibition of imitation, I think, could be justified through Lukácsean theory, particularly if one introduces the concepts of realism and totality. Surely, there cannot be just reproduction and use of a theoretical model. It requires adaptation to and exploration of a specific situation.

RS I do not mean to say that Lukács provides no inspiration. What I say is that you cannot take his outline and apply it to Brazilian reality in the same way you can in Europe. This is not true only for Lukács but for Marx as well. The sequence of feudalism, capitalism, and socialism does not work in Latin America for the simple fact that there has been no feudalism, even if our elite loves to see itself as aristocratic and even if our left loves to insult them as being feudal. The history of Latin America, or more generally of the former colonies, requires new conceptual developments.

ELC Going back to the idea of imitation, in reading you I had the impression that the kind of imitation you recommended could be compared to the one encouraged by the Pléiade during the Renaissance. Du Bellay and his fellow poets studied the classics in the way, I think, you want Brazilian writers to study and imitate Europeans. It is a kind of "innutrition," a studious absorption of a model culture which will allow for a creative development of a new, enriched, and hopefully more typical Brazilian literature.

RS There is a famous modernist writer in Brazil who proposed that Brazilian culture should be anthropophagic. He meant that we should eat up modern European culture so as to enable ourselves to elaborate modern Brazilian literature. I think what he says is funny, even exhilarating, but it does not really clarify what is going on. In fact, all Latin American countries are part of the development of capitalism as a whole, and yet their process is a little bit different from the classical one. This difference must be conceptualized, and it is relevant not only to them, not only to their authenticity or singularity, it is an effective and integral part of contemporary capitalist society, an inner difference. That Latin American countries do not manage to progress and get the same benefits as welfare societies is not simply a fact of backwardness or a lack of culture, it is one aspect of the uneven development of contemporary society which has its official and its unacknowledged faces. This complimentarity must be conceptualized. The difference is not the feature of one country. It is a problem of the whole of modern society. Modern poverty is a problem of modern society and not only of poor countries.

ELC Don't you accept that you have more in common with countries such as Paraguay, Chile, or Argentina than with France and Germany? When you meet theoreticians of other South American countries, don't you share more questions and problems with them than you would with theoreticians from European countries?

RS Yes and no. There is a problematic common to Latin Americans, but it cannot be thought of without reference to Europeans and North Americans, i.e., without reference to the achievements and disasters of the advanced poles of contemporary society.

ELC How about fiction, how about creative work?

RS It also depends on European and American references, which it is foolish to deny. When the dependence is productive, there is nothing diminishing about it.

ELC Surrealism has flourished in South America, particularly in Mexico.

RS All modernism has been very influential: futurism, cubism, expressionism, surrealism, and so on. Fascism and Marxism as well.

ELC It would be interesting to observe what a given country has made of the model, how it changed it. This would reveal the country's specificity and ideology. Such an investigation could be quite Lukácsean: the analysis of a developing form within a social and historical context. I find no conflict here with the Lukácsean method. It would be historical, social, situational, structural. . . .

RS To a certain extent one might say that Lukácsean analysis supposes, in his work of the thirties especially, a sort of unity of the nation. He speaks, for instance, of the German people, or the French people, and of national developments. This may have been a tribute to socialism—or capitalism—in one country. What happens in countries like ours in Latin America is that the meaningful unity is not national. As they come from a colonial matrix, they belong to a unity that is transnational from the beginning, and in order to understand them well you must also understand that one pole, one significant pole of all Latin American countries, is abroad. The cultural forms come from abroad, at least in part, and the economic dependency has one pole abroad by definition. The national closure did not complete itself, and it probably never will. To a certain extent, these experiences are truer than the European ones because European nations are not closed unities either. The sort of inner, organic necessity that Lukács works out so well for the European nations and their class struggle and culture was an active and inevitable model for Latin American nation-building. Yet as these nations are falling apart before attaining completion, they force you to acknowledge the delusion that was in that model. If you go one step further, as national autonomy loses force in the advanced countries as well, Latin American perplexities about it begin to ring truer than the national confidence that still may exist in the First World.

ELC Are you still searching for an "inner necessity"!

RS Yes, but not on a national scale. I am looking for a sort of international system without which you do not understand Brazil.

ELC You see Brazil very much as being part of the modern world. This is somewhat surprising to me. It is my first trip to South America and to me, naturally, Brazil is very different from all other countries I have experienced in North America and Europe. I have lived in several "old" countries and then in the United States. Because of the masses of poor people, Brazil seems very much like a socially raw or virgin country, whichever one prefers, but in which Lukács's theories could fall on a very fertile ground. There is a need to bring up a large segment of the population if not to an equal at least to a living level. As I see it, Hegelian-Marxist dialectics would probably have great appeal for the poor majority of the Brazilian population.

Do you see yourself as a dialectician?

RS Yes, I do.

ELC I do, too. But I think that your dialectics are quite unusual, very interesting. For instance, you oppose the local and the universal, you superimpose incongruous coordinates, things that clash, even linguistically, for instance, when this rather primitive man uses the imperfect of the subjunctive to make fun, sarcastically, of the upper class.* It is a kind of linguistic dialectic that is different, surprising. Have you been told about this?

RS No. I am thankful for your remark.

ELC When I first began to read your book *Misplaced Ideas* I was wondering what you meant by "misplaced." Then I found more such expressions, for instance "maladjustment," "displacement," etc., and in each case the negative term turned into a positive notion. There are many such linguistic upside-down examples in your work. To me, they seem to be quite typical of your writing: dialectics within the linguistic system itself; an ironical approach to its own law and order, one could say. From the very title of your book, you put the logic and the power of linguistic signs into question.

What do you wish to achieve with such dialectics? Your dialectics are quite different from the ones of Lukács, the Hegelian-Marxist dialectics, particularly in the sense that you do not seem to put great emphasis on synthesis and actually seem to be critical of normative approaches, the kind Lukács adhered to.

RS I agree with you. Terms like "misplaced" and "maladjustment" point to a deviation from the European norm (the norm that Lukács criticizes, values, and represents), and in this first sense they are negative. But they are positive as well in the sense that they point to struc-

---

*In chapter 9 of *Misplaced Ideas*, "The Cart, the Tram, and the Modernist Poet" (pp. 108–125), Roberto Schwarz analyzes what he calls the "poetically successful formula for looking at Brazil" (p. 108) invented by Oswald de Andrade. This Brazilian modernist poet juxtaposes in his "Brazil-wood" poetry (*Poesia Pau-Brasil*, 1924) elements characteristic of colonial prebourgeois Brazil with those of postcolonial bourgeois Brazil to satirize, for instance, the obsession of the erudite upper class with "correct" linguistic convention. If an uneducated man of the lower classes uses the imperfect subjunctive, he symbolizes the sociologically and linguistically disjointed reality of the country and becomes the expert subverter of linguistic conventions. According to Schwarz, Oswald de Andrade's Brazil-wood poetry thus quite optimistically prefigures the possibility of a *postbourgeois humanity* (p. 111).

tural realities which must be thought through or taken up as artistic materials. They present objective difficulties of Brazilian culture. All the countries on the periphery of capitalism have strongly dissonant cultures. The dissonance results from the historical need to incorporate what is new in the modern, advanced countries from the no less historical need to be true to the local social relations. This makes for a permanent awkwardness, for a permanent lack of organicity in cultural life. The better writers discover that the dissonances are not simply artistic errors but that they are very substantive, that the substance of the national process is there. So they begin to elaborate them by creating a sense of humor which depends on these dissonances.

ELC Speaking of social reality and the possibility of its transformation, I should like to inject here a question about the function and value of work—we talked about this a bit yesterday. Lukács admired in Lenin the importance attributed to the revolutionary function of work and its being instrumental in the social transformation that would eventually lead to a more egalitarian state and a general betterment of society. You provide a wonderful example in the character of Dona Placida ("The Poor Old Woman and Her Portraitist," *Misplaced Ideas*, pp. 94–99) in whom you analyze what you call "the Brazilian slave mentality" as problematic in relation to the value of work. You introduce the concept of "favor" as being typical of this type of social relation. Do you think that work in Brazil can be rehabilitated—since in a slave society the value of work and work ethics do not exist in the way we know and idealize them in modernized countries—and do you think that work can become useful, valued, and ultimately helpful to the Brazilian poor in their attempt to break out of the vicious circle of their present subhuman existence? If so, what is necessary?

RS As everything else, work should be considered in historical terms. What Lenin had in mind was the educational value of the discipline in the factory. At that time it sounded likely that industrial work would become dominant at large. Yet today's process of production took a shape that is excluding rather than all-embracing. So the whole question lost actuality to a certain degree. If you turn to Brazil, you will feel intensely that the poor would like to work in order to enter the market and to get a minimum of social recognition. But there is no work for them. In the modern workplace, they need fewer and fewer people, and the jobs require a degree of education and specialization which is not accessible to the large masses of the poor in Brazil. So one can say that work in the abstract might be imagined as a great educator but that it will not happen here. There will not be work for everybody.

ELC I am thinking of the poor in the United States where, for instance, black women at an early age, as young girls, were often able to find work in wealthy households and, within that environment, could acquire quite refined manners and skills that subsequently enabled them to integrate more easily into the work force than was the case for black males. Does anything like that happen in Brazil? Do any of the people in the cardboard shacks I saw coming in from the airport break out of that environment and become, for instance, maids? Do the men work as gardeners or chauffeurs? Do they come to work in bourgeois families?

RS A part does, but it is a small part. If there were decent work in society, their lives would be much better. The problem is precisely that the modern work process has taken a form which is dispensing with them. In advanced countries those who do not find work are still citizens and are taken care of in one way or another by social security and so on. But in countries where this does not exist, the consequences are much more catastrophic.

ELC You do not have social legislation with regard to the poor?

RS A little bit, but it is much, much less than in advanced countries. Besides, not all laws are supposed to carry their full practical consequence.

ELC It is interesting to note that the very rich don't work and the very poor don't work; only the middle class does.

Is poverty in Brazil tied to a racial problem?

RS Well, it includes a racial problem, no doubt. The blacks are much more numerous among the poor.

ELC How do you explain the fact that the relatively wide dissemination of Marxist, socialist, and Lukácsean ideas in Brazil has not led to a better social environment, especially for the poor?

RS The years in which the left opposition gained strength in Brazil, say, from 1960 to 1964, was a time linked to the pressure for structural reforms, especially with regard to land distribution. The movement was beaten militarily. In fact, in 1964, we had a conservative military takeover. The dictatorship was definitely antipopular.

ELC You mean, it was antipopular in the sense that it was against the poor?

RS Yes, it was against all the organizations of the people: unions, the movement of the students, peasant leagues, popular culture groups, and so on.

ELC In reading your book I found fascinating your idea of a rich man going down the social ladder toward a complete marginalization. It was in your discussion of Chico Buarque's novel.* I thought about this possibility in relation to the role of the intellectual who wants to speak for the poor. Should the intellectual go down that ladder, and can he really do so? Both Lukács and Sartre were criticized for being bourgeois writers locked into their studies and not knowing much of what was going on in the street below their windows. How do you feel about this? You told me yesterday that in the upcoming Brazilian election you are endorsing a candidate for the presidency who is a worker himself and that you prefer him, although he may not be as ready for the charge as the other candidate. Do you believe in a sort of chaos theory, in the sense that an initial, nonsystematized society, a somewhat chaotic environment, would allow the creation and emergence of a more just and more natural social form that could be the solution to the economic problems of the nation and, in particular, the masses of the poor?

RS It is true that any energetic change is linked to certain risks and a bit of chaos, especially in a very conservative and privilege-minded society. As to the opposition you mention between the people's streets and the intellectual's studies, it may have lost its actuality. The lack of reality in present-day intellectual life is due to real changes, to the difficulty of keeping up critically with the new development of global capitalism. I don't think it should be attributed to a lack of contact with everyday life on the streets.

ELC Let's talk a bit more about your literary views. You often mention realism, and I find your analyses of Machado de Assis fascinating, but I think that what you call "realism" is really closer to "naturalism." In some ways, Machado de Assis's realism made me think of García Márquez's "magic realism." At one point you refer to Machado's realism as an "intensive realism," which, I think, is an acceptable term to someone who has been strongly influenced by Lukácsean concepts. I was

---

*The editor of *Misplaced Ideas* decided to include Schwarz's review of Chico Buarque's novel *Estorvo* (*Veja*, August 1991) as the final chapter of his book, "since it gives an insight (admittedly a pessimistic one) into Schwarz's view of the present direction of his country" (*Misplaced Ideas*, p. 197). Chico Buarque is one of Brazil's most famous popular singers and composers who has repeatedly spoken of the drama of exile, repression, and exploitation. He is also the son of an important historian, Sérgio Buarque de Holande. His novel *Estorvo*, an immediate best-seller, narrates the apocalyptic experiences of an alienated offspring of a wealthy family whose life as a bum leads to suspension of moral judgment, apathy, and complete social marginalization (198). His flight from bourgeois society has no positive outcome. "Monstrosity takes over . . . the absurd readiness to carry on in just the same way in impossible circumstances" (201). Schwarz recognizes in the hopeless situation portrayed in the novel a "potent metaphor" of contemporary Brazil.

wondering how much you agreed with Lukács's limits of realism and naturalism defined, for instance, in the essay you mentioned before, "Narrate or Describe." Have there been "realists" in the Lukácsean sense in Brazil?

RS Yes, there have been novelists who imitated Balzac and who on the surface would be realists in the Lukácsean sense. But their novels are not first-class and do not work because of the reasons I mentioned earlier. Machado de Assis was very clear-minded about them. He understood their weakness and worked to avoid it. Machado wrote in a thoroughly realistic spirit.

ELC So did Zola, no?

RS Well, Machado de Assis is very different from Zola whom he certainly had in mind as a competitor he wanted to outdo. Machado understood what Brazilian society was all about and thought that a close imitation of the modern French manner would not be helpful. So he looked for a different form of composition, but in order to be more realistic. He wrote realist novels, but with antirealist techniques. It is quite paradoxical.

ELC You mean antirealist in which sense?

RS At a time of massive predominance of Balzac, Flaubert, and Zola, Machado used techniques of the eighteenth-century novel, especially the manner of Sterne, techniques which looked whimsical and anti-scientific.

ELC Did he appreciate Diderot?

RS Yes. He learned and borrowed from him. So he used prerealist, eighteenth-century techniques, but in a thoroughly realist, nineteenth-century spirit, always without losing sight of Balzacian realities. This is interesting, because you can see at work a sort of reassured policy in the choice of literary forms and models. Besides, forms are put to work in a spirit very different from the original one. It is as if the arbitrary choice of "archaic" narrative techniques allowed for the freedom Machado needed in order to render the specificities of Brazilian society, which the pressure of the contemporary French fashion would suppress.

ELC Is there less detail and exaggeration than in the naturalist novel? Is it less pessimistic? Would you say that it is experimental?

RS It certainly is full of experiments. And extremely pessimistic.

ELC But you still think that it is not like the novels of Zola?

RS No, it is not, although Machado had a very scientific bent of mind. His novels look at once prerealist, postnaturalist, and avant-garde. Yet their spirit is realistic, and their point is to capture the specific aspect of Brazilian actuality and social life.

188

ELC So the difference Lukács makes between narration and description cannot be applied here. Do you find that Machado narrated rather than described, in the Lukácsean sense?

RS I think Machado put together a form which Lukács would say is good but which does not fit into the alternatives Lukács describes in "Narrate or Describe."

ELC Do you know whether Lukács read him?

RS I think he did not. But this difficulty with critical terms we were just talking about is very interesting and telling in itself. Naturalism in Brazil does not mean the same thing it did in Europe, nor do realism, Parnassianism, or modernism. This is a general point one should not lose sight of when writing literary history and criticism in Latin America. It is necessary to study what becomes of the European models once they go through the filter of new circumstances. It is wise to imagine that they change substantially, which would be only natural, since the colonial or ex-colonial societies differ in structure from the metropolitan ones.

ELC You have then no use for the Lukácsean concepts?

RS Quite to the contrary, but you must use them differentially. Because they are apt and very explicit about their presuppositions in European history, they may be helpful, precisely in order to make us aware of the differences which are our essential problem. These differences are of truly world-historical significance. They are at the heart of Latin American literature, and the task of our criticism is to work them out. You must know the European meaning of the model, the changes it went through in America, and you must find a convincing, global interpretation of the difference. Of course, these questions exist for the literature of North America as well.

ELC For Lukács it was very important that a realist novel should project a totality. Do you think that Machado was preoccupied with projecting a realist totality?

RS To a certain degree. His novels are well-rounded in a hidden way. In spite of their ostensibly erratic and fragmentary course, which so to say leads nowhere, they have a sort of sociological completeness, a complete system of social types. The absence of a definite direction, which looks so modernist and which is really disconcerting, may be one of their great realistic (Balzacian) features.

ELC Are there critics who do accept and use the Lukácsean concepts for the analysis of Brazilian literature?

RS You mean critics who take him at face value? Yes, there are. We disagree, and we are very good friends.

ELC I did find some difference but also some similarity in your work to

Lukács's use of irony as the constitutive element of the novel form. Irony, as we know, proceeds on a double level, it has a double structure. But whereas for Lukács irony was a very serious element, a dead-serious critical tool, I found that in your analyses, particularly of Machado de Assis, irony was often replaced by humor. Humor seemed to assume the constitutive but also critical function of irony in the Lukácsean sense. I enjoyed reading it. It reminded me of Voltaire's humorous use of irony. Do you agree with this assessment?

RS Maybe. There is a certain distance Machado will always keep in relation to his subject. This distance, half playful, half nasty, allows him to see all situations from different angles, once from the European point of view, once from a local point of view, once from the top, once from below. These shifts make for vertiginous irony, which is quite objective and realist in spirit because it gives successive and subtle expression to the essential positions of the social process.

ELC It seems humorous, lightly put, but it is really seriously meant.

RS Well, it is actually terrible once you understand it better.

ELC Before coming here, I was told that the Brazilians have a wonderful sense of humor. And I think it is true, and when they use humor—as they did at the gathering last night—it is really like irony at the same time. It is just a different approach. Or maybe they do not take themselves as seriously as Lukács did, who was a very serious man.

RS Machado de Assis was certainly serious, even dead serious. A Brazilian poet, who did not feel in sympathy with him, considered him to be too Protestant, too much of a soul-searcher. In this sense he is really an untypical Brazilian, and there are not many Brazilian writers who are like him.

ELC To bring in a few other terms you use: "volatility," and also the "to-and-fro that epitomizes the vexation of a nation," "the ideological and moral incongruity imposed by the contemporary world," the typical rhythm of the Brazilian novel as you describe it, even its "capriciousness" (*Misplaced Ideas*, p. 92), could be linked to the dialectic structure of irony. Maybe this somewhat light, humorous, and vacillating movement is precisely the form of the Brazilian dialectic, the dialectic of the Brazilian novel.

RS Yes, and again, this irony is realistic because it shifts between points of view which are substantial to the life of the country: you have the European or "liberal" or "modern" point of view, which goes together with the ostensibly civilized ruling classes and yet makes them look like caricatures because of their inadequacy; of course, the European point of view looks like a caricature as well, because of its pompous shallowness, still underscored by the occasional presence of slaves; you have the point of view of the poor who float in a terrible social void, since they are neither slaves nor wage earners, i.e., nothing of substance, and depend on the hazardous sympathies of the people of property, a sort of uncertainty that weighs like an iron law. Etc., etc. So there is this shifting of the points of view, which makes for an extraordinary sort of ironic prose. Each in his own way, there are several Brazilian writers who actually cultivated such "volatility," which may well be complementary, in a perverse way, to the awful stability of our social inequality. It is a very mobile and debunking prose, artistically very interesting.

ELC Musicality and theater seem very important in your analyses as well. You know that Lukács, as early as 1904, was one of the founders of an experimental theater in Budapest, the Thalia, where they staged the socially critical plays of Hauptmann and Ibsen. Lukács wanted to do this in order to improve the social awareness of the population. Do you think that Brazilians privilege music, dance, and theater as a means of popular communication, as a way of expressing what is wrong in their lives? This may be just another typically Brazilian expression, but you say somewhere that music has the advantage of avoiding the "word." I found this interesting considering the recent deconstructive critique of the linguistic sign. It can also be linked to the tradition of Antonin Artaud's "theater of cruelty." I thought that particularly in Brazil this form of nonverbal communication and critique may be very appropriate, much more so than it was in Lukács's socially well-established, early twentieth-century Vienna or Budapest. Dance, music, and theatrical gestures constitute a different form of communicating thought, inspired by the needs or preferences of a particular people or situation.

RS In fact, the use of music and dance as an important form of social criticism was not a private preference of mine. It flourished immediately after the establishment of the dictatorship in 1964. People wanted to express their opposition in a manner that would not land them in prison. So music, dance, and an oblique kind of political theater became flags of opposition. Censorship had to adapt to them first, so as to decide what things were not acceptable and why. So the absence of words was a camouflage which furthermore allowed for a convergence between local artistic developments and the international fashion of the nonverbal theater.

ELC Theater often flourishes at times of revolution, for instance at the time of the 1789 Revolution in France, and again in 1968, during the May crisis, when, Minouchkine and others developed the *théâtre du soleil* in Avignon. I find the parallel with the Brazilian phenomenon interesting.

There is another one of Lukács's revolutionary concepts, the concept of fetishism, developed from Marx's theory of the fetishism of merchandise or commodities, which I think you have updated and taken a bit further by putting it into a typically modern context, using the all-intrusive milieu of the media. You write: "What would popular culture be like if it were possible to isolate it from commercial interests and particularly from mass media?" (*Misplaced Ideas*, p. 3) Has Lukács influenced you in this thought?

RS The question you quoted on the preservation of the culture of the poor was meant to render the point of view of a part of the left (not my own) whom you could classify as the purists of popular culture, a point of view that developed from the revolutionary hopes of the sixties. The idea was quite mythical. There was the hope that once you barred the imperialist influence (commodification, new technologies, American way of life) as well as the elitist prejudices against the people, you would allow for an independent blooming of pure and national popular culture, free from all the sins and alienations of modern life. I may be simplifying the argument a bit, but on the whole this is what it was about. Still, it is interesting to note that at that time, since the media had not yet exercised its pull on high culture, intellectuals felt free to "liberate" the poor from the dictatorship and from radio and TV. Today the idea of a culture that is not commodified or that is weakly commodified has become unthinkable in itself.

ELC In our postmodern era we are totally enslaved by the media and commodities.

RS Yes, and that is why it is so interesting to see that not so long ago, say thirty years ago, the outlook in backward countries such as Brazil was completely different. There were still forms of culture that were relatively free from commodification. But when you talk to students about this now, they cannot imagine how those popular forms that were to be enshrined could point to socialism or to freedom. Having said this, Lukács's theory of the fetishism of commodities in *History and Class Consciousness* is certainly his most important contribution and the most modern one. The theoretical aspect seems to me completely alive. On the other hand, the writings about class consciousness sound rather mythical today, as they are linked to a view of the proletariat that has received a historical dementi.

ELC One of the most striking chapters of your book *Misplaced Ideas* is the one entitled "Is There a Third World Aesthetic?" It is very brief (pp. 173–174). You essentially say that there is *no* Third World aesthetic. Is there a Brazilian aesthetic? Are you opposed to notions of aesthetics as you are, I think, opposed to norms and systems?

RS Actually, there was a Third World aesthetic. It was a mix of libertarian and authoritarian features, of nationalism and internationalism, of avant-garde and artistic regression, and it hoped to escape the alternative between capitalism and socialism. Its libertarianism depended on the better motives of anti-imperialism: it demanded self-determination and respect for downtrodden nations; it expressed their desire to escape stagnation and backwardness, and, to this extent, it had something of the epic of humanity, as opposed to the individualistic and somewhat irrelevant scope of bourgeois culture. On the other hand, as it was closely linked to strong nationalist efforts, it had something definitely authoritarian about itself, something ostensibly positive and anticritical, a readiness to sacrifice the individual, a deep sympathy for brutalities exerted in the name of History, etc. So it is not that a Third World aesthetic did not exist, but that it should be looked at critically.

ELC I thought your reservations were maybe linked to the fact that you do not like norms. In this respect you must also disapprove of Lukács since he always tries to fit ideas and developments into norms. An aesthetic is in a way a norm.

RS This is yet another matter. I am not for the normative aesthetic of Lukács, this is certain. It is *so* distant from modern art and modern society that it is really hard to be earnestly in touch with it. Something similar is true for his general theory of genres, according to which all modern literature developed against the classical norm. For some abstruse reasons—but there he was not alone—Lukács remained a classicist in the midst of social revolution, miles away from all that happened. In fact, this is intriguing and a surprise, coming from such a great historical mind, from a man who has understood and explained more than most others the historical character of literary forms.

ELC He is normative and rigid.

RS But his good pieces of criticism do not suffer from this abstract normativity. They look out for the effective organization of novels or dramas and are most ingenious about their historical character and significance. There he is really excellent. In fact, this normativity probably endeared him to Latin American critics. As I told you before, by the very nature of things, we take European developments as being norms. For us, their shape is canonical: English parliamentarianism, the rationalization of labor, French poetry, and such developments inevitably have a sort of "classical" status for peripheral societies. I may be wrong, but I think that in Brazil such tendencies make for a considerable elective affinity with Lukács's aesthetic doctrinarianism.

ELC As to models, I think that you found in Anatol Rosenfeld, to whom you devote a chapter in *Misplaced Ideas* (pp. 175–86), to a certain extent your own model. He is a bit your soul brother, it seems to me, who would also take you away from Lukács and the normative world.

RS You are right, he was very irritated by Lukács.

ELC I bet he was, since he strongly laments the importance Lukács attached to the so-called loss of perspective of the modern "irrational" novel (p. 180). Rosenfeld, as you describe him, was "free of the social humbug," free of norms, schools, and anything that would limit his own individuality. In this, I feel, he is close to you, in an "elementary rationality" that is informed by enormous learning and understanding of connections but at the same time is guided by a deep commitment to and need for freedom. You yourself seem to practice a kind of theoretical "innutrition," but then you come up with your own independent thought and judgment. You do not seem to subscribe to one theory or the other, as is so often the case with scholars today, but rather stick to your own.

RS You flatter me. Leaving myself aside, you described something that really happened. It is true that for a whole period in Brazil, Marxists would be either Lukácsean, Althusserian, or Trotskyite and that they would evaluate each other and themselves according to these affiliations. Then, after a period of elaboration, a part, not all, showed up with objective problems dictated by history and demanding specific studies and uncharted answers. When you have identified a problem and try to solve it on your own instead of affiliating yourself with this or that school, then you have taken a step forward.

ELC Today, we have talked a great deal about Lukács and not at all about the Frankfurt School, which may well have influenced you much more than Lukács. Do you feel closer to Adorno, Benjamin, and the Frankfurt School in general rather than to Lukács?

RS I certainly do. Nevertheless, I feel greatly indebted to Lukács to whom on the whole I owe my outline of the European novel. As I told you, his construction does not correspond to Brazilian realities. Yet, as it is a remarkable formulation of the great lines of European social and literary history, it allows you to sense the points where Brazilian society and culture *deviate* from their very cherished European models. These deviations were sorely felt by contemporaries, who saw them as national faults and, in the better cases, transformed them into dynamic elements of social criticism and artistic production. As I tried to examine these questions, Lukács's studies on the novel entered in a very substantial even though negative manner into my work. But coming back to your question, at present I feel more inclined to look for a certain complementarity between Lukács, Benjamin, and Adorno rather than throwing away one or two of them. In his work in the 1950s, if you put aside the tribute to Stalinism, Lukács has interesting things to say about the relations between class struggle and literary composition. Adorno meanwhile concentrated on the progress of fetishism, in line with the central chapter of *History and Class Consciousness.* To my mind, Adorno's description of modern society is much keener than Lukács's, although seemingly a less political one. He was also younger, one must note, and belonged to a later moment in the history of capitalism, of socialism, and of art. Benjamin in his turn made a pathbreaking discovery about the artistic consequences of the development of productive forces. It may sound Solomonic, but it is true that each had a different focus. One was keen on the development of productive forces, the other on alienation, and the third on class struggle. The three aspects still exist, all have changed considerably, and I do not think it productive to take sides exclusively.

ELC What I found in your book is that you take each one a step further. For instance you have incorporated into your critique the lessons derived from more recent linguistic theories which were not available to Lukács. You are very style-conscious. Lukács was not.

RS This is a problem with Lukács. He does not really care for prose. He is very good on composition but not on prose. Yet, one must look at prose, in particular in modern literature where everything goes on in the writing itself, to a certain degree at the expense of action.

ELC Yes, Lukács excels in analyses of content, even though he does not really want to admit this. He says that he works with form more than content. I think Lukács is particularly good at producing a global awareness of developments and pitching literary movements against each other. To me he was very important in defining European romanticism, realism, and naturalism, not so much in his providing convincing literary examples, but in his general characterization of the movements in relation to their historical context.

RS I think Lukács is right when he stresses that he works with form. His analysis of content always leads to compositional consequences. In this sense he is looking for the formal energies of content and checking the consistency of their literary realization. Also on Balzac, his analyses of the "types" and their compositional value are often very interesting.

ELC Do you mean his analyses of the "problematic hero"? This leads me into my next question. I find that in much of your work you seem to assume the role of a trans-individual hero, a Lukácsean hero who sets out to find what Lukács would call a "home" for Brazil in the form of a more authentic Brazilian identity, a "harmony," as you say, "between the spirit and vital necessity" (*Misplaced Ideas*, p. 183). It is a down-to-earth goal, and in that sense I feel that your work represents very much what I should like to call a functional critique. Your interest in linguistic theories does not seem to get lost in the nihilism of recent linguistic conclusions. Derrida's deconstructions usually result in statements that imply that one cannot really touch the truth or say anything real and truthful about man and society because of the restrictive limitations of the linguistic system. On the other hand, your critique clearly expresses a human and ethical concern. You address human suffering and social injustice.

RS Well, yes.

ELC As we are coming to the end of our discussion, I should like to ask you how much, in this critical effort, you have felt inspired by Lukács and whether you think that Lukács will continue to be useful to Brazilian critics and still inspire what I should like to call "functional critique" in the future?

RS I know from my own experience that reading Lukács can have a great impact. The young reader may learn that the decisive thing to be interpreted in a work of art is form rather than subject matter and that form, in its turn, should be interpreted in social terms. This is a great saying, difficult to put into practice, but it is a great saying. He may see also that it is worthwhile to interpret form. If you interpret it in terms of social history, you discover relationships between artistic beauty and social questions which are truly interesting and worth looking for. Lukács has a very demanding and strong conception of what constitutes a work of literature. The gestalten, the inventive search for the appropriate form for a subject matter, is considered a difficult task and a high accomplishment. And if the critic is able to interpret artistic and literary form and render it conceptually, he will be saying relevant things. So I think that Lukács gives the critic a high mission, which I like very much.

ELC What comes to your mind when you think of Lukács? Which of his theories? What has he given us that will continue to be seminal for the future?

RS Well, as I said before, I think his chapter on reification has not been exhausted at all. The point that the whole of modern society turns around commodity fetishism and that this is a sort of "rational" form that blinds us to reality and which it is dangerous to trespass continues to be very true. Of course, like everything else, fetishism has changed since then. For instance, if you take Latin American countries, but Europe as well, nobody thinks anymore that commodities are "natural" in the sense Marx or Lukács would still speak of them. Many countries have tampered with the laws of the economy, and innumerable economic plans have been tried out. Brazil has just now changed its monetary unity. So there is nothing "natural" to capital anymore; its man-made nature is obvious to all children, and yet with every day that passes and in spite of all catastrophes, capital looks more and more insurmountable. Nobody dares to think beyond the exchange of commodities. It is an extreme situation when people do not respect the basic forms of the economy but do not allow themselves to think of alternatives. So it seems to be the limit of limits in our society, and its criticism is possibly a radical task for which Lukács's chapter on fetishism may still provide useful inspiration.

ELC Have you read and used Lukács's early work or have you limited yourself to his later theories?

RS I have read *Soul and Form* and *The Theory of the Novel*, and I am aware of course of their superior inspiration. But still what was more helpful to my work with nineteenth-century Brazilian literature were his essays from the 1930s on the European nineteenth century. The sentences expressing tough communist propaganda that Lukács deliberately added to his text are hard to swallow, but the essays are also packed with knowledge and insights. There are not many critics who can stand up to Lukács.

ELC Do you think that Lukács will continue to be of value to you and Brazilian literary criticism in general?

RS One thing that impresses me very much, and I think should be written about, is his conception of nineteenth-century realism. The present fashion is to see realism as a simple trompe l'oeil, as a rhetorical *effet de réalité*, as an outcome of some tricks of prose. This is poor indeed. Lukács's view of realism not as a kind of photographic rendering but rather as a complex formal construction invented in view of the new forms of society is much more interesting. It is a deep, important thought to which very little scholarship has been devoted.

ELC Yes, that is true for the past ten to fifteen years, but I think it is coming back now.

RS In fact, it is not easy to guess what will become of such an outstanding communist critic once communism is not there anymore. I continue to think that Lukács's discussions about form will remain a source of inspiration. On reading them, you feel like trying a hand at it yourself. They stimulate you to imagine what form would be fit to render this or that aspect of modern life. The clear-minded and knowledgeable discussions about the appropriateness of form to subject matter awaken the artistic intelligence in the reader. Although the writings are often a little dry, "professional" as Adorno has rightly put it, they are not sterile.

ELC I find your comments very interesting, particularly since I have just completed a study entitled "The Seductions of Realism" in which I analyze the development of realism from Flaubert, who wanted to overcome his romanticism with the help of realism, to Lukács for whom it was the ideal form of literature. Contemporary linguists and pragmatists such as Richard Rorty dismiss realism as a simple *fait linguistique.* You, to the contrary, seem to believe that language can be helpful in identifying and in elucidating social problems and can have a realist function. Lukács never even asked the question.

RS It would sound silly to him!

ELC Yes, well, he never questioned language as a means of communication. So I find it very interesting that you, who are very familiar with contemporary linguistic theories, should have selected Lukács's concept of realism as his most lasting and inspiring contribution to the future of literary criticism. Thank you very much for your thoughts.

RS I do thank you.

NOTES ON CONTRIBUTORS

ETIENNE BALIBAR is Professor of Philosophy at the University of Paris I, France, where he teaches courses in epistemology and in political philosophy. He has written extensively on Marxism and political theory and is coauthor with Louis Althusser of *Reading Capital* (1985). Among his books are *Spinoza et la politique* (1985), *Race, Nation, Class: Ambiguous Identities* (coauthored with Immanuel Wallerstein, 1988), *Ecrits pour Althusser* (1991), *Les Frontières de la démocratie* (1992), *Masses, Classes, Ideas: Studies on Politics and Philosophy Before and After Marx* (1993), and *The Philosophy of Marx* (1995).

PETER BÜRGER is Professor of French and Comparative Literature at the University of Bremen, Germany. Among his numerous publications on the relation between politics and aesthetics are his much-noted *Theory of the Avant-Garde* (1984), *Prosa der Moderne* (1988; *La Prose de la modernité,* 1994), *The Institutions of Art* (coauthored with Christa Bürger, 1992), *The Decline of Modernism* (1992), *Das Denken des Herrn* (1992), *Die Tränen des Odysseus* (1993), and *Der Französische Surrealismus. Studien zur Avantgardischen Literatur* (1996).

EVA CORREDOR is Professor of French and German at the United States Naval Academy. She has written extensively on the theories of György Lukács, particularly with regard to fiction and drama, and has compared Lukács's views and concepts to those of other twentieth-century theoreticians such as Bakhtin, Goldmann, Sartre, Foucault, and Derrida. Some of her work has appeared in *Diacritics, New German Critique, The French Review, Comparative Literature, The University of Ottawa Quarterly,* and *Philosophy and Literature.* She contributed a chapter to *Tracing Literary Theory,* ed. Joseph Natoli (1987), and is the author of *György Lukács and the Literary Pretext* (1987).

TERRY EAGLETON is Warton Professor of English Literature at St. Catherine's College, Oxford. Among his many books on literary criticism and political theory are *Marxism and Literary Criticism* (1976), *Criticism and Ideology: A Study in Marxist Literary Theory* (1978), *Walter Benjamin* (1981), *Literary Theory: An Introduction* (1983), *The Function of Criticism: From the Spectator to Poststructuralism* (1984), *Against the Grain: Essays 1975–1985* (1986), *The Ideology of the Aesthetic* (1990), *Nationalism, Colonialism, and Literature* (coauthored with Fredric Jameson and Edward Said, 1990), and *Ideology: An Introduction* (1991). He is the editor of *Ideology: Selected Texts* (1994), and coeditor of *Marxist Literary Theory*

(1996). He wrote the preface to *Cultural Politics at the 'Fin de siècle'*, ed. S. Ledger and S. MacCracken (1995).

FREDRIC JAMESON is William A. Lane Professor of Comparative Literature and Director of the Graduate Program in Literature and the Duke Center for Critical Theory at Duke University. Among his most influential books on Marxism and contemporary critical theory are *Marxism and Form: Twentieth-Century Dialectical Theories of Literature* (1971), *The Prison-House of Language: A Critical Account of Poststructuralism and Russian Formalism* (1972), *The Political Unconscious* (1981), *The Ideologies of Theory: Essays 1971–1986—Volume I, Situations of Theory* and *Volume II, Syntax of History* (1988), *Late Marxism: Adorno, or, The Persistence of the Dialectic* (1990), *Postmodernism, or, The Cultural Logic of Late Capitalism* (1991), and *Seeds of Time* (1994). With Kang Lieu and Xiaobing Tang, he coedited *Politics, Ideology, and Literature: Discourse in Modern China* (1994).

JACQUES LEENHARDT succeeded Lucien Goldmann as Director of the Sociology of Literature at the Ecole des Hautes Etudes en Sciences Sociales, Sorbonne, France. He has written extensively on the sociology of literature and art and the origin of aesthetic creation. Among his books are *Lecture politique du roman: "La Jalousie" d'Alain Robbe-Grillet* (1973), *Lire la lecture* (coauthored with Pierre Józsa, 1982), *La Force des mots: Le rôle des intellectuels* (coauthored with Barnaba Maj, 1982), *Existe-t-il un lecteur européen? Etude de lecture du roman "Le Grand Cahier" d'Agota Kristof* (in collaboration with Martine Burgos and Brigitte Navelet-Noualhier, 1989), and *Dans les jardins de Roberto Burle Marx* (1994).

MICHAEL LÖWY, Centre National de la Recherche Scientifique, Paris, France, has published widely on Marxism and political theory. His books include *Pour une sociologie des intellectuels révolutionnaires: L'Evolution politique de Lukács, 1902–1929* (1976). He edited and introduced *Littérature, philosophie, marxisme, 1922–1923* (1978). More recently he published *On a Changing World: Essays in Political Philosophy from Karl Marx to Walter Benjamin* (1992), *Marxism in Latin America from 1909 to the Present: An Anthology* (1992), *Redemption and Utopia—Jewish Libertarian Thought in Central Europe: A Study in Elective Affinity* (1992), *Révolte et mélancholie: Le romantisme à contre-courant de la modernité* (with Robert Sayre, 1992), and *The Theory of Revolution in the Young Marx* (1995).

ROBERTO SCHWARZ is Professor Emeritus of Literary Theory at the University of Campinas, São Paulo, Brazil. He has written extensively on Brazilian literature, art, and political theory, and is particularly well known for his highly original political analyses of the work of the famous nineteenth-century Brazilian novelist Machado de Assis. *Misplaced Ideas*

(1992) made available for the first time in English some of his brilliant essays in critical theory. Among his books published in Brazil are *Um Mestre na Periferia do Capitalismo: Machado de Assis* (1990), *Que Horas São?* (1987), *O Pai de Familia* (1978), and *Ao Vencedor as Batatas* (1977).

GEORGE STEINER is Extraordinary Fellow at Churchill College, Cambridge, and Professor of English and Comparative Literature at the University of Geneva. Called one of the last true "men of letters," he has written brilliantly on questions of literary criticism, philosophy, and linguistic theory. His publications include *The Death of Tragedy* (1961), *Language and Silence: Essays on Language, Literature, and the Inhuman* (1967), *In Bluebeard's Castle: Some Notes Towards the Redefinition of Culture* (1974), *After Babel: Aspects of Language and Translation* (1975), *Martin Heidegger* (1978), *The Portage to San Cristobal of AH* (1981), *Antigones* (1984), *Real Presences* (1991), *Proofs and Three Parables* (1993), and *No Passion Spent: Essays 1978–1995* (1996). He wrote the introduction to Franz Kafka, *The Trial* (1995).

SUSAN RUBIN SULEIMAN is Professor of Romance and Comparative Literature at Harvard University. She has published widely on modern fiction and theories of feminism. With Inge Crosman, she is coeditor of *The Reader in the Text: Essays on Audience and Interpretation* (1980). She is the editor of *The Female Body in Western Culture* (1986), and wrote the introduction to Hélène Cixous, *Coming to Writing and Other Essays* (1991). Her books include *Authoritarian Fictions: The Ideological Novel as a Literary Genre* (1983), *Subversive Intent: Gender, Politics, and the_ Avant-Garde* (1990), and *Risking Who One Is* (1996).

CORNEL WEST is Professor of Afro-American Studies and the Philosophy of Religion at Harvard University. Among his numerous publications on philosophy, political theory, and race relations are *Prophetic Fragments* (1988), *The American Evasion of Philosophy: A Genealogy of Pragmatism* (1989), *Breaking Bread* (1991), *The Ethical Dimension of Marxist Thought* (1991), *Race Matters* (1993), *Keeping Faith: Philosophy and Race in America* (1993), and *Jews and Blacks: The Hard Hunt for Common Ground* (with Michael Lerner, 1995). He is coeditor of *Encyclopedia of African-American Culture and History* (1995), and wrote the foreword to *Critical Race Theory: The Key Writings That Formed the Movement*, ed. K. Crenshaw, N. Gotanda, G. Peller, and K. Thomas (1995), and to Jim Wallis, *The Soul of Politics: Beyond Religious Right and Secular Left* (1995).